STAR WARS™
GALAXY'S EDGE

BLACK SPIRE OUTPOST is a haven for smugglers, merchantsand travelers from every corner of the galaxy — all looking to make the score of a lifetime on the infamous black market.

War. The fall of the Republic. The rise of the Empire. Black Spire has endured. And the mysterious trader Dok-Ondar has weathered it all, thriving on the unique opportunities that abound in the lawless pockets of the galactic fringes.

But a new evil rises in the galaxy, one that may threaten even Dok-Ondar and Black Spire...

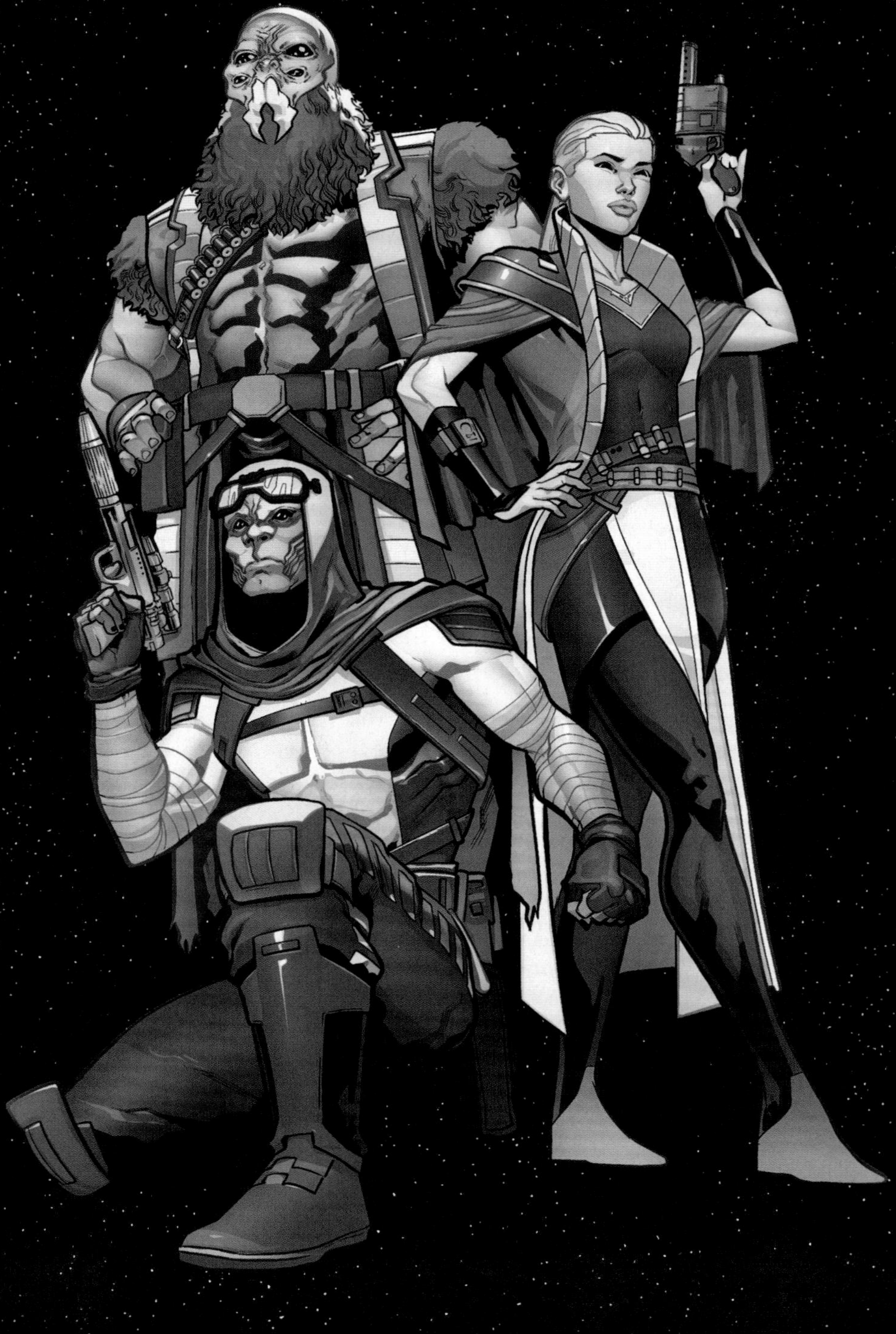

STAR WARS
GALAXY'S EDGE

Writer	**ETHAN SACKS**
Artist	**WILL SLINEY**
Color Artists	**DONO SÁNCHEZ-ALMARA** WITH **PROTOBUNKER**
Letterer	**VC's TRAVIS LANHAM**
Cover Art	**ROD REIS** (#1) & **TOMMY LEE EDWARDS** (#2-5)
Assistant Editor	**TOM GRONEMAN**
Editor	**MARK PANICCIA**
Editor in Chief	**C.B. CEBULSKI**
Chief Creative Officer	**JOE QUESADA**
President	**DAN BUCKLEY**

For Lucasfilm:

Assistant Editor	**BEATRICE KILAT**
Senior Editor	**ROBERT SIMPSON**
Creative Director	**MICHAEL SIGLAIN**
Lucasfilm Story Group	**PABLO HIDALGO, MATT MARTIN & EMILY SHKOUKANI**
Lucasfilm Art Department	**PHIL SZOSTAK**

Walt Disney Imagineering:

Creative Executive	**SCOTT TROWBRIDGE**
Assistant Producer	**STACEY LEONG**
Managing Story Editor	**MARGARET KERRISON**
Asset Specialist	**CARTER TATA**
Producer	**RACHEL SHERBILL**
Producer	**RAINA ROSS**

Collection Editor **JENNIFER GRÜNWALD**
Assistant Editor **CAITLIN O'CONNELL**
Associate Managing Editor **KATERI WOODY**
Editor, Special Projects **MARK D. BEAZLEY**

VP Production & Special Projects **JEFF YOUNGQUIST**
SVP Print, Sales & Marketing **DAVID GABRIEL**
Director, Licensed Publishing **SVEN LARSEN**
Book Designer **ADAM DEL RE**

STAR WARS: GALAXY'S EDGE. Contains material originally published in magazine form as STAR WARS: GALAXY'S EDGE #1-5. First printing 2019. ISBN 978-1-302-91786-9. Published by MARVEL WORLDWIDE, INC., a subsidiary of MARVEL ENTERTAINMENT, LLC. OFFICE OF PUBLICATION: 135 West 50th Street, New York, NY 10020. STAR WARS and related text and illustrations are trademarks and/or copyrights, in the United States and other countries, of Lucasfilm Ltd. and/or its affiliates. © & ™ Lucasfilm Ltd. No similarity between any of the names, characters, persons, and/or institutions in this magazine with those of any living or dead person or institution is intended, and any such similarity which may exist is purely coincidental. Marvel and its logos are TM Marvel Characters, Inc. **Printed in Canada.** DAN BUCKLEY, President, Marvel Entertainment; JOHN NEE, Publisher; JOE QUESADA, Chief Creative Officer; TOM BREVOORT, SVP of Publishing; DAVID BOGART, Associate Publisher & SVP of Talent Affairs; DAVID GABRIEL, SVP of Sales & Publishing, Publishing; JEFF YOUNGQUIST, VP of Production & Special Projects; DAN CARR, Executive Director of Publishing Technology; ALEX MORALES, Director of Publishing Operations; DAN EDINGTON, Managing Editor; SUSAN CRESPI, Production Manager; STAN LEE, Chairman Emeritus. For information regarding advertising in Marvel Comics or on Marvel.com, please contact Vit DeBellis, Custom Solutions & Integrated Advertising Manager, at vdebellis@marvel.com. For Marvel subscription inquiries, please call 888-511-5480. **Manufactured between 8/16/2019 and 9/17/2019 by SOLISCO PRINTERS, SCOTT, QC, CANADA.**

10 9 8 7 6 5 4 3 2 1

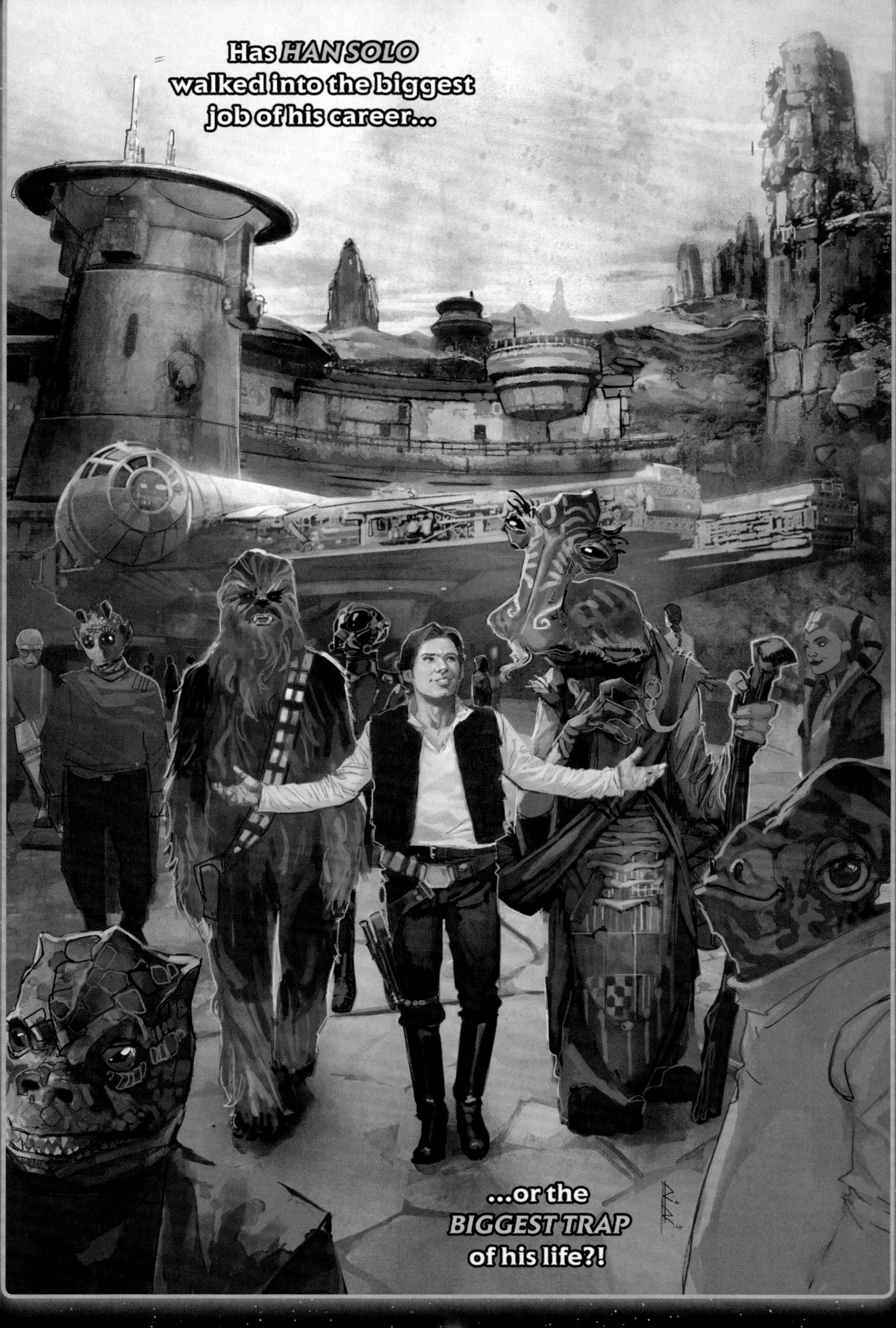
Has HAN SOLO walked into the biggest job of his career...
...or the BIGGEST TRAP of his life?!

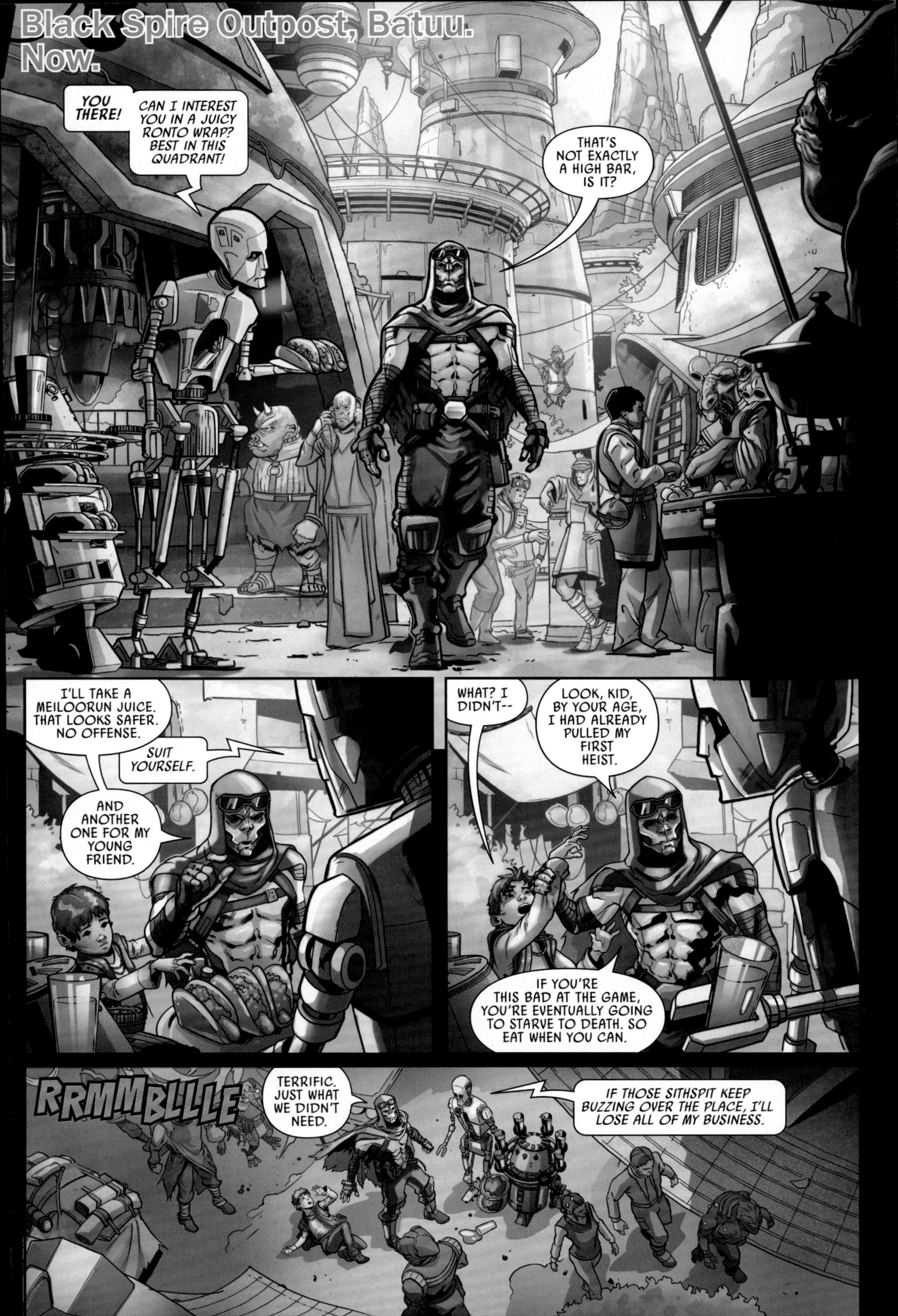
Black Spire Outpost, Batuu.
Now.
YOU THERE!
CAN I INTEREST YOU IN A JUICY RONTO WRAP? BEST IN THIS QUADRANT!
THAT'S NOT EXACTLY A HIGH BAR, IS IT?
I'LL TAKE A MEILOORUN JUICE. THAT LOOKS SAFER. NO OFFENSE.
SUIT YOURSELF.
AND ANOTHER ONE FOR MY YOUNG FRIEND.
WHAT? I DIDN'T--
LOOK, KID, BY YOUR AGE, I HAD ALREADY PULLED MY FIRST HEIST.
IF YOU'RE THIS BAD AT THE GAME, YOU'RE EVENTUALLY GOING TO STARVE TO DEATH. SO EAT WHEN YOU CAN.
RRMMBLLLE
TERRIFIC. JUST WHAT WE DIDN'T NEED.
IF THOSE SITHSPIT KEEP BUZZING OVER THE PLACE, I'LL LOSE ALL OF MY BUSINESS.

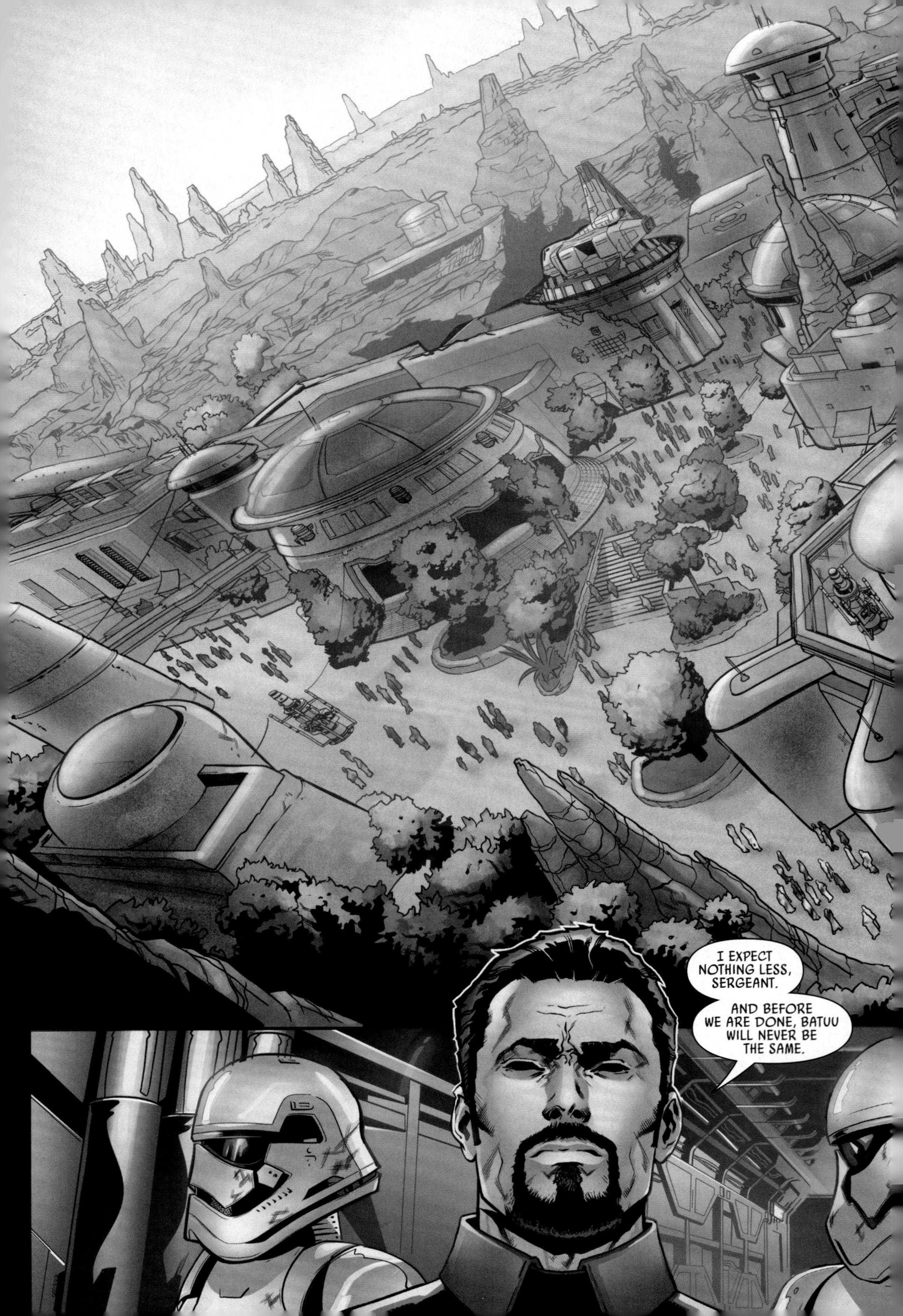
I EXPECT NOTHING LESS, SERGEANT.
AND BEFORE WE ARE DONE, BATUU WILL NEVER BE THE SAME.

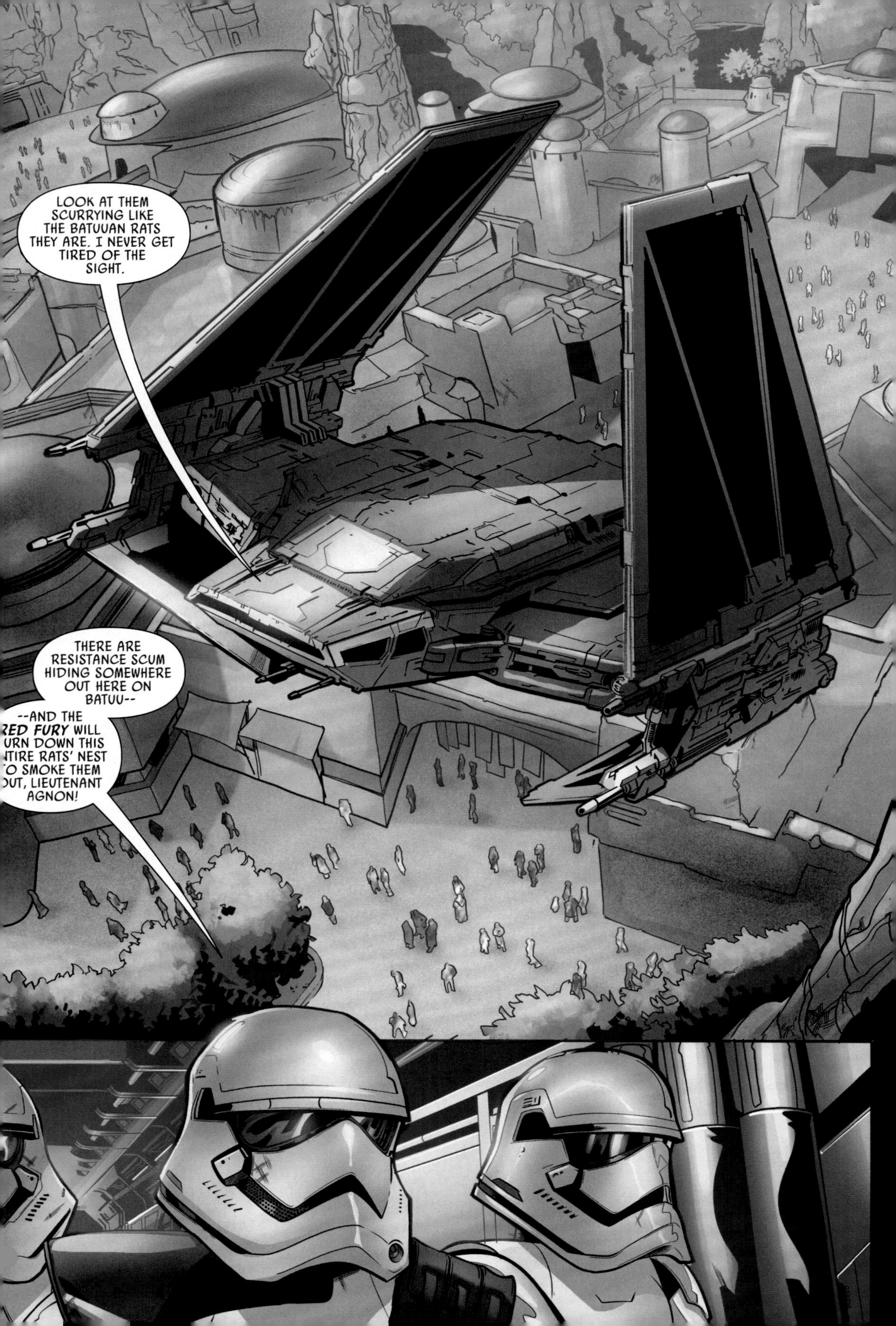
LOOK AT THEM SCURRYING LIKE THE BATUUAN RATS THEY ARE. I NEVER GET TIRED OF THE SIGHT.
THERE ARE RESISTANCE SCUM HIDING SOMEWHERE OUT HERE ON BATUU--
--AND THE RED FURY WILL URN DOWN THIS NTIRE RATS' NEST O SMOKE THEM UT, LIEUTENANT AGNON!

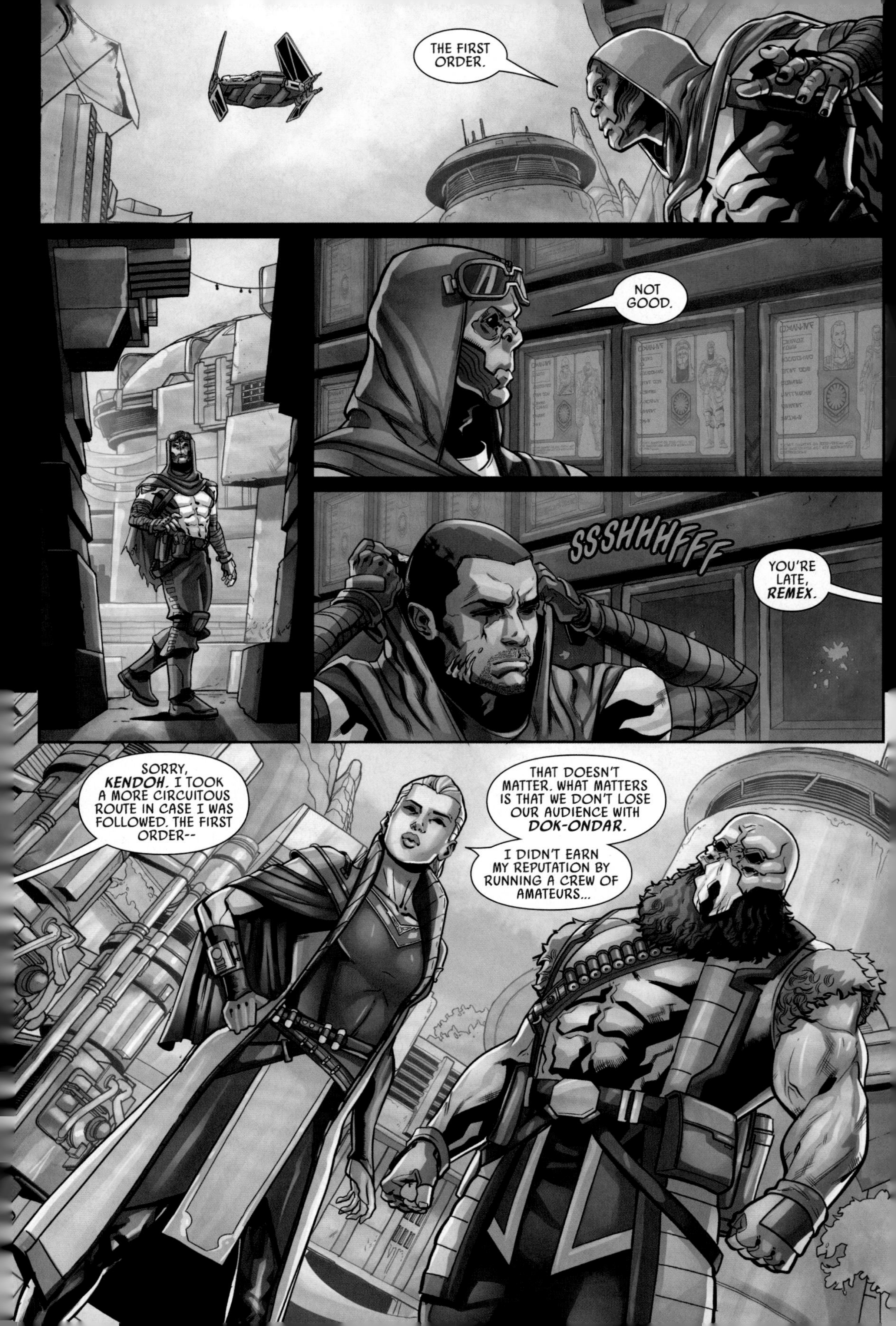
THE FIRST ORDER.
NOT GOOD.
SSSHHHFFF
YOU'RE LATE, REMEX.
SORRY, KENDOH. I TOOK A MORE CIRCUITOUS ROUTE IN CASE I WAS FOLLOWED. THE FIRST ORDER--
THAT DOESN'T MATTER. WHAT MATTERS IS THAT WE DON'T LOSE OUR AUDIENCE WITH DOK-ONDAR.
I DIDN'T EARN MY REPUTATION BY RUNNING A CREW OF AMATEURS...

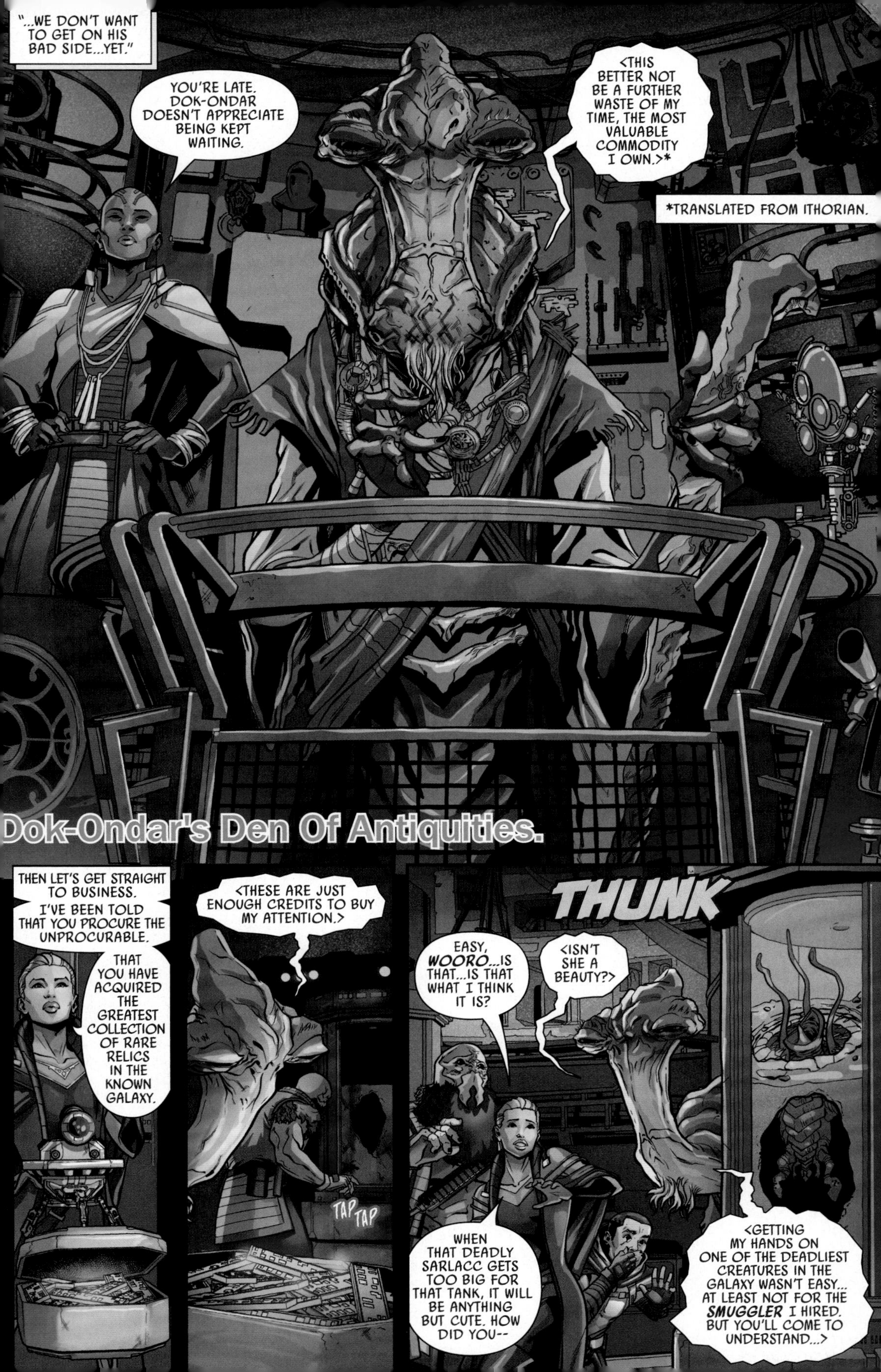
"...WE DON'T WANT TO GET ON HIS BAD SIDE...YET."
YOU'RE LATE. DOK-ONDAR DOESN'T APPRECIATE BEING KEPT WAITING.
<THIS BETTER NOT BE A FURTHER WASTE OF MY TIME, THE MOST VALUABLE COMMODITY I OWN.>*
*TRANSLATED FROM ITHORIAN.
Dok-Ondar's Den Of Antiquities.
THEN LET'S GET STRAIGHT TO BUSINESS.
I'VE BEEN TOLD THAT YOU PROCURE THE UNPROCURABLE.
THAT YOU HAVE ACQUIRED THE GREATEST COLLECTION OF RARE RELICS IN THE KNOWN GALAXY.
<THESE ARE JUST ENOUGH CREDITS TO BUY MY ATTENTION.>
TAP TAP
THUNK
EASY, WOORO...IS THAT...IS THAT WHAT I THINK IT IS?
<ISN'T SHE A BEAUTY?>
WHEN THAT DEADLY SARLACC GETS TOO BIG FOR THAT TANK, IT WILL BE ANYTHING BUT CUTE. HOW DID YOU--
<GETTING MY HANDS ON ONE OF THE DEADLIEST CREATURES IN THE GALAXY WASN'T EASY... AT LEAST NOT FOR THE SMUGGLER I HIRED. BUT YOU'LL COME TO UNDERSTAND...>

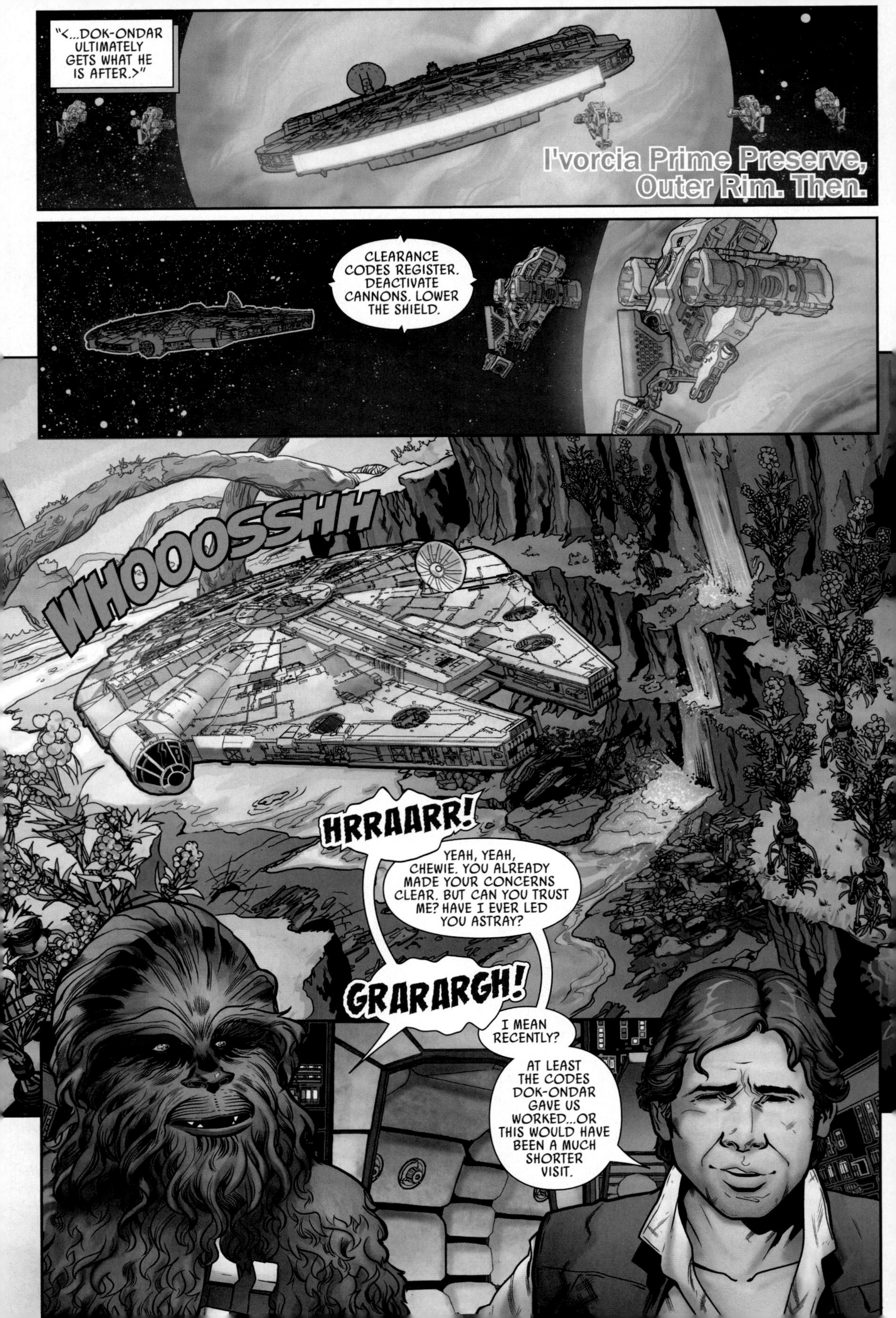

"<...DOK-ONDAR ULTIMATELY GETS WHAT HE IS AFTER.>"
I'vorcia Prime Preserve, Outer Rim. Then.
CLEARANCE CODES REGISTER. DEACTIVATE CANNONS. LOWER THE SHIELD.
WHOOOSSHH
HRRAARR!
YEAH, YEAH, CHEWIE. YOU ALREADY MADE YOUR CONCERNS CLEAR. BUT CAN YOU TRUST ME? HAVE I EVER LED YOU ASTRAY?
GRARARGH!
I MEAN RECENTLY?
AT LEAST THE CODES DOK-ONDAR GAVE US WORKED...OR THIS WOULD HAVE BEEN A MUCH SHORTER VISIT.

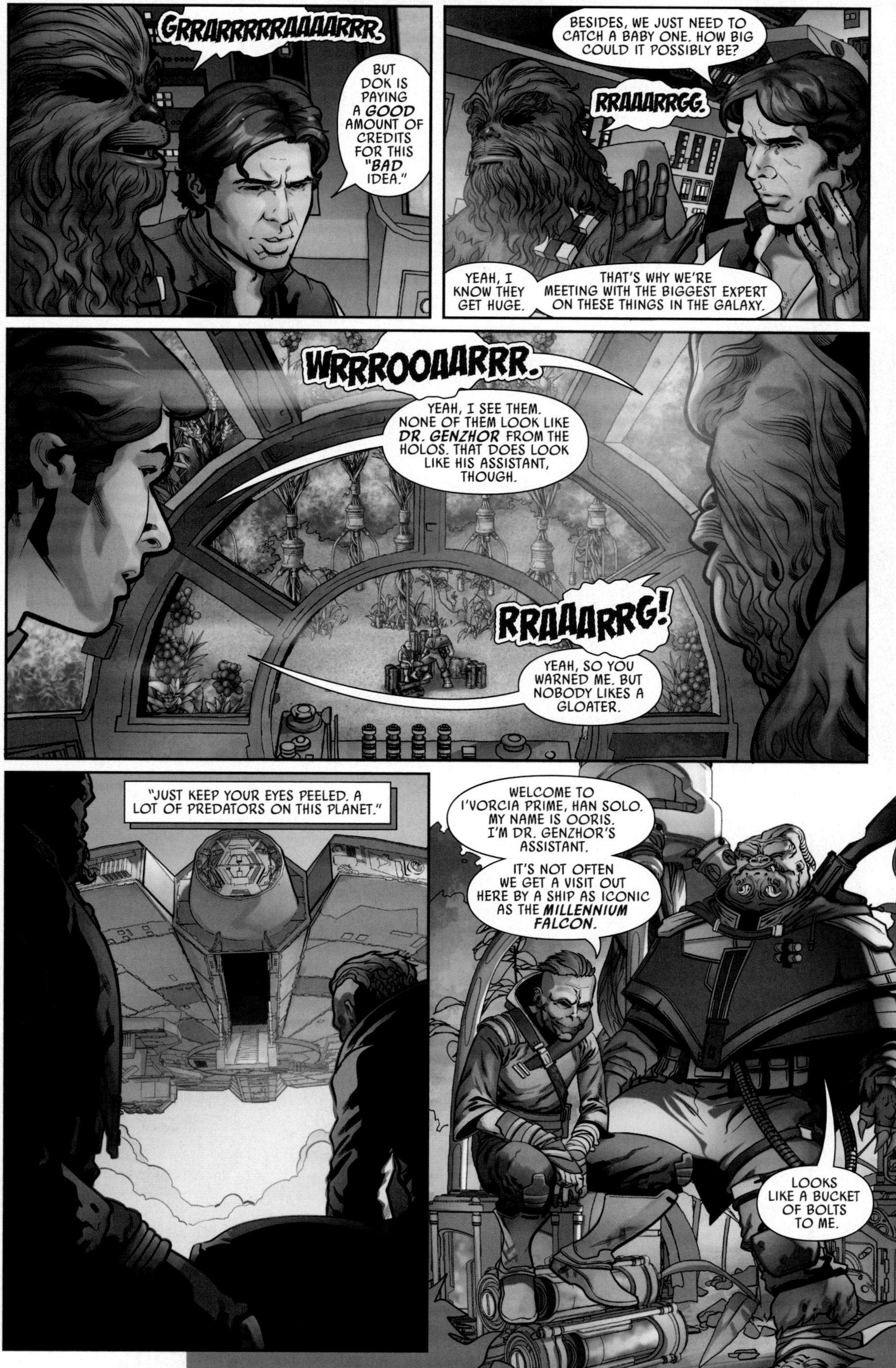
GRRARRRRRAAAARRR.
BUT DOK IS PAYING A *GOOD* AMOUNT OF CREDITS FOR THIS "*BAD* IDEA."
BESIDES, WE JUST NEED TO CATCH A BABY ONE. HOW BIG COULD IT POSSIBLY BE?
RRAAARRGG.
YEAH, I KNOW THEY GET HUGE.
THAT'S WHY WE'RE MEETING WITH THE BIGGEST EXPERT ON THESE THINGS IN THE GALAXY.
WRRROOAARRR.
YEAH, I SEE THEM. NONE OF THEM LOOK LIKE *DR. GENZHOR* FROM THE HOLOS. THAT DOES LOOK LIKE HIS ASSISTANT, THOUGH.
RRAAARRG!
YEAH, SO YOU WARNED ME. BUT NOBODY LIKES A GLOATER.
"JUST KEEP YOUR EYES PEELED. A LOT OF PREDATORS ON THIS PLANET."
WELCOME TO I'VORCIA PRIME, HAN SOLO. MY NAME IS OORIS. I'M DR. GENZHOR'S ASSISTANT.
IT'S NOT OFTEN WE GET A VISIT OUT HERE BY A SHIP AS ICONIC AS THE *MILLENNIUM FALCON.*
LOOKS LIKE A BUCKET OF BOLTS TO ME.

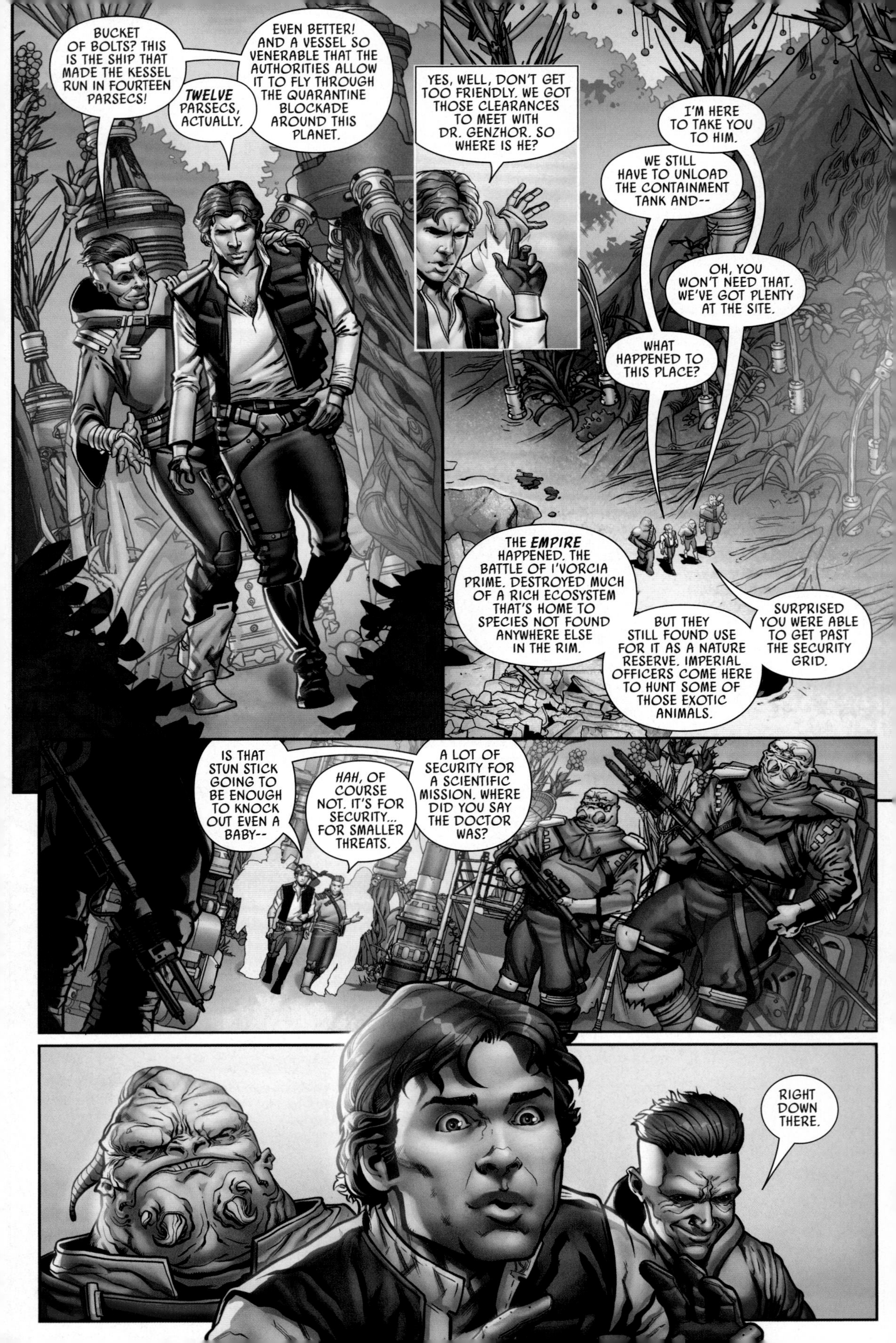
BUCKET OF BOLTS? THIS IS THE SHIP THAT MADE THE KESSEL RUN IN FOURTEEN PARSECS!
TWELVE PARSECS, ACTUALLY.
EVEN BETTER! AND A VESSEL SO VENERABLE THAT THE AUTHORITIES ALLOW IT TO FLY THROUGH THE QUARANTINE BLOCKADE AROUND THIS PLANET.
YES, WELL, DON'T GET TOO FRIENDLY. WE GOT THOSE CLEARANCES TO MEET WITH DR. GENZHOR. SO WHERE IS HE?
I'M HERE TO TAKE YOU TO HIM.
WE STILL HAVE TO UNLOAD THE CONTAINMENT TANK AND--
OH, YOU WON'T NEED THAT. WE'VE GOT PLENTY AT THE SITE.
WHAT HAPPENED TO THIS PLACE?
THE EMPIRE HAPPENED. THE BATTLE OF I'VORCIA PRIME. DESTROYED MUCH OF A RICH ECOSYSTEM THAT'S HOME TO SPECIES NOT FOUND ANYWHERE ELSE IN THE RIM.
BUT THEY STILL FOUND USE FOR IT AS A NATURE RESERVE. IMPERIAL OFFICERS COME HERE TO HUNT SOME OF THOSE EXOTIC ANIMALS.
SURPRISED YOU WERE ABLE TO GET PAST THE SECURITY GRID.
IS THAT STUN STICK GOING TO BE ENOUGH TO KNOCK OUT EVEN A BABY--
HAH, OF COURSE NOT. IT'S FOR SECURITY... FOR SMALLER THREATS.
A LOT OF SECURITY FOR A SCIENTIFIC MISSION. WHERE DID YOU SAY THE DOCTOR WAS?
RIGHT DOWN THERE.

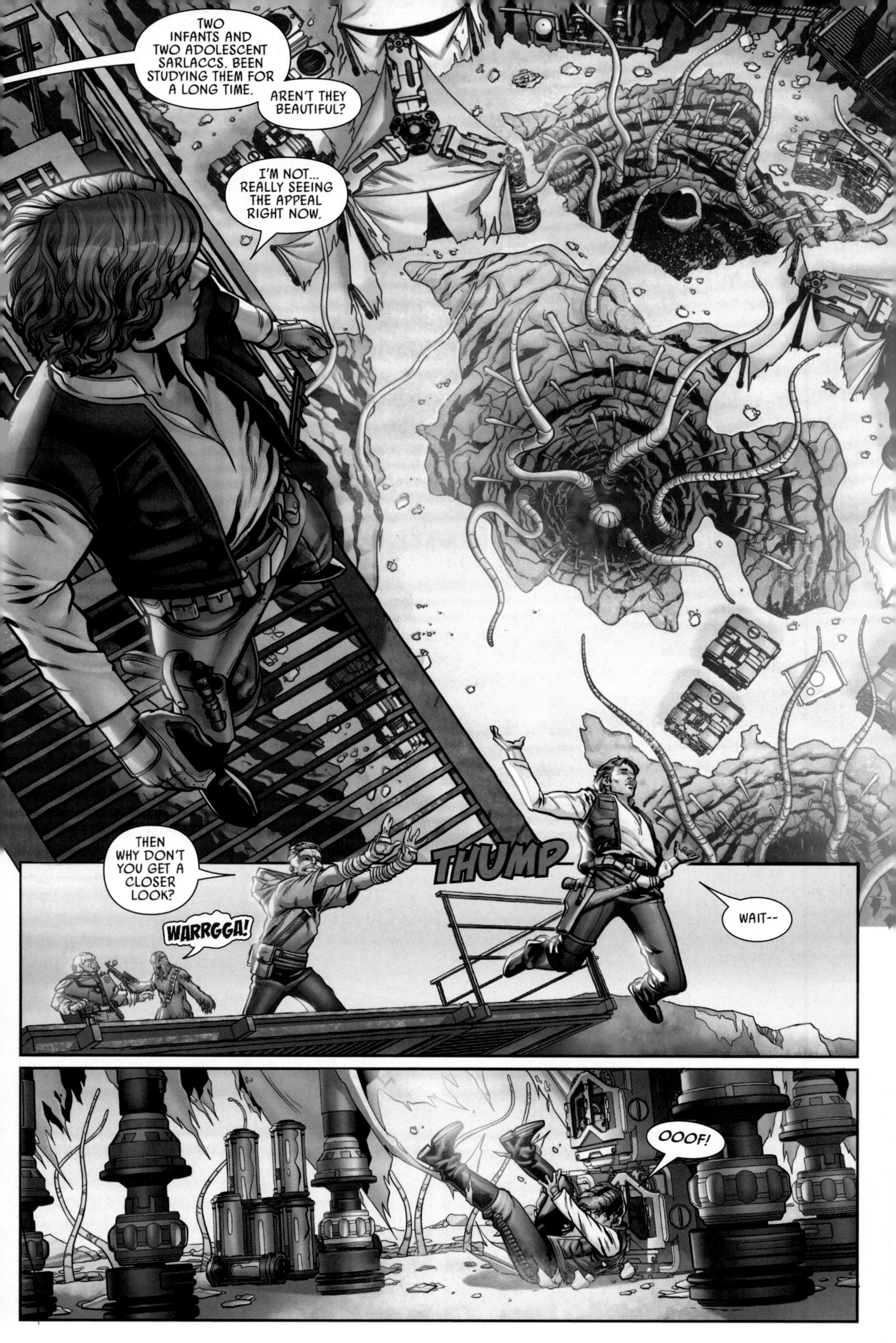
TWO INFANTS AND TWO ADOLESCENT SARLACCS. BEEN STUDYING THEM FOR A LONG TIME.
AREN'T THEY BEAUTIFUL?
I'M NOT... REALLY SEEING THE APPEAL RIGHT NOW.
THEN WHY DON'T YOU GET A CLOSER LOOK?
THUMP
WARRGGA!
WAIT--
OOOF!

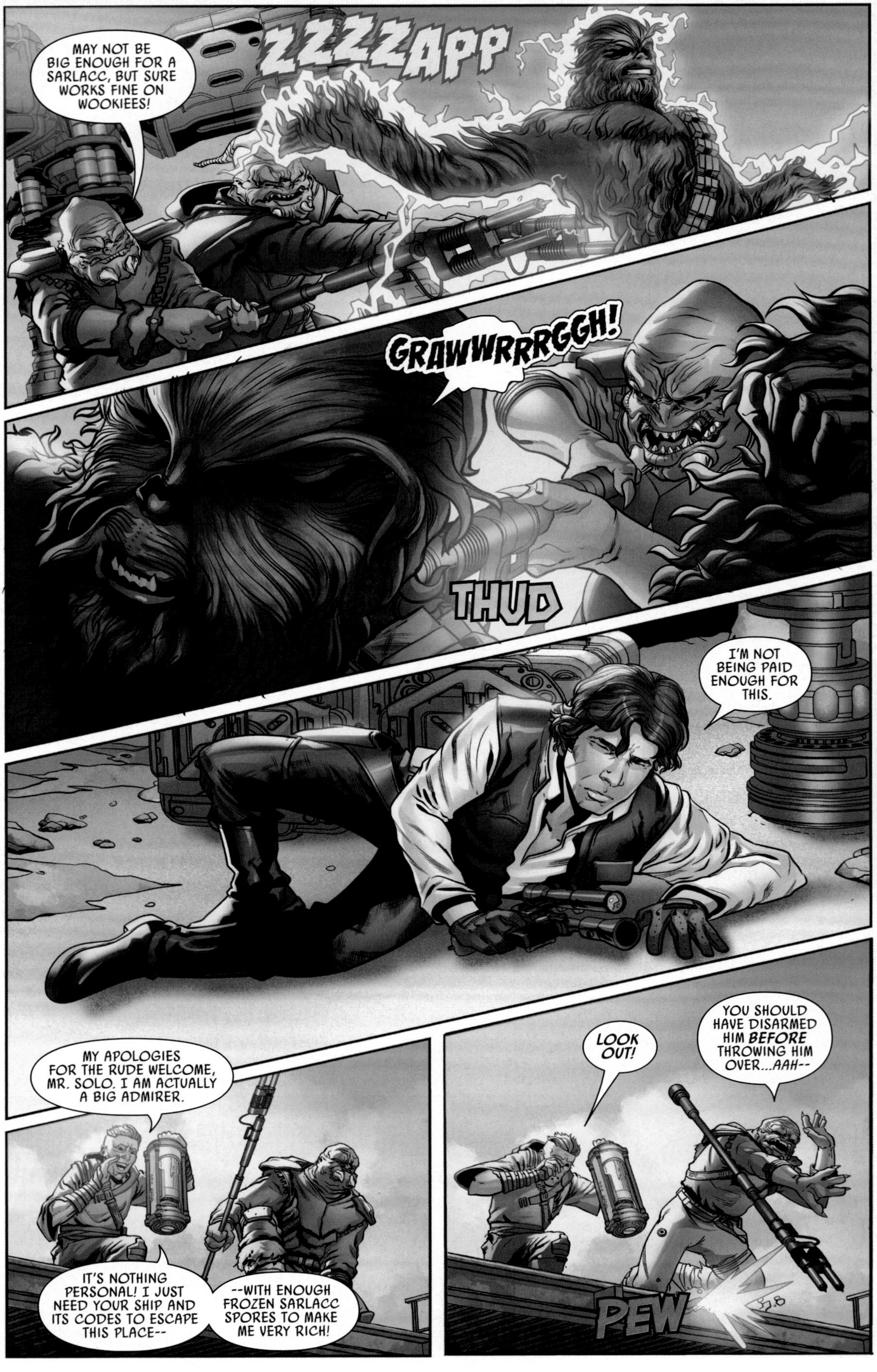

ZZZZAPP
MAY NOT BE BIG ENOUGH FOR A SARLACC, BUT SURE WORKS FINE ON WOOKIEES!
GRAWWRRRGGH!
THUD
I'M NOT BEING PAID ENOUGH FOR THIS.
MY APOLOGIES FOR THE RUDE WELCOME, MR. SOLO. I AM ACTUALLY A BIG ADMIRER.
IT'S NOTHING PERSONAL! I JUST NEED YOUR SHIP AND ITS CODES TO ESCAPE THIS PLACE--
--WITH ENOUGH FROZEN SARLACC SPORES TO MAKE ME VERY RICH!
LOOK OUT!
YOU SHOULD HAVE DISARMED HIM *BEFORE* THROWING HIM OVER...AAH--
PEW

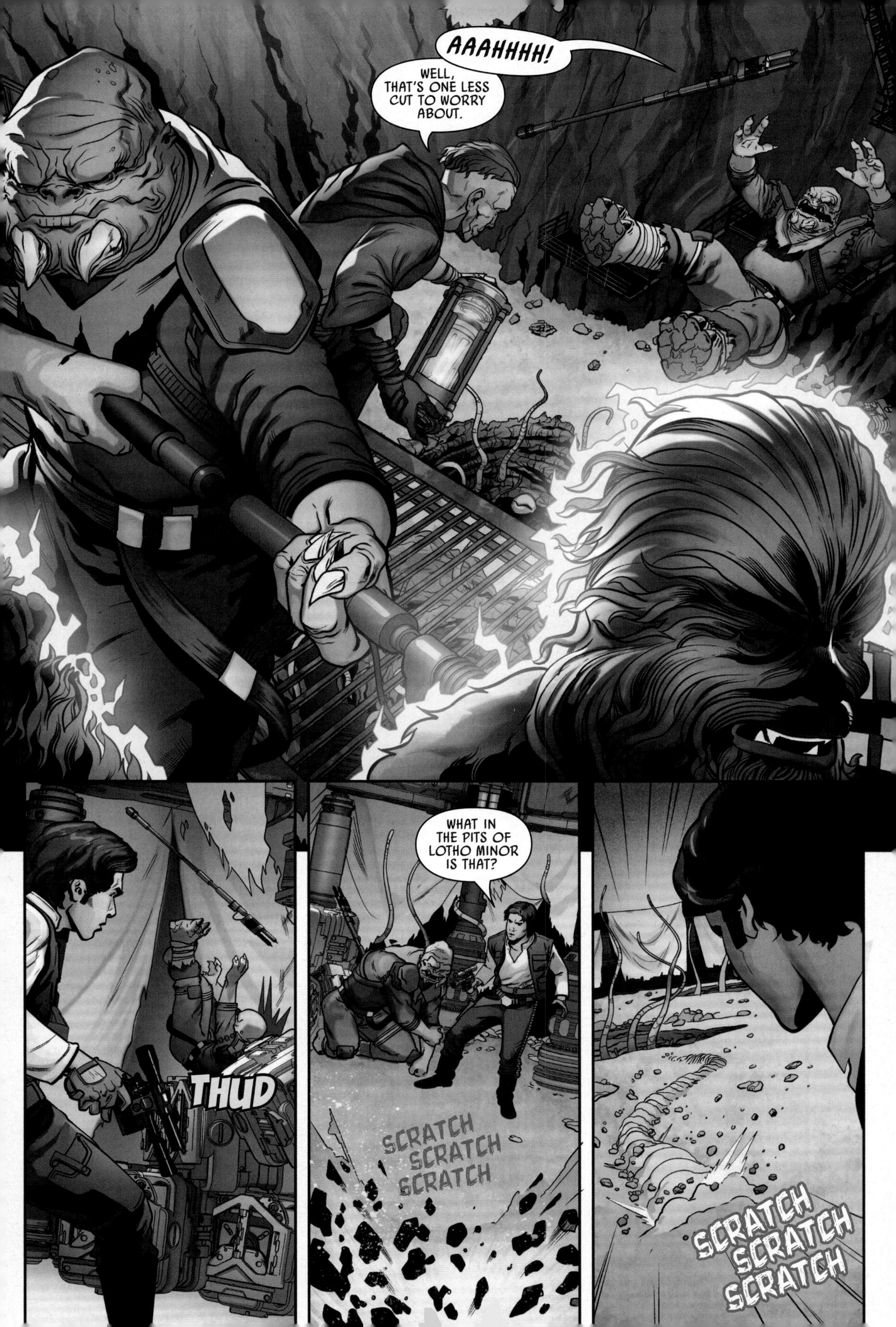
AAAHHHH!
WELL, THAT'S ONE LESS CUT TO WORRY ABOUT.
THUD
WHAT IN THE PITS OF LOTHO MINOR IS THAT?
SCRATCH SCRATCH SCRATCH
SCRATCH SCRATCH SCRATCH

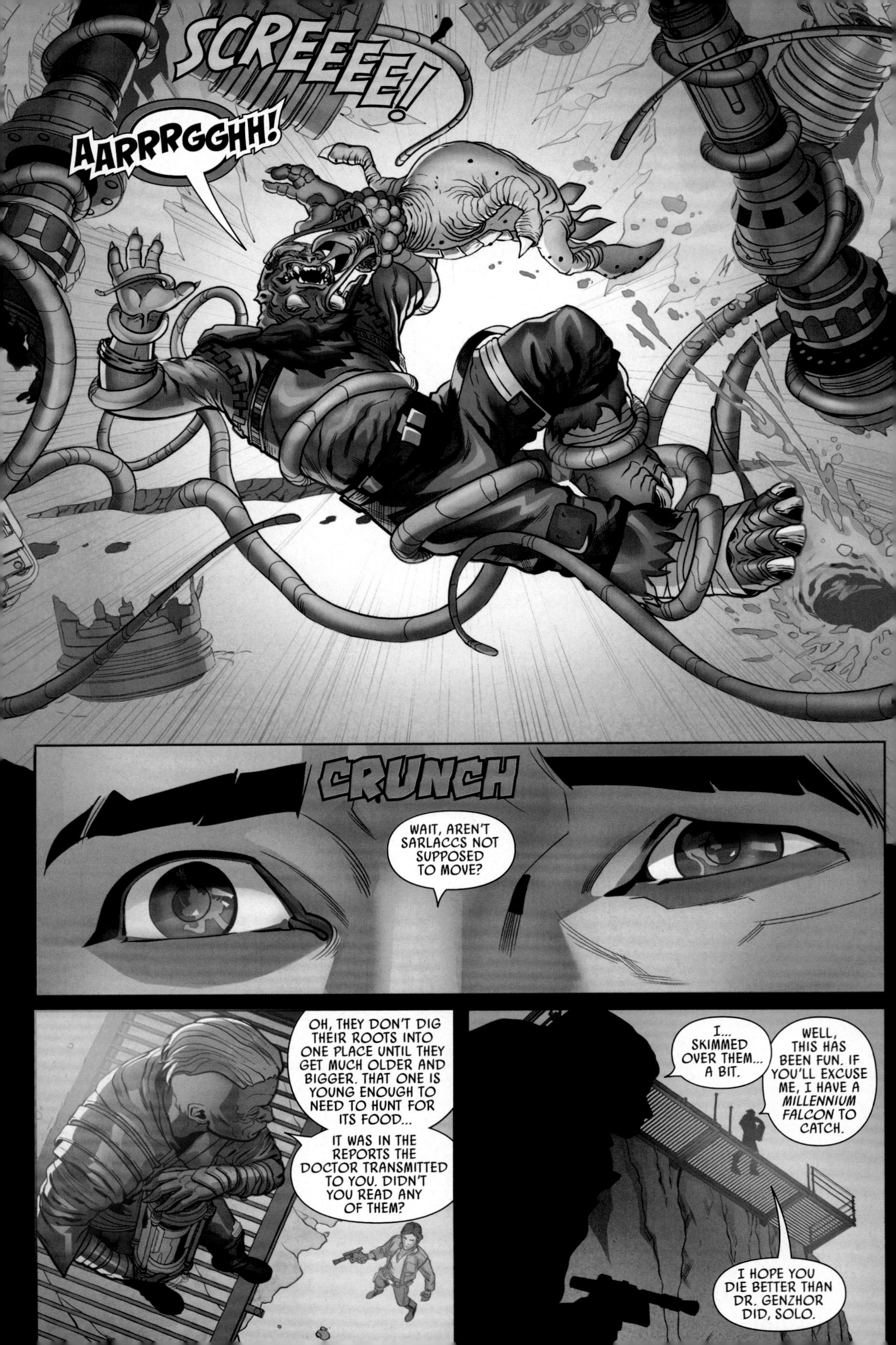
SCREEEEE!
AARRRGGHH!
CRUNCH
WAIT, AREN'T SARLACCS NOT SUPPOSED TO MOVE?
OH, THEY DON'T DIG THEIR ROOTS INTO ONE PLACE UNTIL THEY GET MUCH OLDER AND BIGGER. THAT ONE IS YOUNG ENOUGH TO NEED TO HUNT FOR ITS FOOD...
IT WAS IN THE REPORTS THE DOCTOR TRANSMITTED TO YOU. DIDN'T YOU READ ANY OF THEM?
I... SKIMMED OVER THEM... A BIT.
WELL, THIS HAS BEEN FUN. IF YOU'LL EXCUSE ME, I HAVE A *MILLENNIUM FALCON* TO CATCH.
I HOPE YOU DIE BETTER THAN DR. GENZHOR DID, SOLO.

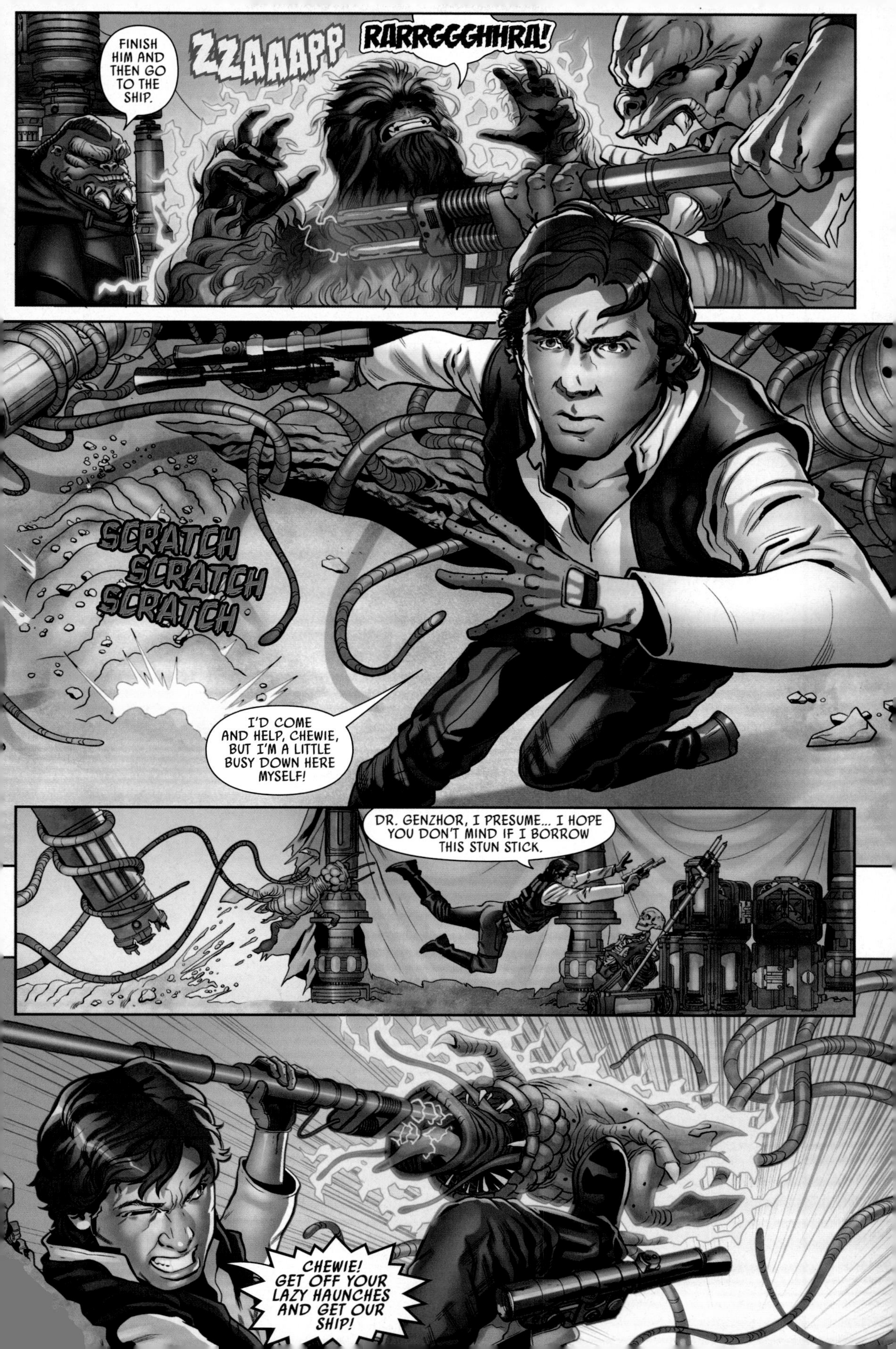
FINISH HIM AND THEN GO TO THE SHIP.
ZZAAAPP
RARRGGGHHRA!
SCRATCH SCRATCH SCRATCH
I'D COME AND HELP, CHEWIE, BUT I'M A LITTLE BUSY DOWN HERE MYSELF!
DR. GENZHOR, I PRESUME... I HOPE YOU DON'T MIND IF I BORROW THIS STUN STICK.
CHEWIE! GET OFF YOUR LAZY HAUNCHES AND GET OUR SHIP!

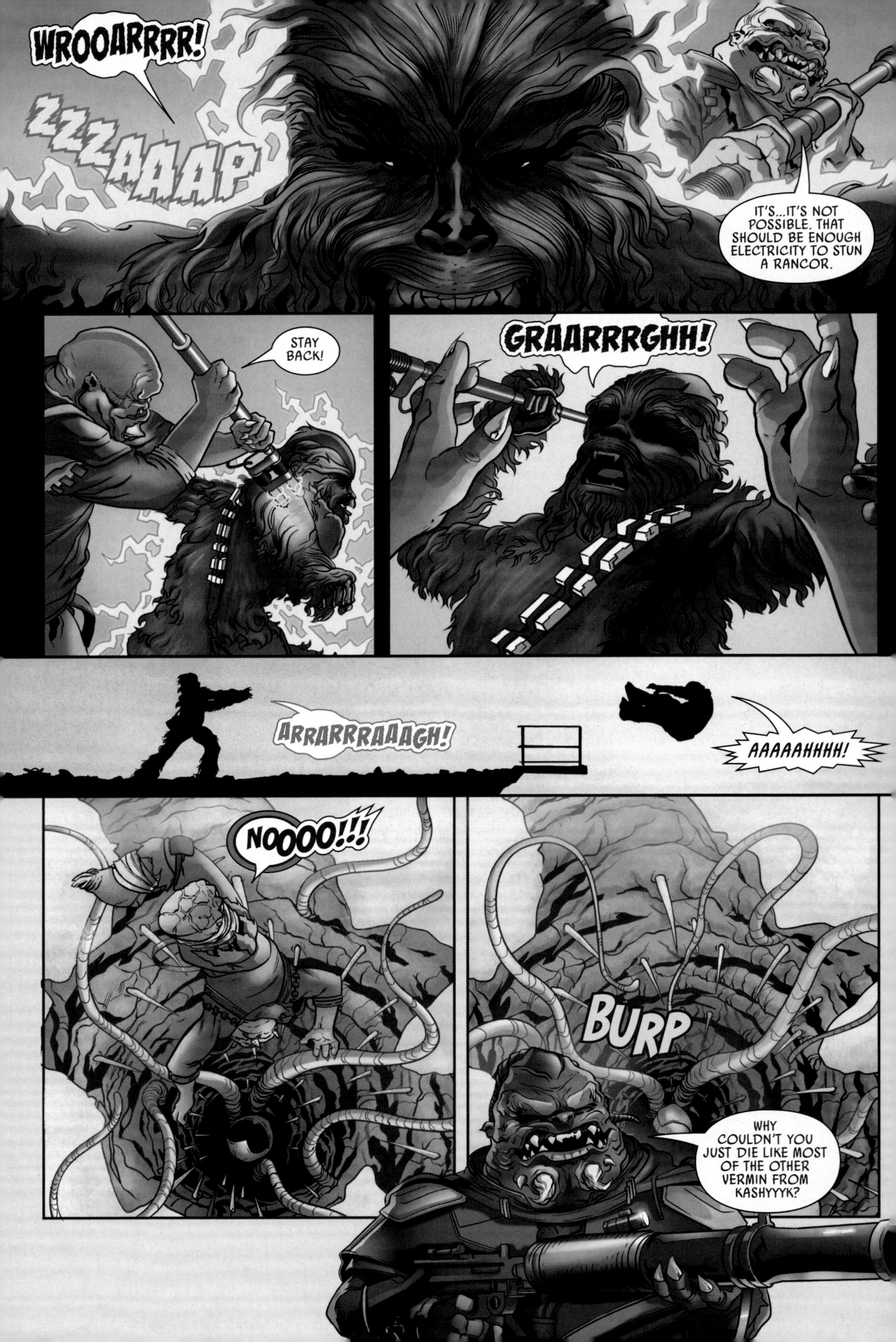

WROOARRRR!
ZZZAAAAP
IT'S...IT'S NOT POSSIBLE. THAT SHOULD BE ENOUGH ELECTRICITY TO STUN A RANCOR.
STAY BACK!
GRAARRRGHH!
ARRARRRAAAGH!
AAAAAHHHH!
NOOOO!!!
BURP
WHY COULDN'T YOU JUST DIE LIKE MOST OF THE OTHER VERMIN FROM KASHYYYK?

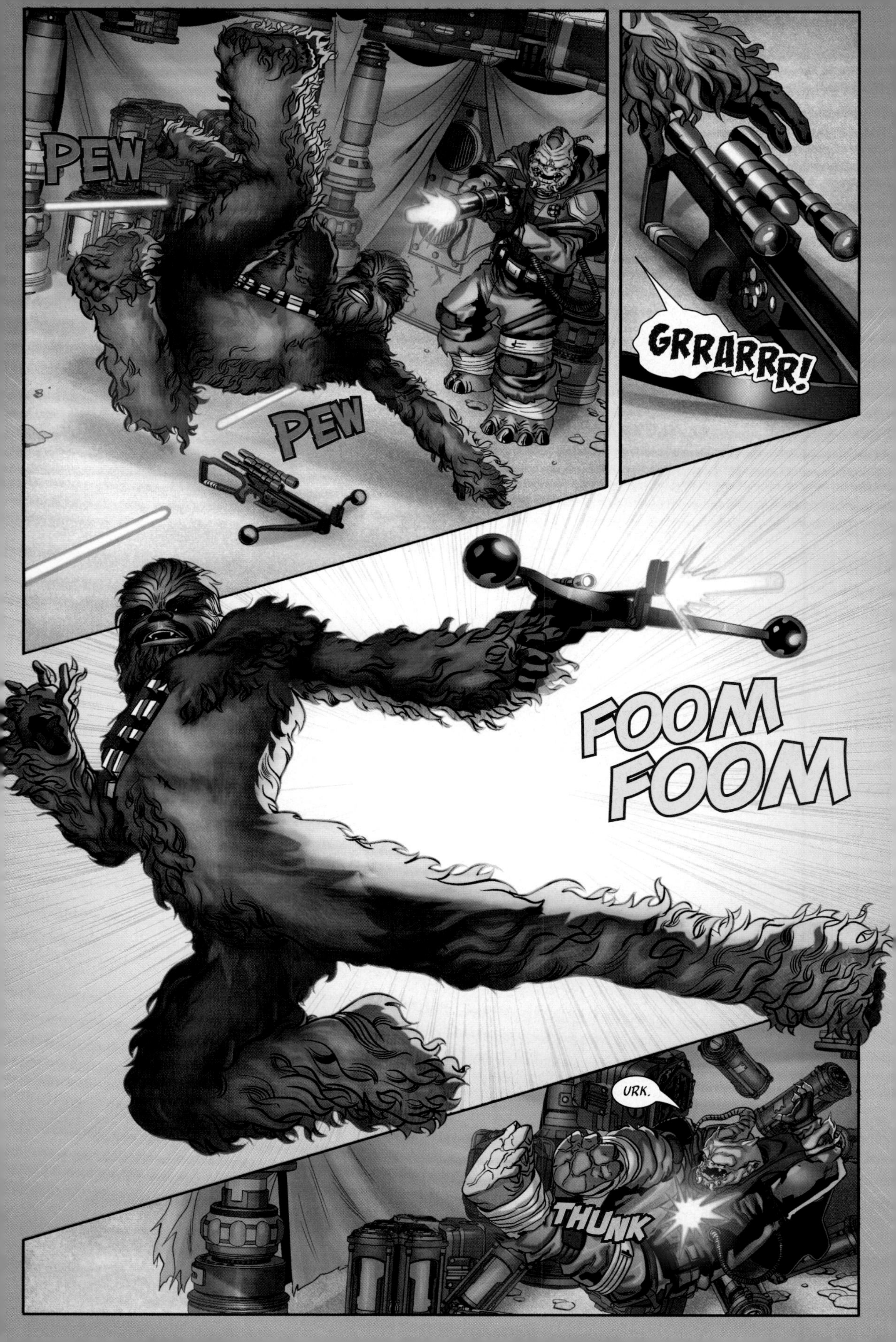
PEW
PEW
GRRARRRR!
FOOM
FOOM
URK.
THUNK

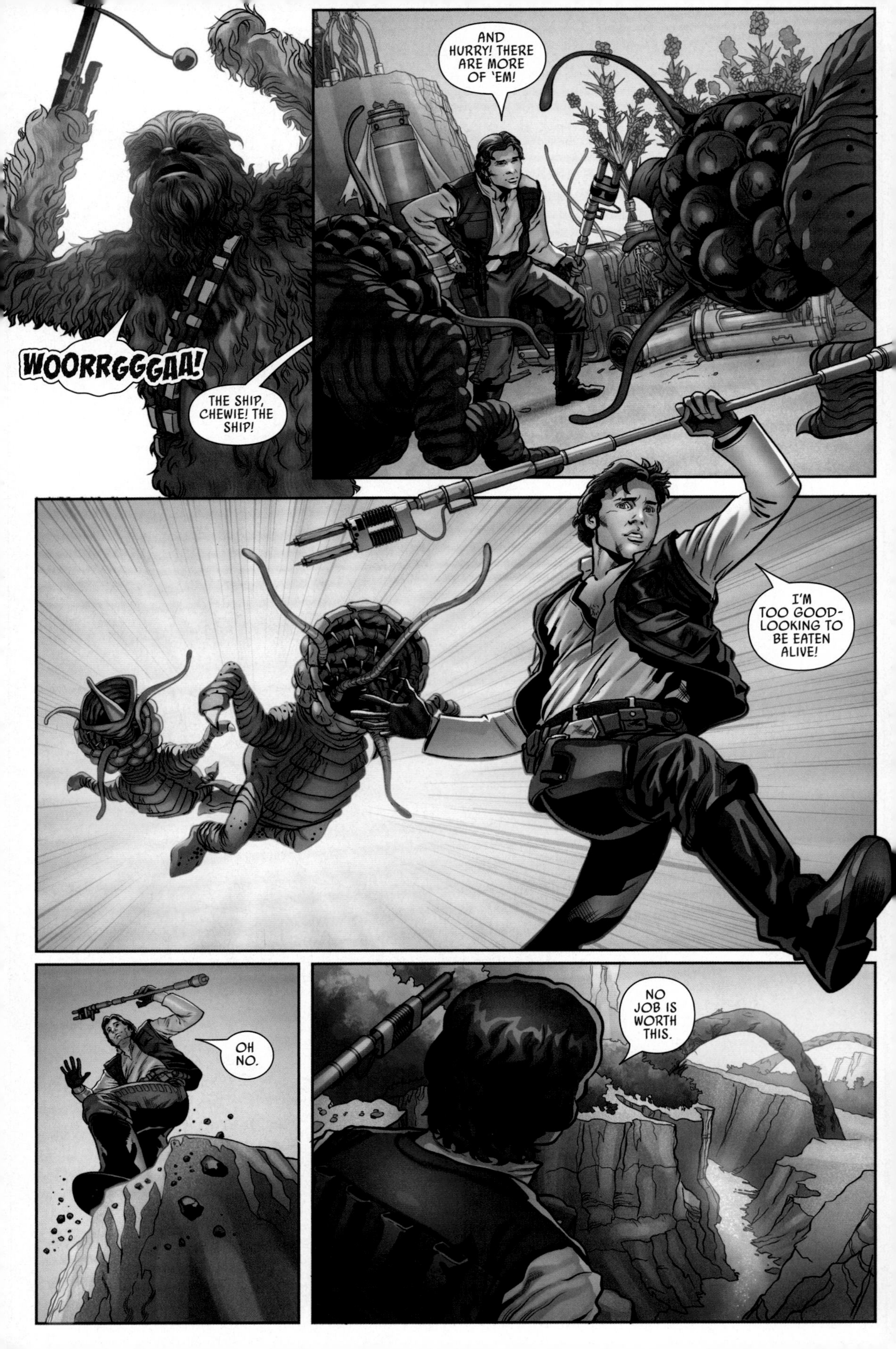
AND HURRY! THERE ARE MORE OF 'EM!
WOORRGGGAA!
THE SHIP, CHEWIE! THE SHIP!
I'M TOO GOOD-LOOKING TO BE EATEN ALIVE!
OH NO.
NO JOB IS WORTH THIS.

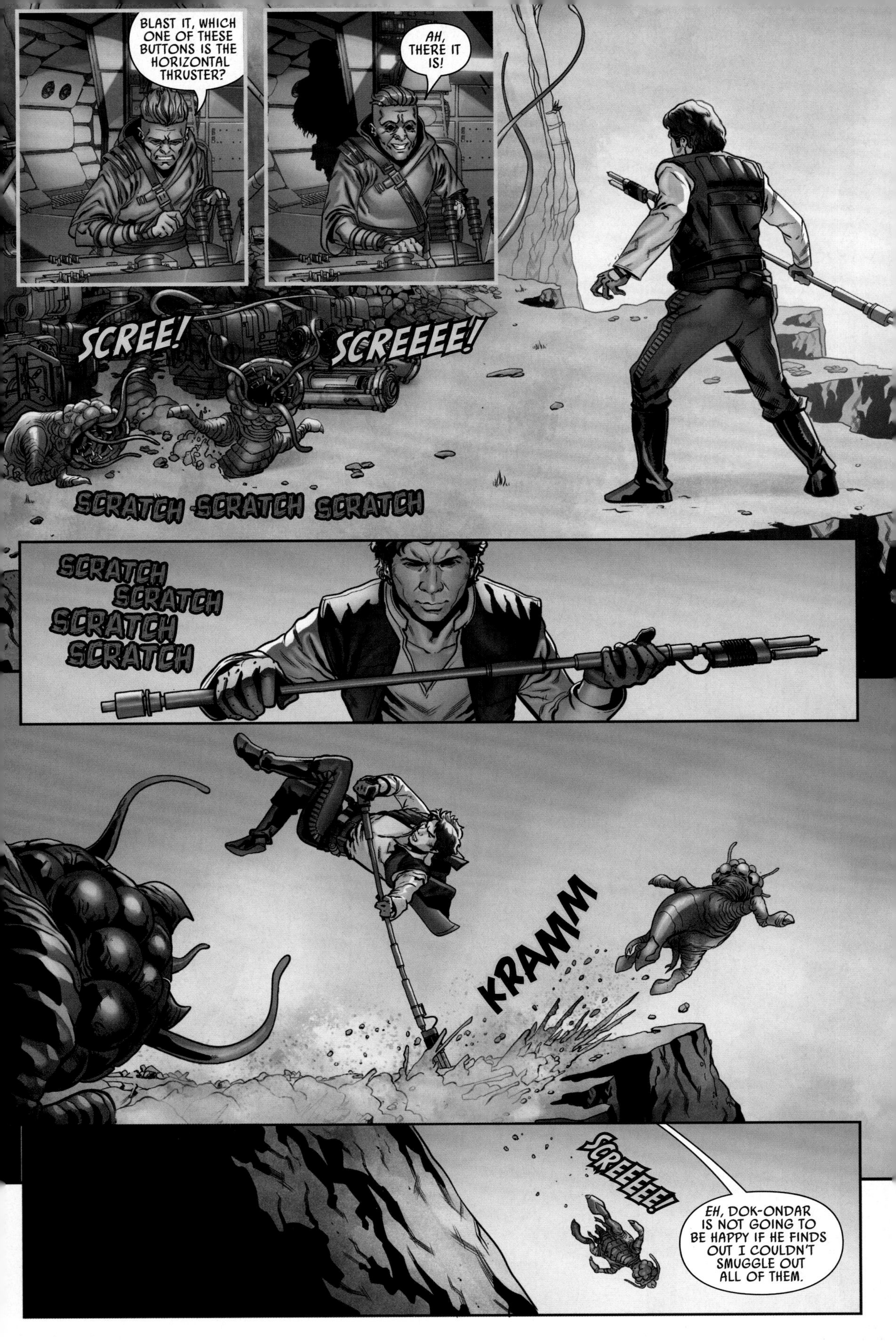

BLAST IT, WHICH ONE OF THESE BUTTONS IS THE HORIZONTAL THRUSTER?
AH, THERE IT IS!
SCREE!
SCREEEE!
SCRATCH SCRATCH SCRATCH
SCRATCH SCRATCH SCRATCH SCRATCH
KRAMM
SCREEEEE!
EH, DOK-ONDAR IS NOT GOING TO BE HAPPY IF HE FINDS OUT I COULDN'T SMUGGLE OUT ALL OF THEM.

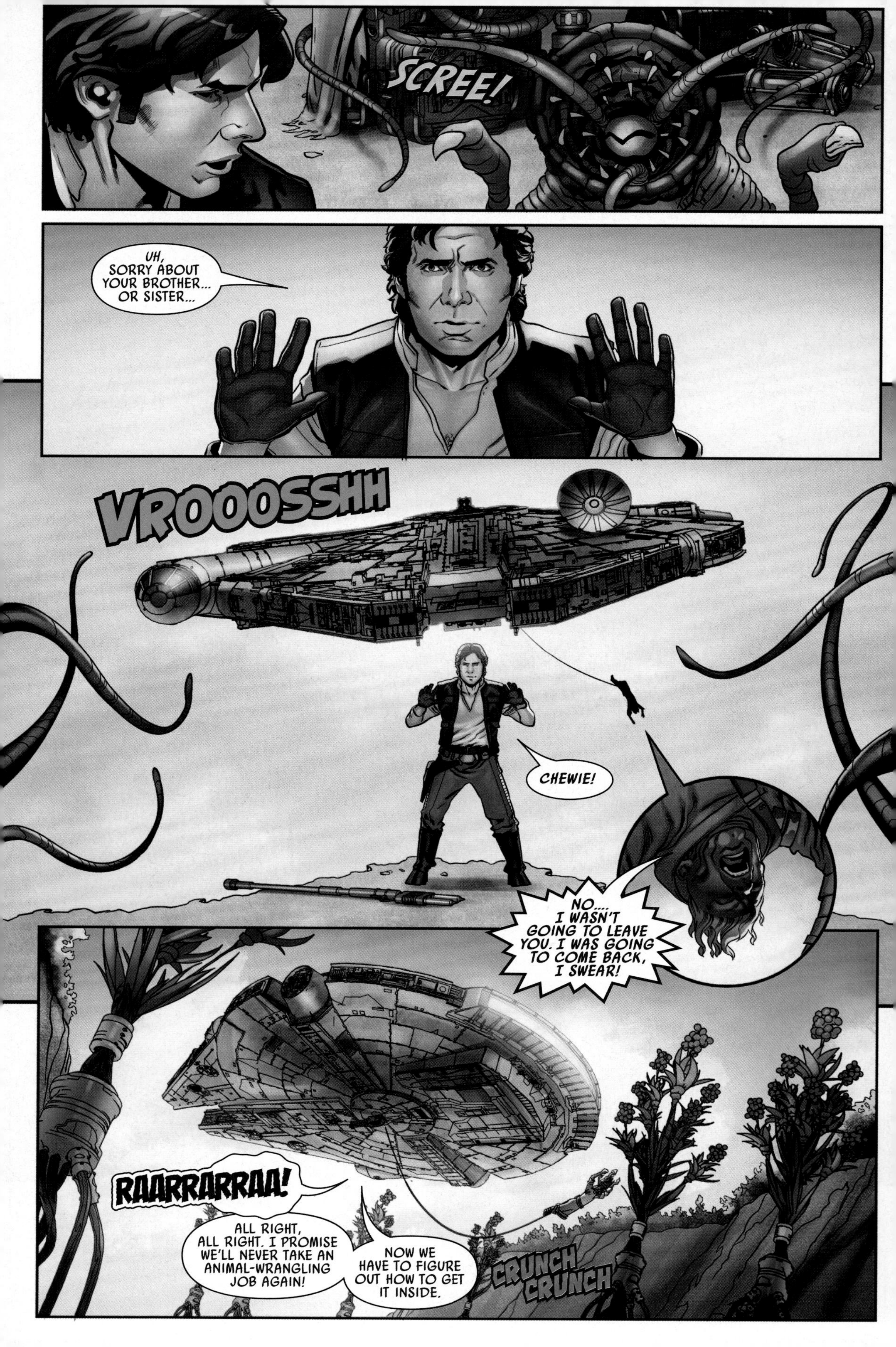
SCREE!
UH, SORRY ABOUT YOUR BROTHER... OR SISTER...
VROOOSSHH
CHEWIE!
NO.... I WASN'T GOING TO LEAVE YOU. I WAS GOING TO COME BACK, I SWEAR!
RAARRARRAA!
ALL RIGHT, ALL RIGHT. I PROMISE WE'LL NEVER TAKE AN ANIMAL-WRANGLING JOB AGAIN!
NOW WE HAVE TO FIGURE OUT HOW TO GET IT INSIDE.
CRUNCH CRUNCH

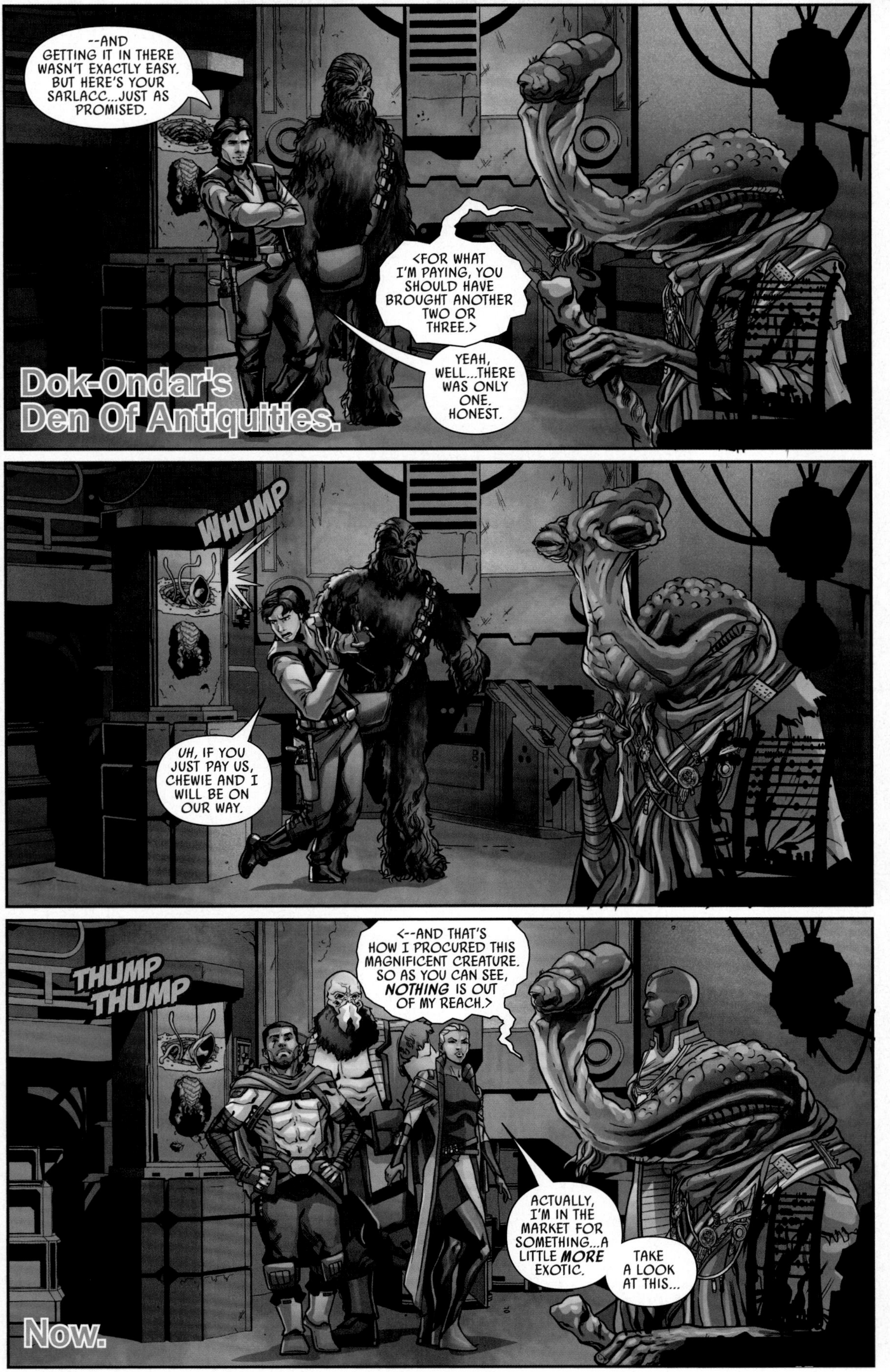
--AND GETTING IT IN THERE WASN'T EXACTLY EASY. BUT HERE'S YOUR SARLACC...JUST AS PROMISED.
<FOR WHAT I'M PAYING, YOU SHOULD HAVE BROUGHT ANOTHER TWO OR THREE.>
YEAH, WELL...THERE WAS ONLY ONE. HONEST.
Dok-Ondar's Den Of Antiquities.
WHUMP
UH, IF YOU JUST PAY US, CHEWIE AND I WILL BE ON OUR WAY.
THUMP THUMP
<--AND THAT'S HOW I PROCURED THIS MAGNIFICENT CREATURE. SO AS YOU CAN SEE, ***NOTHING*** IS OUT OF MY REACH.>
ACTUALLY, I'M IN THE MARKET FOR SOMETHING...A LITTLE ***MORE*** EXOTIC.
TAKE A LOOK AT THIS...
Now.

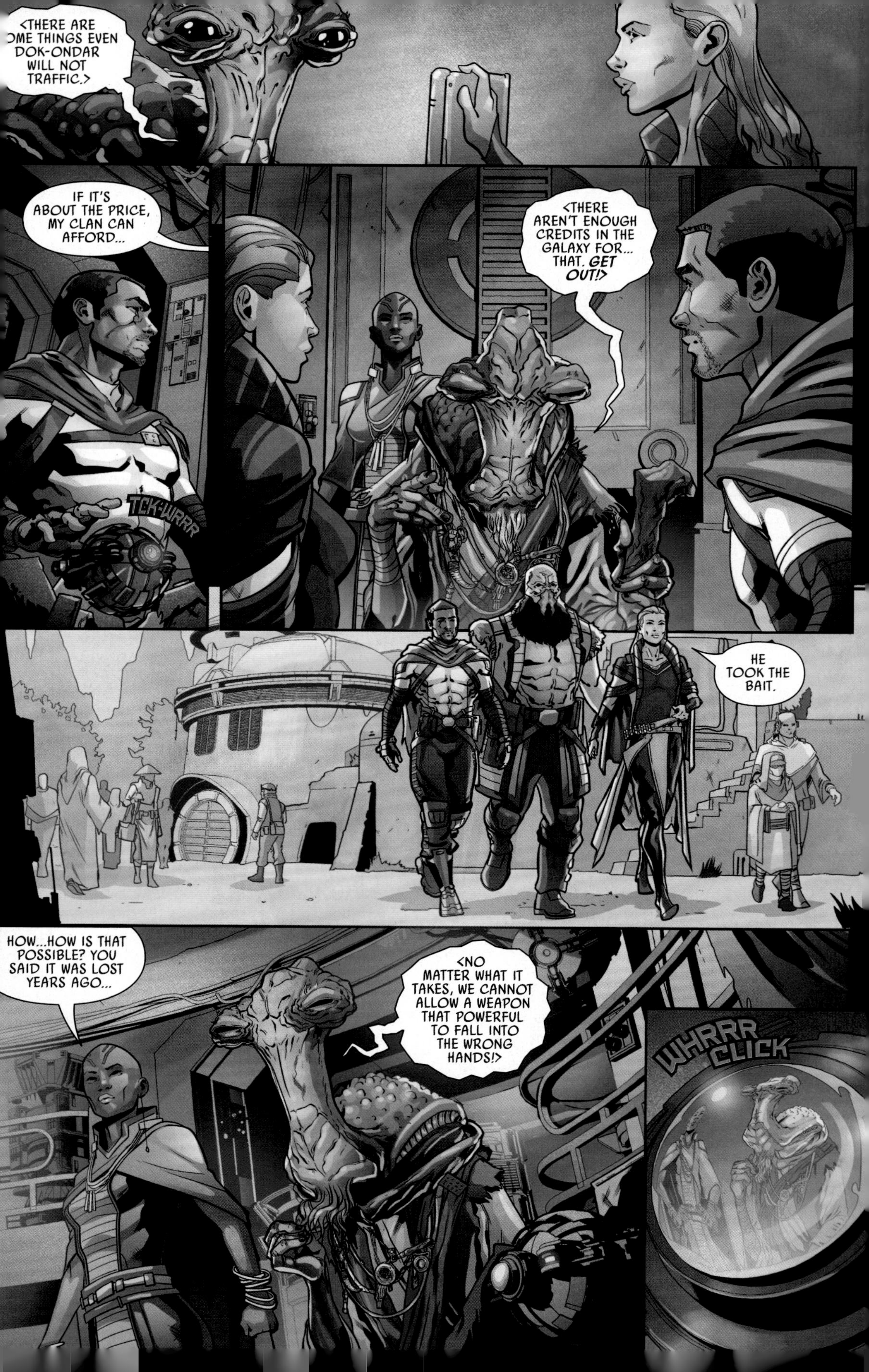
<THERE ARE OME THINGS EVEN DOK-ONDAR WILL NOT TRAFFIC.>
IF IT'S ABOUT THE PRICE, MY CLAN CAN AFFORD...
TCK-WRRR
<THERE AREN'T ENOUGH CREDITS IN THE GALAXY FOR... THAT. **GET OUT!**>
HE TOOK THE BAIT.
HOW...HOW IS THAT POSSIBLE? YOU SAID IT WAS LOST YEARS AGO...
<NO MATTER WHAT IT TAKES, WE CANNOT ALLOW A WEAPON THAT POWERFUL TO FALL INTO THE WRONG HANDS!>
WHRRR CLICK

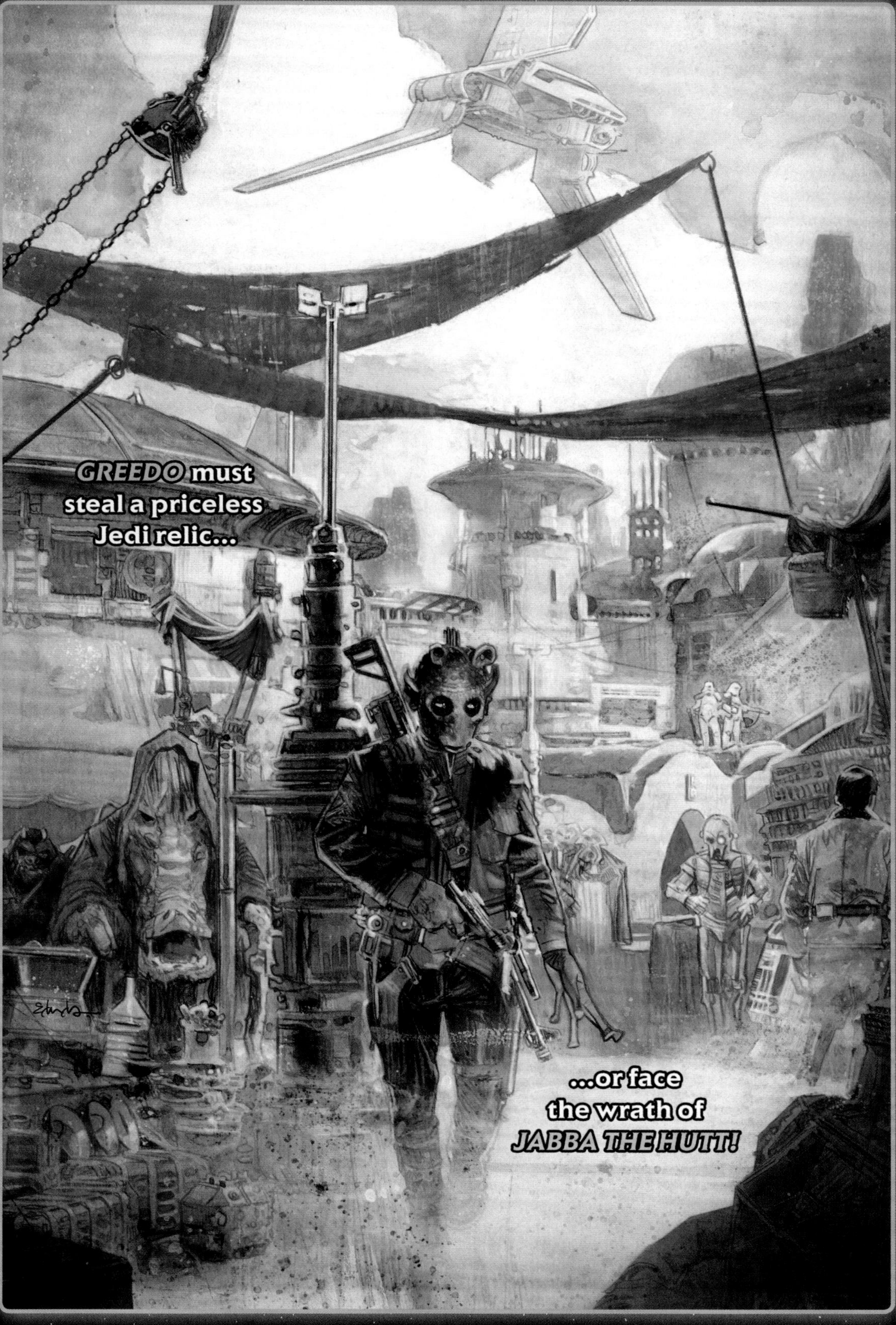
GREEDO must steal a priceless Jedi relic...
...or face the wrath of JABBA THE HUTT!

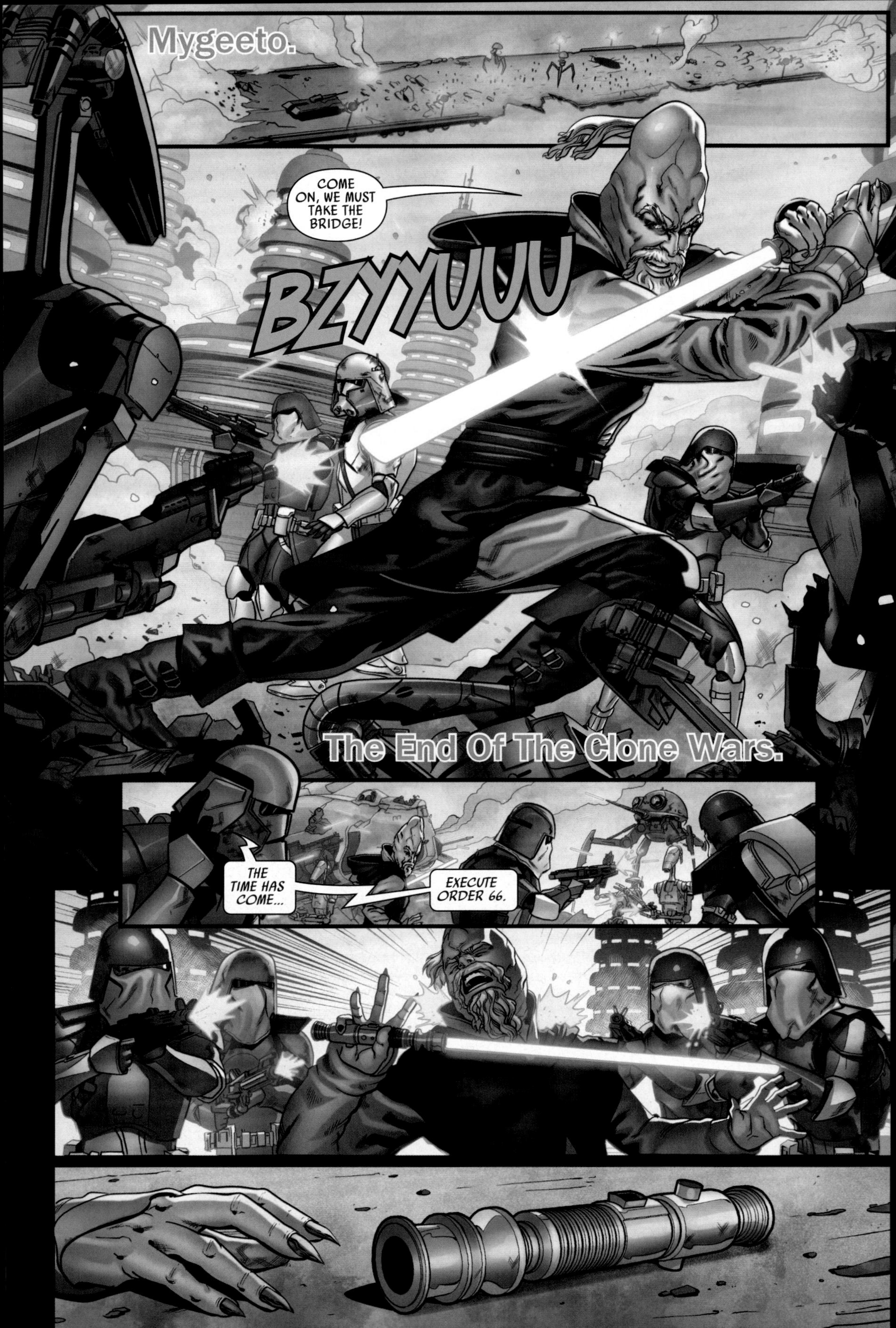
Mygeeto.
COME ON, WE MUST TAKE THE BRIDGE!
BZYYUUU
The End Of The Clone Wars.
THE TIME HAS COME...
EXECUTE ORDER 66.

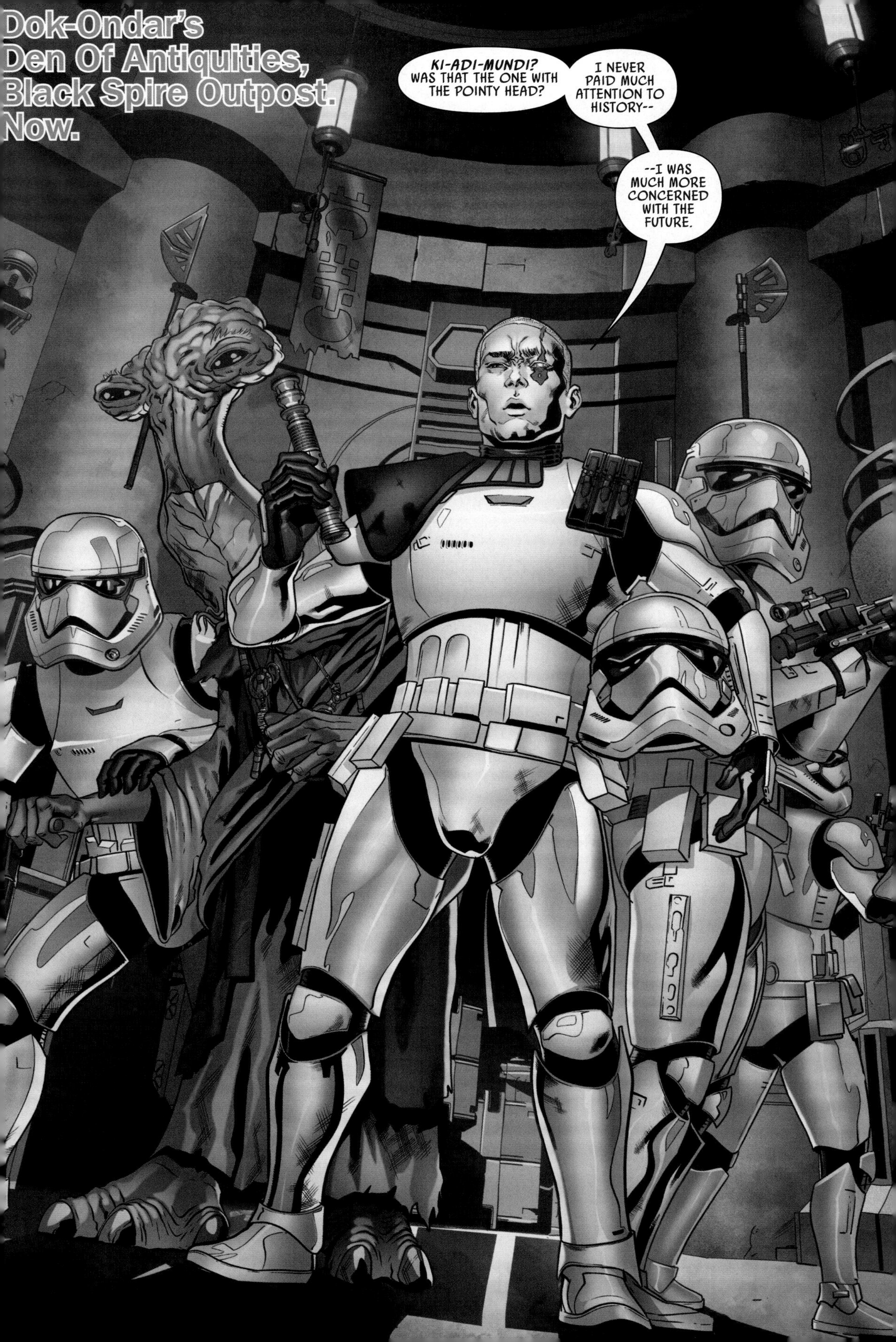
Dok-Ondar's Den Of Antiquities, Black Spire Outpost. Now.
KI-ADI-MUNDI? WAS THAT THE ONE WITH THE POINTY HEAD?
I NEVER PAID MUCH ATTENTION TO HISTORY--
--I WAS MUCH MORE CONCERNED WITH THE FUTURE.

ZZHHOOOM

DO YOU BELIEVE IN THE FUTURE, DOK-ONDAR?

ᴊᴢᴡᴇ ᴇxᴇᴄᴋ ᴊᴇ ᴀᴇ ᴊx ᴇxᴀᴋᴇᴄ x ᴀᴇᴇᴇxᴋ ᴀᴇᴈ, ᴇᴊᴋᴊᴀᴇ ᴀᴇx ᴀᴈᴀ ᴀᴄᴊxᴊᴇᴍ.

I CAN'T SPEAK BLASTED ITHORIAN...

DOK-ONDAR SAYS THERE IS NO NEED FOR THREATS, SERGEANT. HE IS JUST A HUMBLE STORE PROPRIETOR WITH NOTHING BUT... RESPECT...FOR THE FIRST ORDER.

OH, COME NOW, DOK-ONDAR. DO NOT SELL YOURSELF SHORT.

YOUR DEN IS RENOWNED ACROSS THE GALAXY FOR BEING THE PLACE TO ACQUIRE JUST ABOUT ANY RELIC OR SYMBOL OF CONSEQUENCE... FOR THE RIGHT PRICE.

ZYUMM

THE TYPE OF PLACE RESISTANCE SPIES MIGHT SEEK OUT IF THEY WERE LOOKING FOR SOMETHING TO HELP TURN THE TIDE OF THE WAR--

--A JEDI WEAPON PERHAPS.

CLIK-WWRRRR

A NEW DAWN IS COMING, DOK-ONDAR. AND IT WON'T BE LONG BEFORE OWNING JEDI WEAPONS WILL ONCE AGAIN BE A CRIME WITH CONSEQUENCES...

WHRRR

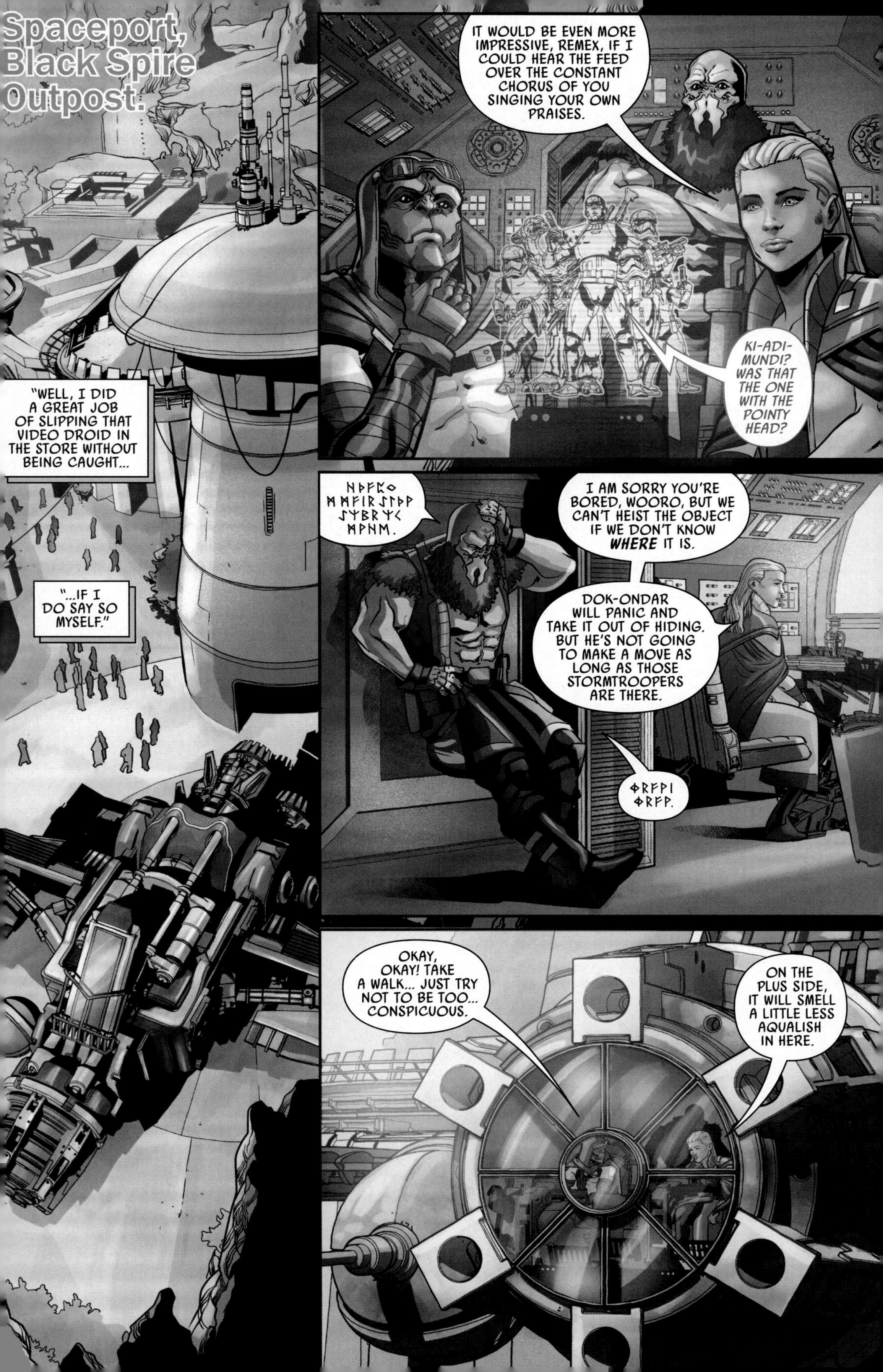

Spaceport, Black Spire Outpost.
"WELL, I DID A GREAT JOB OF SLIPPING THAT VIDEO DROID IN THE STORE WITHOUT BEING CAUGHT...
"...IF I DO SAY SO MYSELF."
IT WOULD BE EVEN MORE IMPRESSIVE, REMEX, IF I COULD HEAR THE FEED OVER THE CONSTANT CHORUS OF YOU SINGING YOUR OWN PRAISES.
KI-ADI-MUNDI? WAS THAT THE ONE WITH THE POINTY HEAD?
I AM SORRY YOU'RE BORED, WOORO, BUT WE CAN'T HEIST THE OBJECT IF WE DON'T KNOW WHERE IT IS.
DOK-ONDAR WILL PANIC AND TAKE IT OUT OF HIDING. BUT HE'S NOT GOING TO MAKE A MOVE AS LONG AS THOSE STORMTROOPERS ARE THERE.
OKAY, OKAY! TAKE A WALK... JUST TRY NOT TO BE TOO... CONSPICUOUS.
ON THE PLUS SIDE, IT WILL SMELL A LITTLE LESS AQUALISH IN HERE.

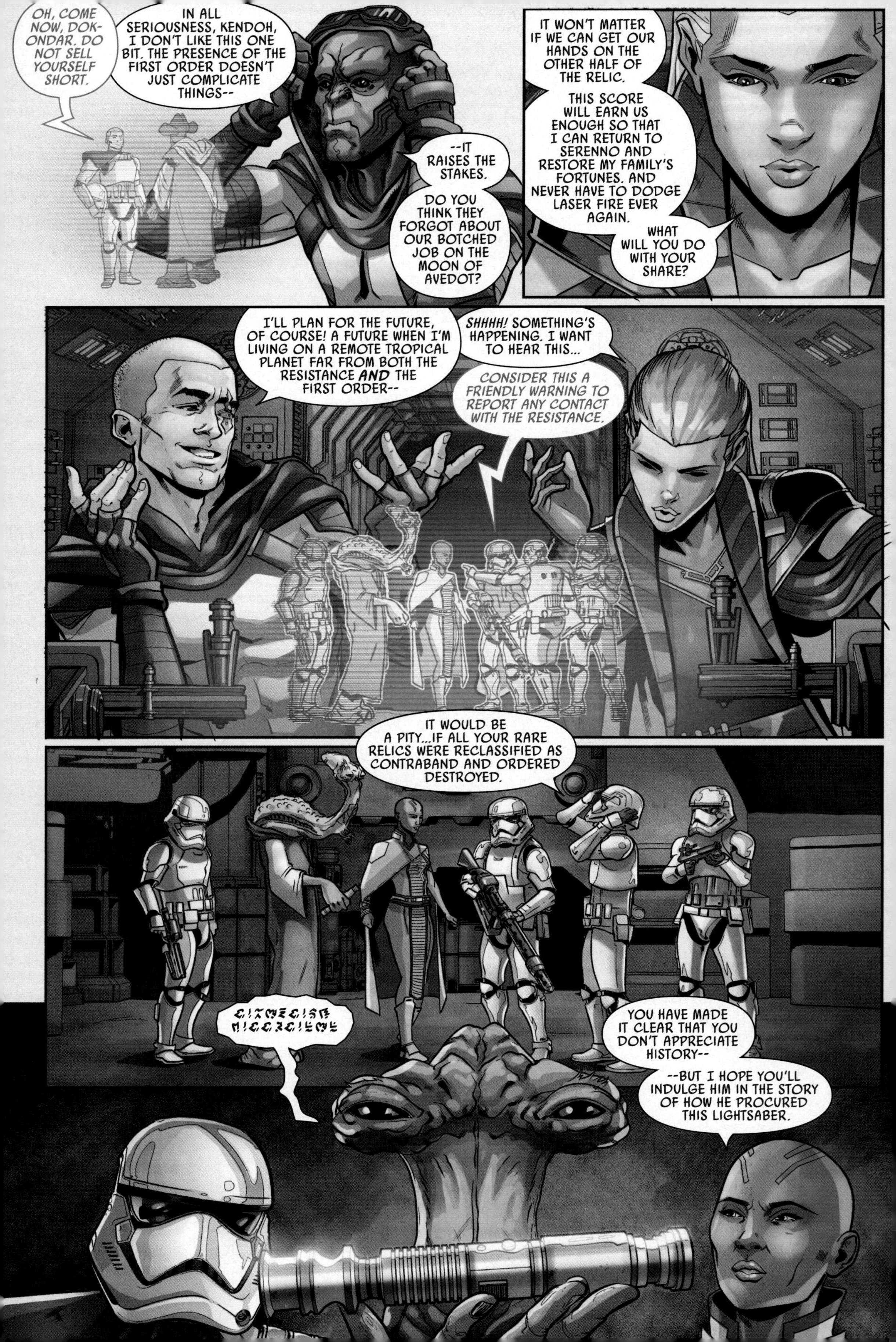

OH, COME NOW, DOK-ONDAR. DO NOT SELL YOURSELF SHORT.
IN ALL SERIOUSNESS, KENDOH, I DON'T LIKE THIS ONE BIT. THE PRESENCE OF THE FIRST ORDER DOESN'T JUST COMPLICATE THINGS--
--IT RAISES THE STAKES.
DO YOU THINK THEY FORGOT ABOUT OUR BOTCHED JOB ON THE MOON OF AVEDOT?
IT WON'T MATTER IF WE CAN GET OUR HANDS ON THE OTHER HALF OF THE RELIC.
THIS SCORE WILL EARN US ENOUGH SO THAT I CAN RETURN TO SERENNO AND RESTORE MY FAMILY'S FORTUNES. AND NEVER HAVE TO DODGE LASER FIRE EVER AGAIN.
WHAT WILL YOU DO WITH YOUR SHARE?
I'LL PLAN FOR THE FUTURE, OF COURSE! A FUTURE WHEN I'M LIVING ON A REMOTE TROPICAL PLANET FAR FROM BOTH THE RESISTANCE AND THE FIRST ORDER--
SHHHH! SOMETHING'S HAPPENING. I WANT TO HEAR THIS...
CONSIDER THIS A FRIENDLY WARNING TO REPORT ANY CONTACT WITH THE RESISTANCE.
IT WOULD BE A PITY...IF ALL YOUR RARE RELICS WERE RECLASSIFIED AS CONTRABAND AND ORDERED DESTROYED.
YOU HAVE MADE IT CLEAR THAT YOU DON'T APPRECIATE HISTORY--
--BUT I HOPE YOU'LL INDULGE HIM IN THE STORY OF HOW HE PROCURED THIS LIGHTSABER.

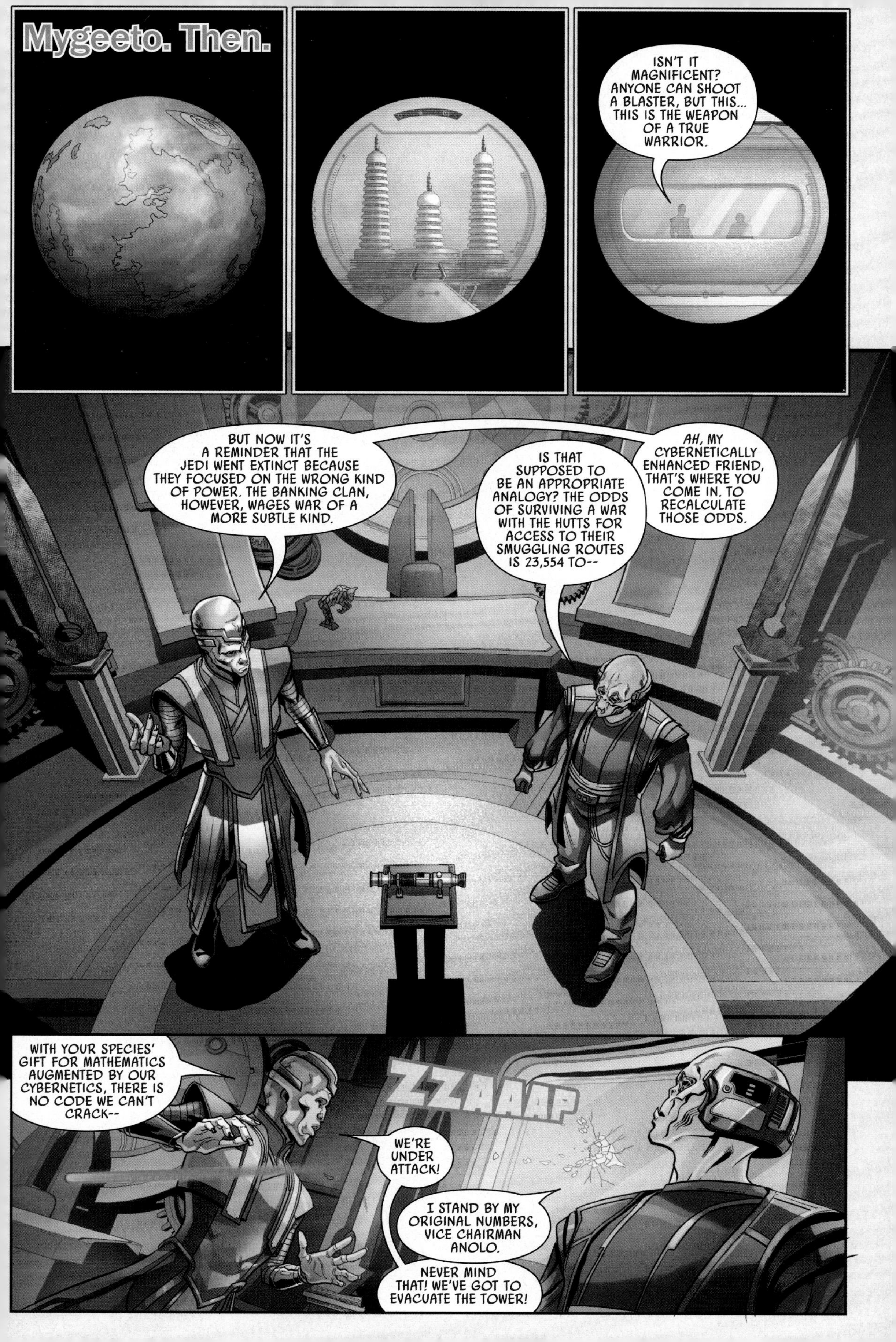
Mygeeto. Then.
ISN'T IT MAGNIFICENT? ANYONE CAN SHOOT A BLASTER, BUT THIS... THIS IS THE WEAPON OF A TRUE WARRIOR.
BUT NOW IT'S A REMINDER THAT THE JEDI WENT EXTINCT BECAUSE THEY FOCUSED ON THE WRONG KIND OF POWER. THE BANKING CLAN, HOWEVER, WAGES WAR OF A MORE SUBTLE KIND.
IS THAT SUPPOSED TO BE AN APPROPRIATE ANALOGY? THE ODDS OF SURVIVING A WAR WITH THE HUTTS FOR ACCESS TO THEIR SMUGGLING ROUTES IS 23,554 TO--
AH, MY CYBERNETICALLY ENHANCED FRIEND, THAT'S WHERE YOU COME IN. TO RECALCULATE THOSE ODDS.
WITH YOUR SPECIES' GIFT FOR MATHEMATICS AUGMENTED BY OUR CYBERNETICS, THERE IS NO CODE WE CAN'T CRACK--
ZZAAAP
WE'RE UNDER ATTACK!
I STAND BY MY ORIGINAL NUMBERS, VICE CHAIRMAN ANOLO.
NEVER MIND THAT! WE'VE GOT TO EVACUATE THE TOWER!

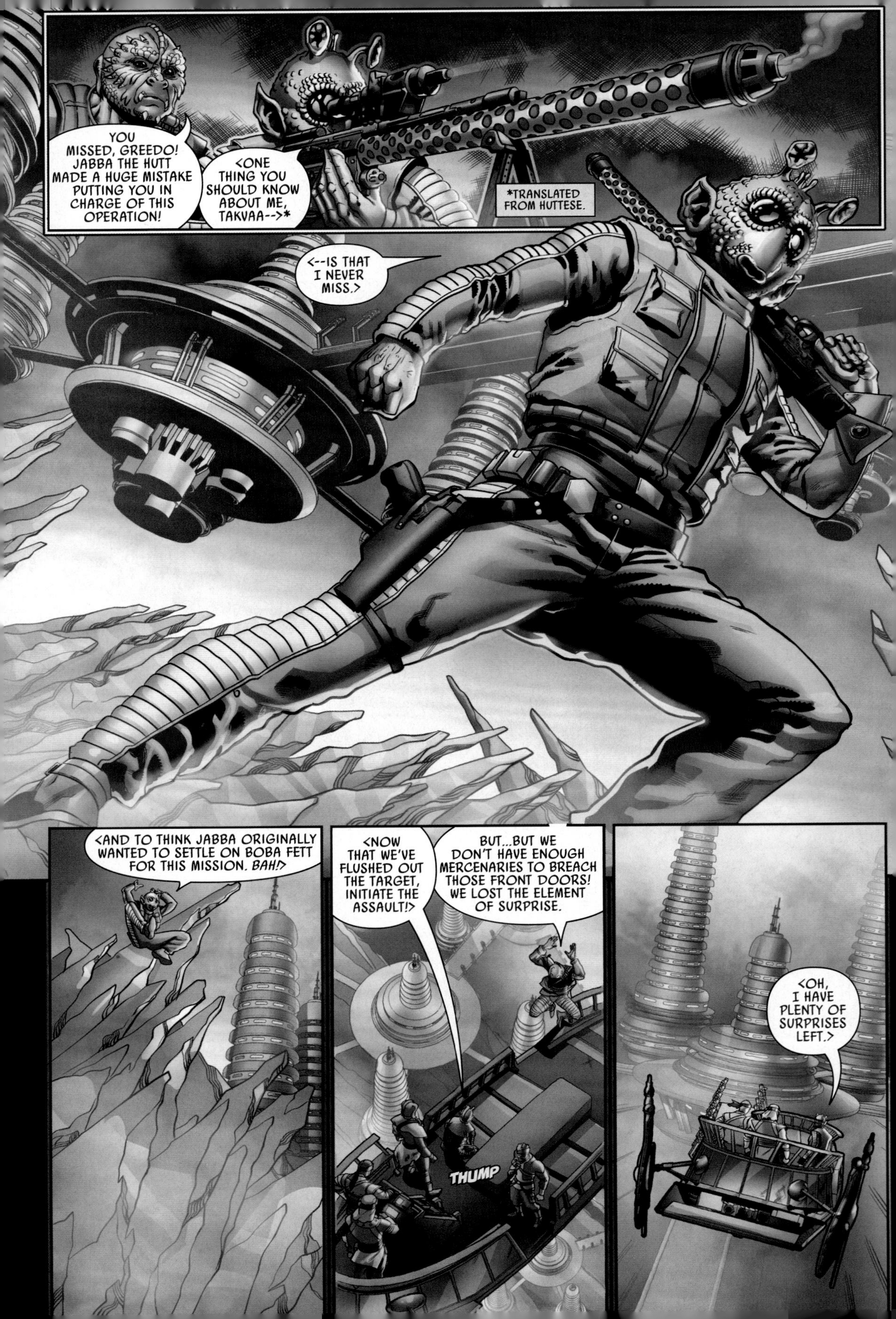
YOU MISSED, GREEDO! JABBA THE HUTT MADE A HUGE MISTAKE PUTTING YOU IN CHARGE OF THIS OPERATION!
<ONE THING YOU SHOULD KNOW ABOUT ME, TAKVAA-->*
*TRANSLATED FROM HUTTESE.
<--IS THAT I NEVER MISS.>
<AND TO THINK JABBA ORIGINALLY WANTED TO SETTLE ON BOBA FETT FOR THIS MISSION. BAH!>
<NOW THAT WE'VE FLUSHED OUT THE TARGET, INITIATE THE ASSAULT!>
BUT...BUT WE DON'T HAVE ENOUGH MERCENARIES TO BREACH THOSE FRONT DOORS! WE LOST THE ELEMENT OF SURPRISE.
THUMP
<OH, I HAVE PLENTY OF SURPRISES LEFT.>

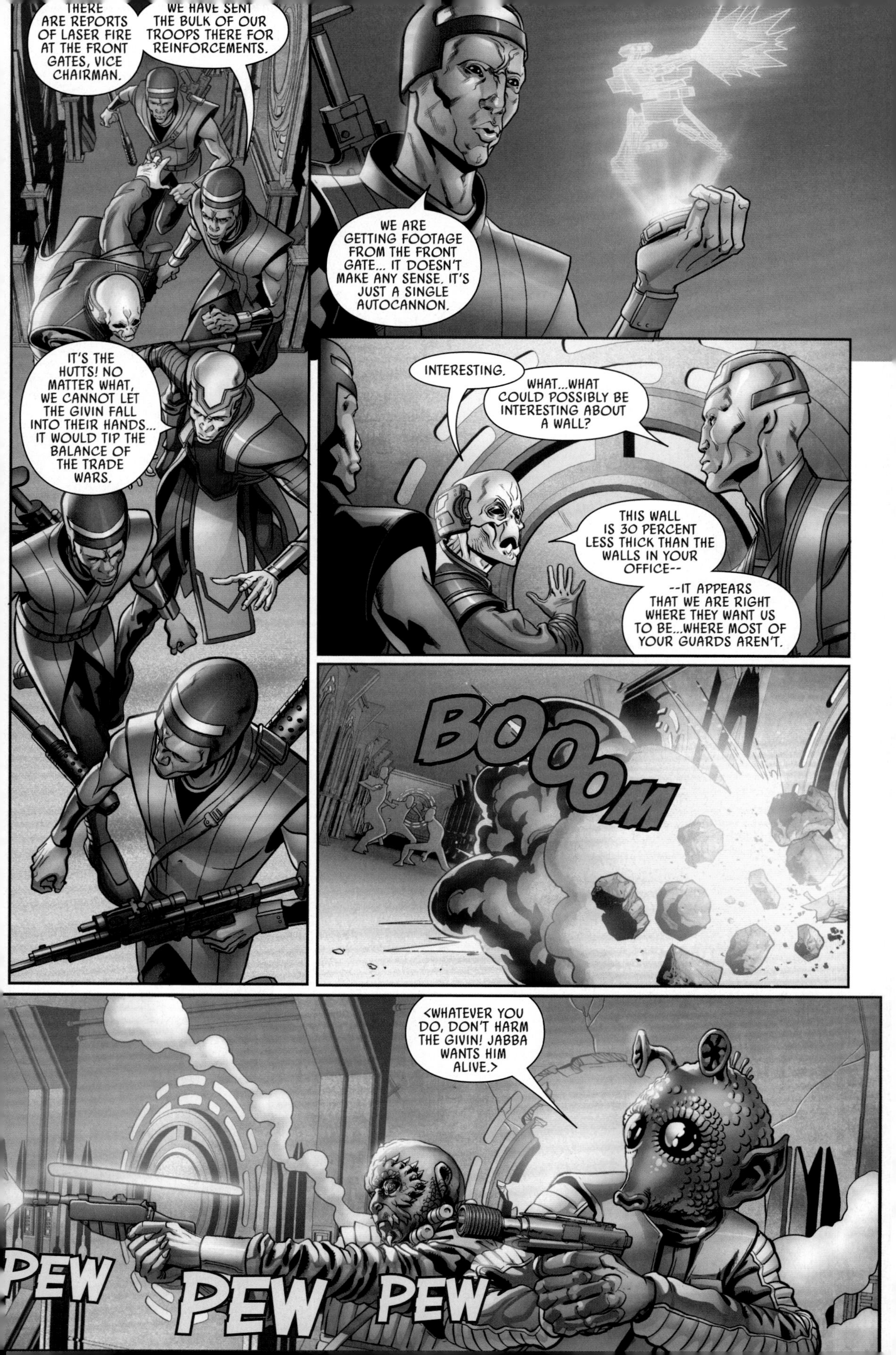
THERE ARE REPORTS OF LASER FIRE AT THE FRONT GATES, VICE CHAIRMAN.
WE HAVE SENT THE BULK OF OUR TROOPS THERE FOR REINFORCEMENTS.
WE ARE GETTING FOOTAGE FROM THE FRONT GATE... IT DOESN'T MAKE ANY SENSE. IT'S JUST A SINGLE AUTOCANNON.
IT'S THE HUTTS! NO MATTER WHAT, WE CANNOT LET THE GIVIN FALL INTO THEIR HANDS... IT WOULD TIP THE BALANCE OF THE TRADE WARS.
INTERESTING.
WHAT...WHAT COULD POSSIBLY BE INTERESTING ABOUT A WALL?
THIS WALL IS 30 PERCENT LESS THICK THAN THE WALLS IN YOUR OFFICE--
--IT APPEARS THAT WE ARE RIGHT WHERE THEY WANT US TO BE...WHERE MOST OF YOUR GUARDS AREN'T.
BOOOOOM
<WHATEVER YOU DO, DON'T HARM THE GIVIN! JABBA WANTS HIM ALIVE.>
PEW
PEW
PEW

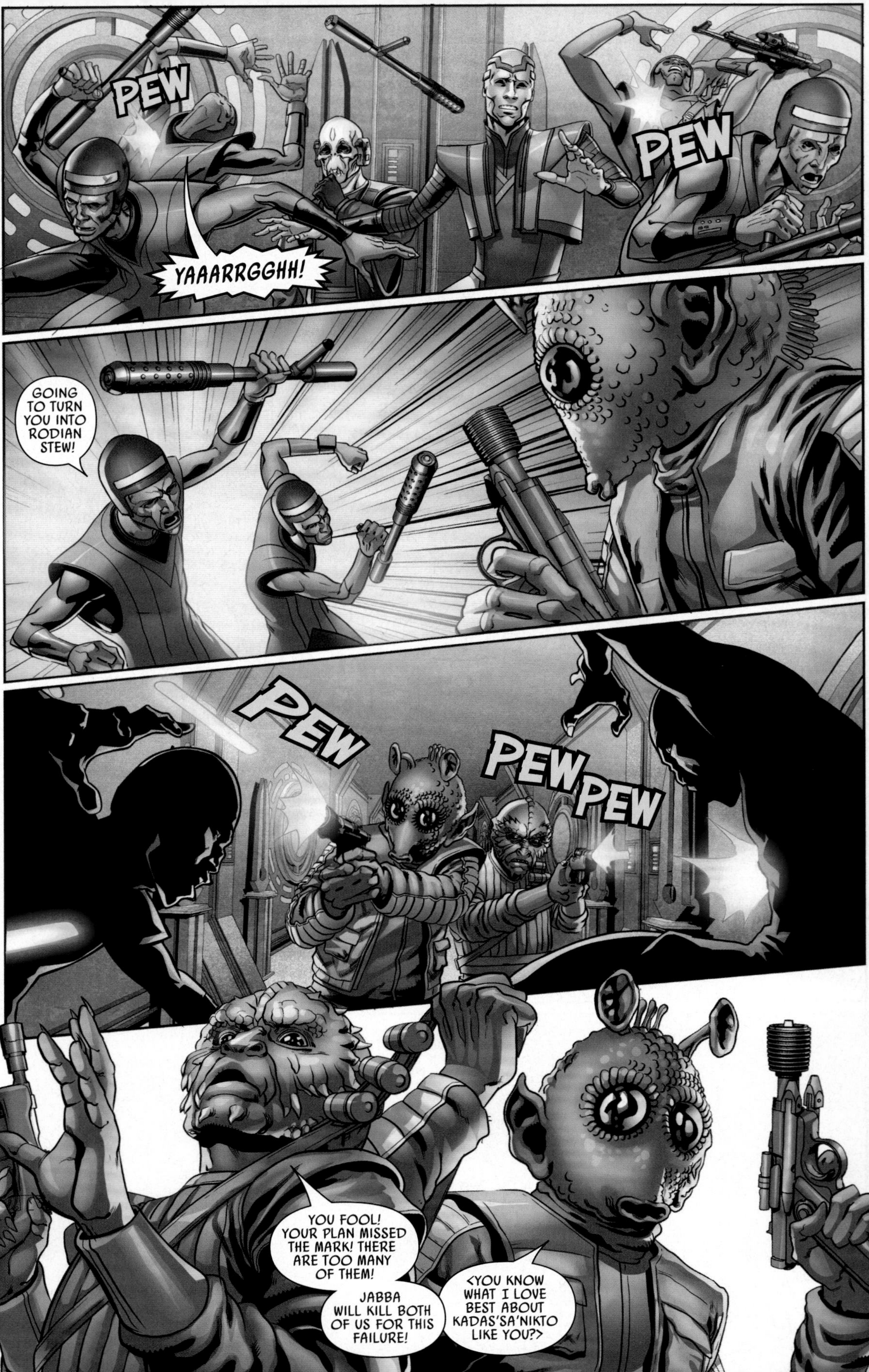
PEW
PEW
YAAARRGGHH!
GOING TO TURN YOU INTO RODIAN STEW!
PEW
PEW PEW
YOU FOOL! YOUR PLAN MISSED THE MARK! THERE ARE TOO MANY OF THEM!
JABBA WILL KILL BOTH OF US FOR THIS FAILURE!
<YOU KNOW WHAT I LOVE BEST ABOUT KADAS'SA'NIKTO LIKE YOU?>

YOUR THICK HIDE.>
SLICE
AAAAAHHH!
<LIKE I SAID...I DON'T MISS.>
PEW
PEW
PEW
DO YOU THINK THE BANKING CLAN WILL ALLOW YOU TO JUST KIDNAP SOMEONE OF MY RANK AND OUR PRIZED CODEBREAKER AND WALK OUT OF HERE ALIVE?
<YOU MAKE A GOOD POINT-->

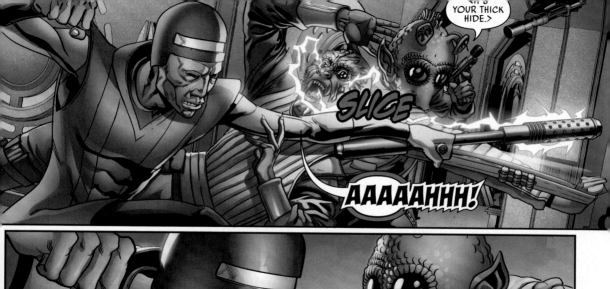

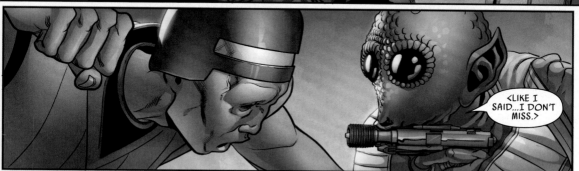

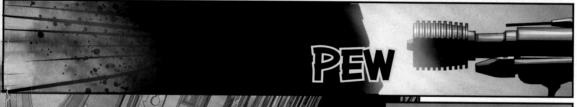

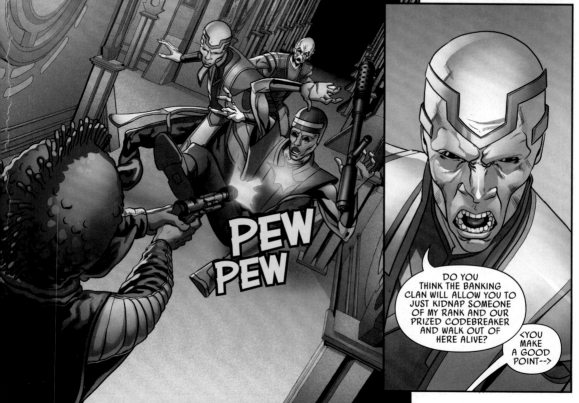

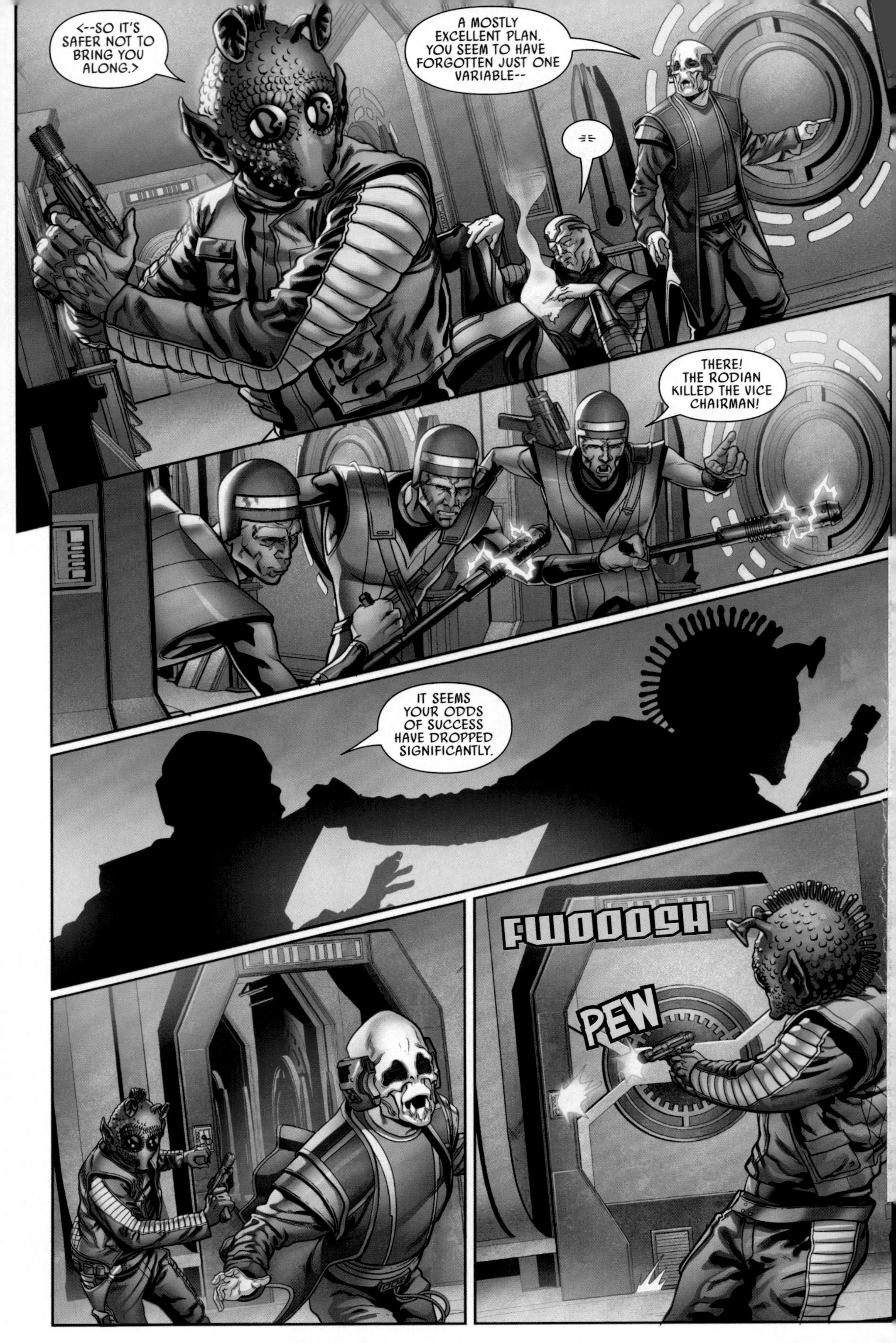

<--SO IT'S SAFER NOT TO BRING YOU ALONG.>
A MOSTLY EXCELLENT PLAN. YOU SEEM TO HAVE FORGOTTEN JUST ONE VARIABLE--
THERE! THE RODIAN KILLED THE VICE CHAIRMAN!
IT SEEMS YOUR ODDS OF SUCCESS HAVE DROPPED SIGNIFICANTLY.
FWOOOSH
PEW

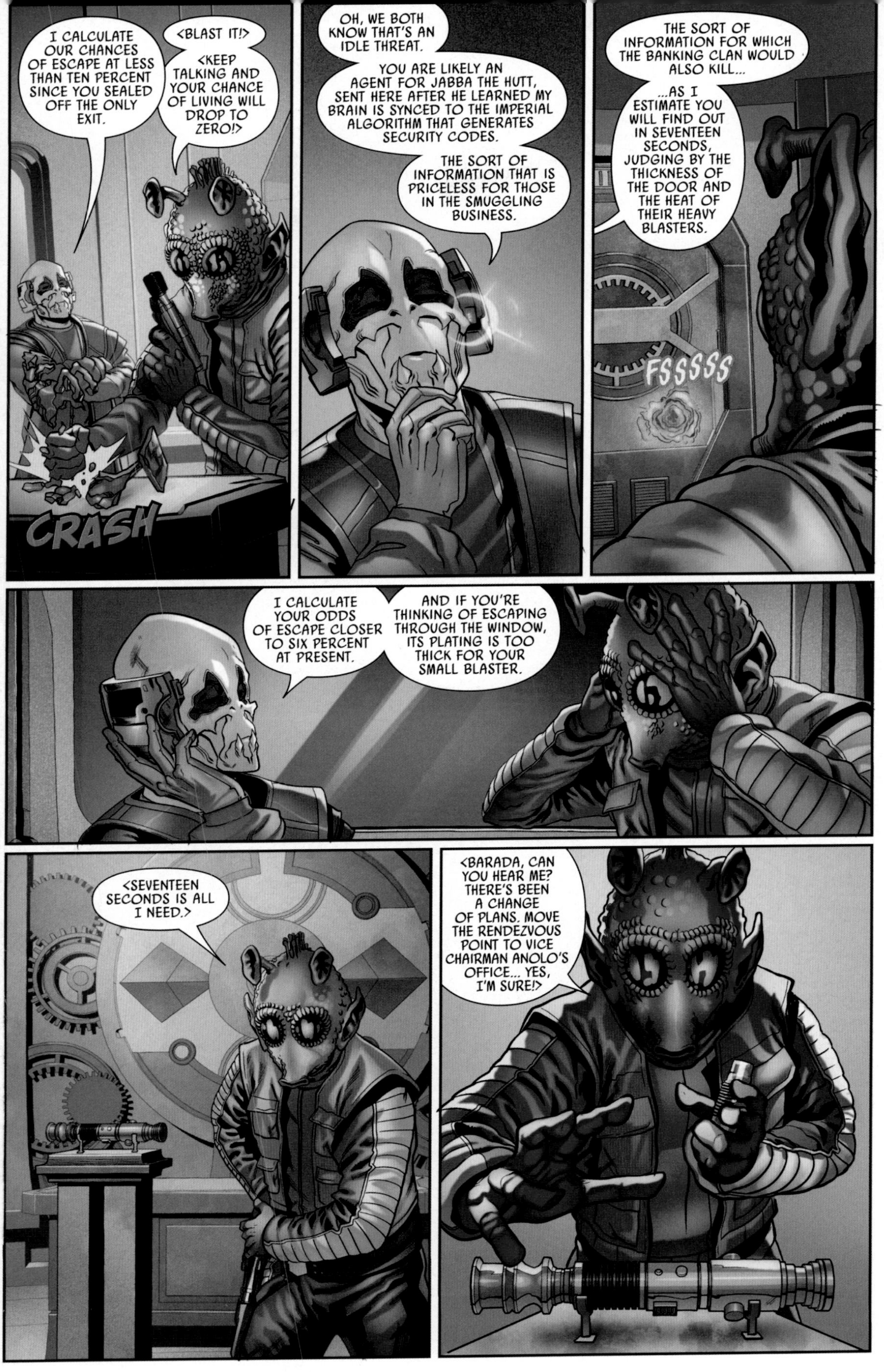
I CALCULATE OUR CHANCES OF ESCAPE AT LESS THAN TEN PERCENT SINCE YOU SEALED OFF THE ONLY EXIT.
<BLAST IT!>
<KEEP TALKING AND YOUR CHANCE OF LIVING WILL DROP TO ZERO!>
CRASH
OH, WE BOTH KNOW THAT'S AN IDLE THREAT.
YOU ARE LIKELY AN AGENT FOR JABBA THE HUTT, SENT HERE AFTER HE LEARNED MY BRAIN IS SYNCED TO THE IMPERIAL ALGORITHM THAT GENERATES SECURITY CODES.
THE SORT OF INFORMATION THAT IS PRICELESS FOR THOSE IN THE SMUGGLING BUSINESS.
THE SORT OF INFORMATION FOR WHICH THE BANKING CLAN WOULD ALSO KILL...
...AS I ESTIMATE YOU WILL FIND OUT IN SEVENTEEN SECONDS, JUDGING BY THE THICKNESS OF THE DOOR AND THE HEAT OF THEIR HEAVY BLASTERS.
FSSSSS
I CALCULATE YOUR ODDS OF ESCAPE CLOSER TO SIX PERCENT AT PRESENT.
AND IF YOU'RE THINKING OF ESCAPING THROUGH THE WINDOW, ITS PLATING IS TOO THICK FOR YOUR SMALL BLASTER.
<SEVENTEEN SECONDS IS ALL I NEED.>
<BARADA, CAN YOU HEAR ME? THERE'S BEEN A CHANGE OF PLANS. MOVE THE RENDEZVOUS POINT TO VICE CHAIRMAN ANOLO'S OFFICE... YES, I'M SURE!>

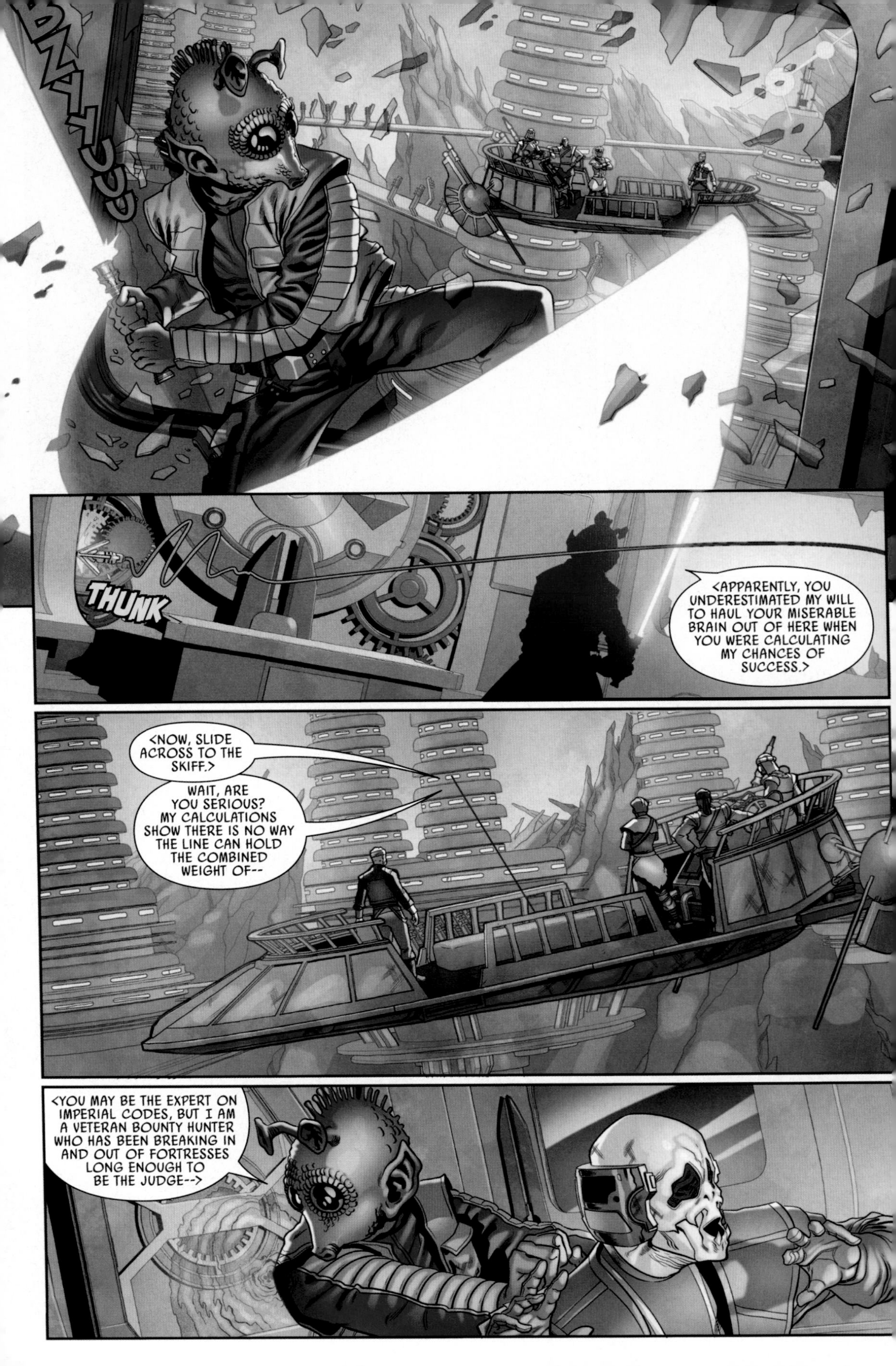
THUNK
<APPARENTLY, YOU UNDERESTIMATED MY WILL TO HAUL YOUR MISERABLE BRAIN OUT OF HERE WHEN YOU WERE CALCULATING MY CHANCES OF SUCCESS.>
<NOW, SLIDE ACROSS TO THE SKIFF.>
WAIT, ARE YOU SERIOUS? MY CALCULATIONS SHOW THERE IS NO WAY THE LINE CAN HOLD THE COMBINED WEIGHT OF--
<YOU MAY BE THE EXPERT ON IMPERIAL CODES, BUT I AM A VETERAN BOUNTY HUNTER WHO HAS BEEN BREAKING IN AND OUT OF FORTRESSES LONG ENOUGH TO BE THE JUDGE-->

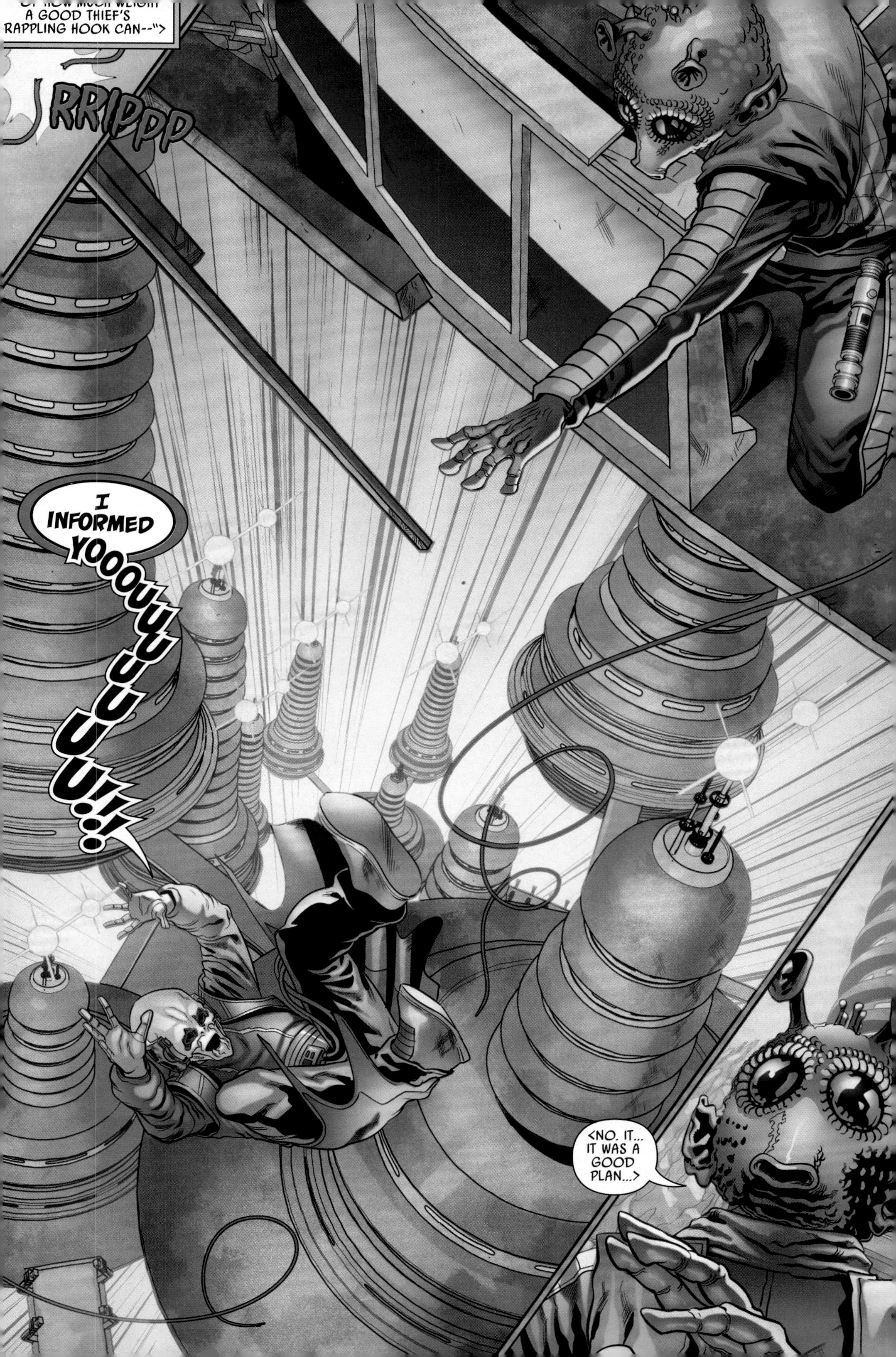
A GOOD THIEF'S RAPPLING HOOK CAN--">
RRIPPP
I INFORMED YOOOUUUUUUU!!!
<NO. IT... IT WAS A GOOD PLAN...>

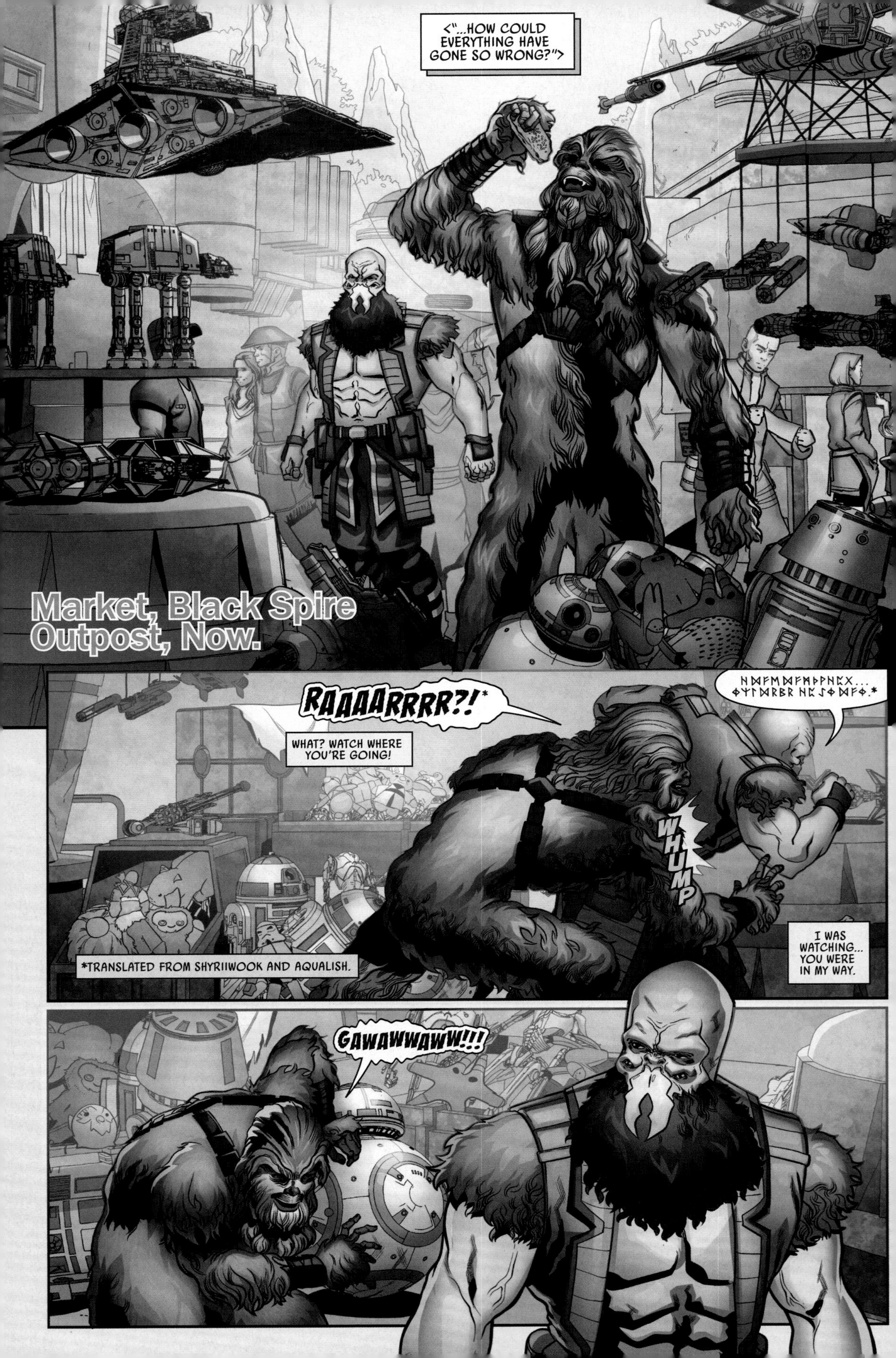
<"...HOW COULD EVERYTHING HAVE GONE SO WRONG?">
Market, Black Spire Outpost, Now.
RAAAARRRR?!*
WHAT? WATCH WHERE YOU'RE GOING!
WHUMP
I WAS WATCHING... YOU WERE IN MY WAY.
*TRANSLATED FROM SHYRIIWOOK AND AQUALISH.
GAWAWWAWW!!!

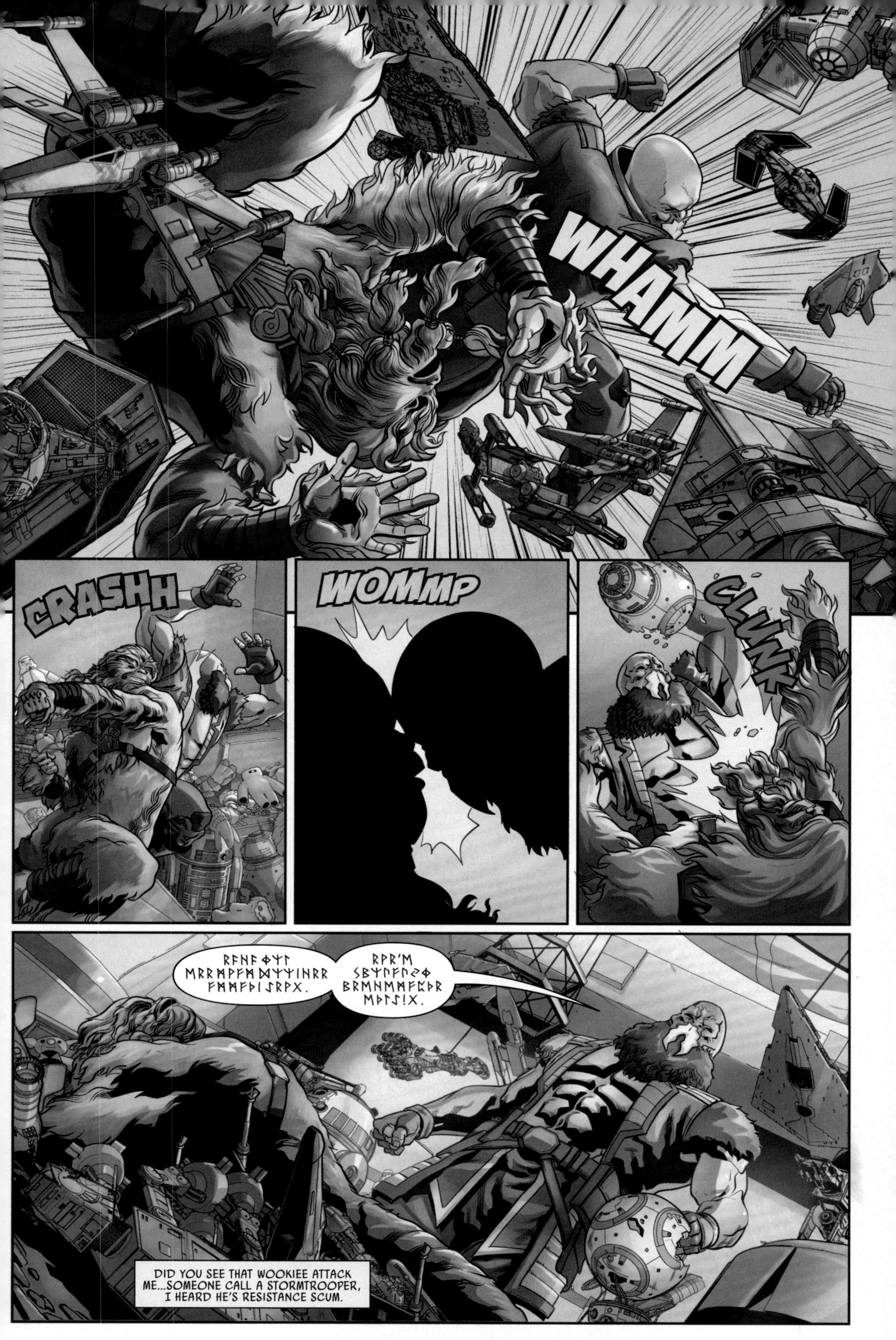
WHAMM
CRASHH
WOMMP
CLUNK
DID YOU SEE THAT WOOKIEE ATTACK ME...SOMEONE CALL A STORMTROOPER, I HEARD HE'S RESISTANCE SCUM.

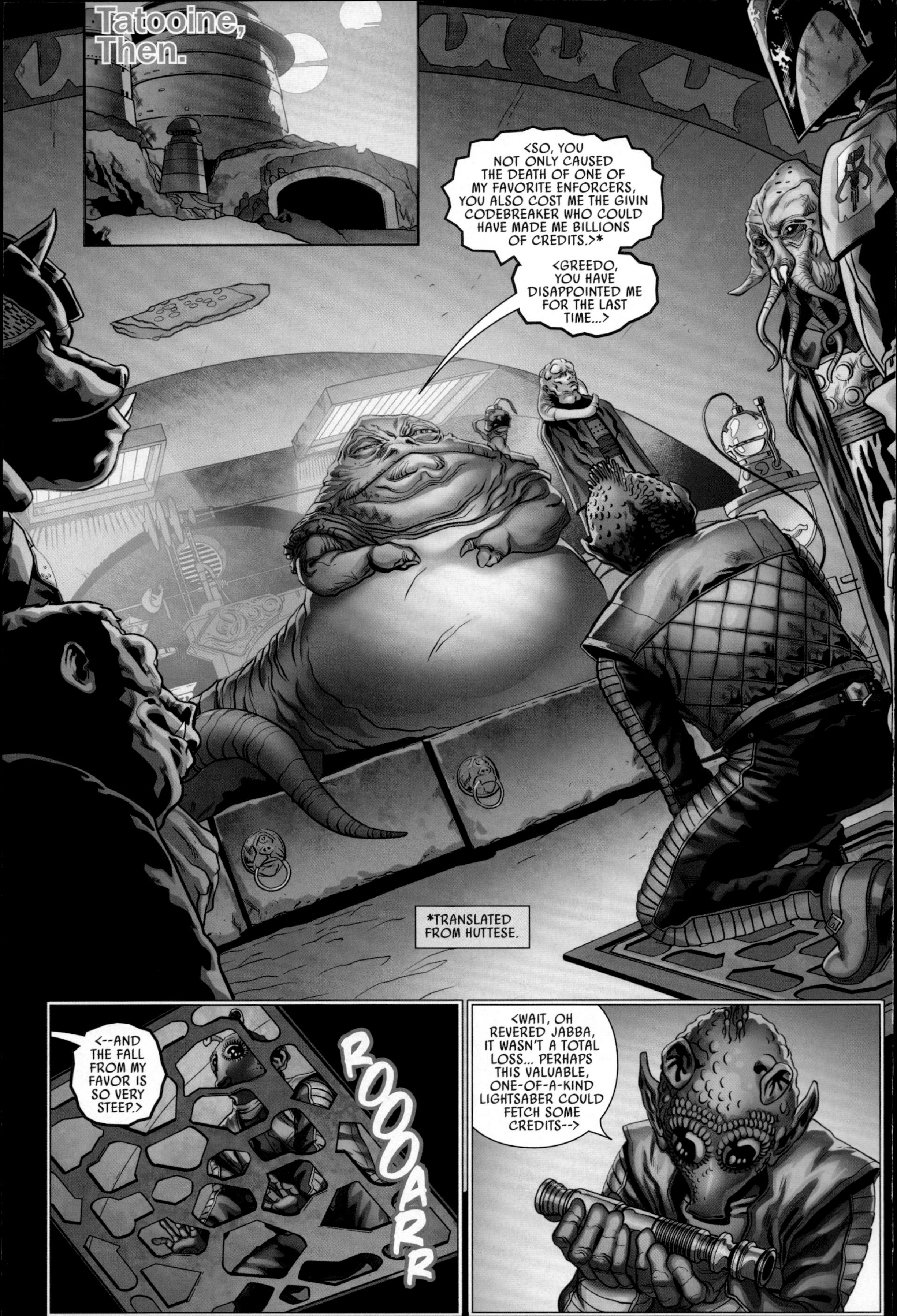
Tatooine, Then.
<SO, YOU NOT ONLY CAUSED THE DEATH OF ONE OF MY FAVORITE ENFORCERS, YOU ALSO COST ME THE GIVIN CODEBREAKER WHO COULD HAVE MADE ME BILLIONS OF CREDITS.>*
<GREEDO, YOU HAVE DISAPPOINTED ME FOR THE LAST TIME...>
*TRANSLATED FROM HUTTESE.
<--AND THE FALL FROM MY FAVOR IS SO VERY STEEP.>
ROOOARR
<WAIT, OH REVERED JABBA, IT WASN'T A TOTAL LOSS... PERHAPS THIS VALUABLE, ONE-OF-A-KIND LIGHTSABER COULD FETCH SOME CREDITS-->

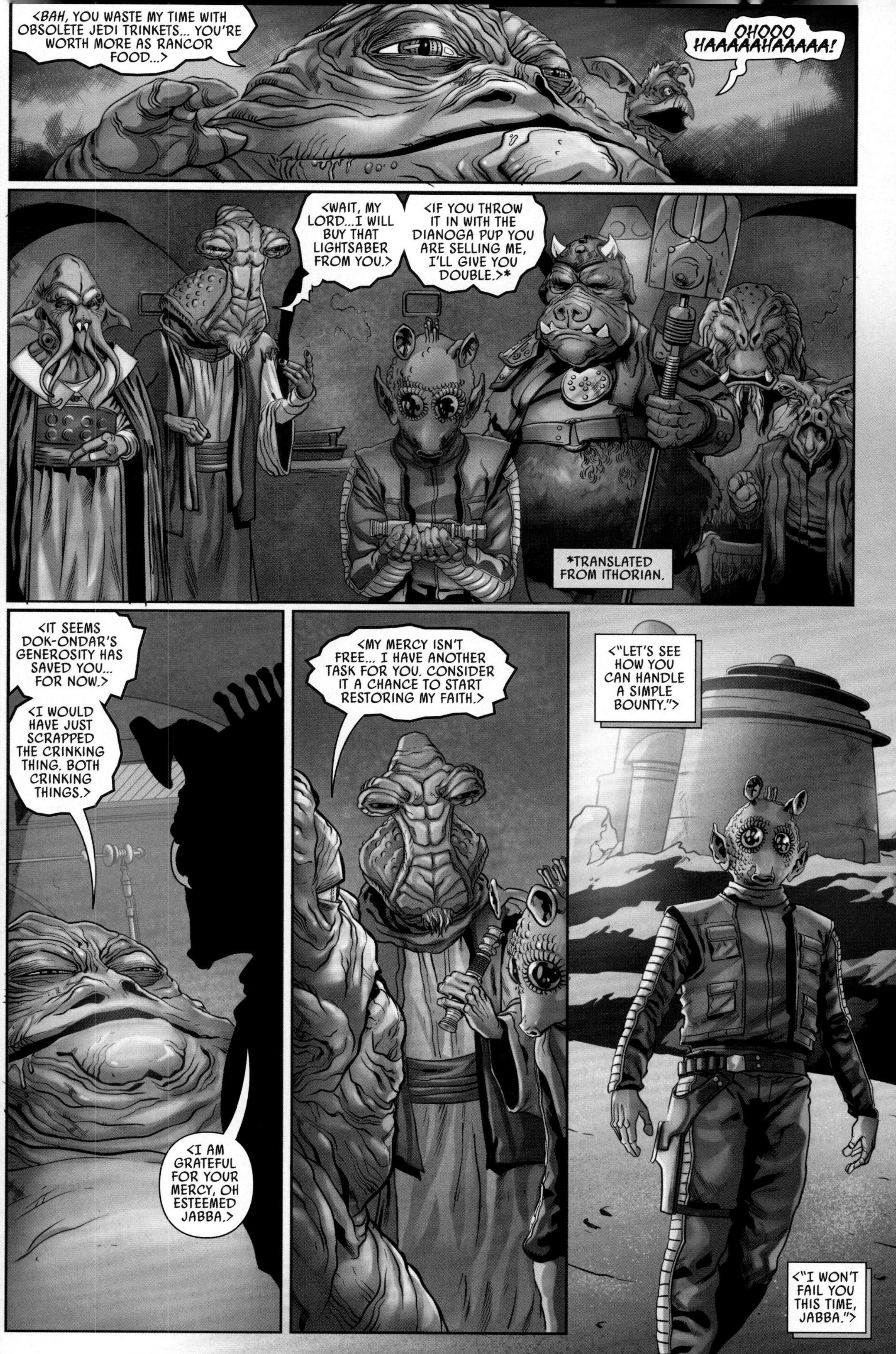
<BAH, YOU WASTE MY TIME WITH OBSOLETE JEDI TRINKETS... YOU'RE WORTH MORE AS RANCOR FOOD...>
OHOOO HAAAAAHAAAAA!
<WAIT, MY LORD...I WILL BUY THAT LIGHTSABER FROM YOU.>
<IF YOU THROW IT IN WITH THE DIANOGA PUP YOU ARE SELLING ME, I'LL GIVE YOU DOUBLE.>*
*TRANSLATED FROM ITHORIAN.
<IT SEEMS DOK-ONDAR'S GENEROSITY HAS SAVED YOU... FOR NOW.>
<I WOULD HAVE JUST SCRAPPED THE CRINKING THING. BOTH CRINKING THINGS.>
<I AM GRATEFUL FOR YOUR MERCY, OH ESTEEMED JABBA.>
<MY MERCY ISN'T FREE... I HAVE ANOTHER TASK FOR YOU. CONSIDER IT A CHANCE TO START RESTORING MY FAITH.>
<"LET'S SEE HOW YOU CAN HANDLE A SIMPLE BOUNTY.">
<"I WON'T FAIL YOU THIS TIME, JABBA.">

AH, YOU'RE BACK. YOU MISSED QUITE THE STORY.

ᚠᚤᚱ'ᛒ ᚱᛈᚱᚼᚠᚤᛋᚱ ᚳᚤᛒᛗᛈᚱᛈᚱᚼᛋ ᛗᚼᛗᛈᛗᛈᚠᛗ ᛗᚤᚤᛁᚾᚱ.

WHAT DO YOU MEAN "YOU'RE WELCOME"? WHAT DISTRACTION? WHAT WOOKIEE?

WHY HAVE YOU WASTED MY TIME WITH THIS TALE? WHAT DOES IT HAVE TO DO WITH THE RESISTANCE?

ᛉ.ᛋᚴᛁᛖᛉ ᛏᚼᛉ ᛖᛉᛏ! ᛗᛉᛋᚵᛖᛒᚵ

HE ASKS YOU TO LOOK CLOSELY AT THE LIGHTSABER, SERGEANT...

"ALL THAT POWER LOCKED INSIDE, LAYING DORMANT UNTIL CALLED FORTH WITH A GREATER PURPOSE...

"IT HAS SURVIVED LONG AFTER ITS GREAT WIELDER HAS FALLEN. IT HAS OUTLASTED THE FALL OF REPUBLICS AND EMPIRES. IT HAS OUTLASTED THE SCHEMES OF ALL THOSE WITH BIG AMBITIONS AND SMALL MINDS.

"IT WILL OUTLAST YOUR FIRST ORDER TOO."

ᛗᛉᛋᚵ ᛗᚳᛁᚵ ᛗᚳᛉᛗᛖ ᛗᛉᛋᛁᚵ

ᛗᛉᛋᚳᛉ ᛒᛖᛗᚳ ᛖᚳ ᛉᛗᛖᛉ.

HE SAYS YOUR HOLD ON BLACK SPIRE OUTPOST IS TENUOUS AT BEST... YOU NEED THE COOPERATION OF ITS LEADERS TO KEEP IT.

SO DON'T COME INTO HIS STORE AND THREATEN HIM EVER AGAIN.

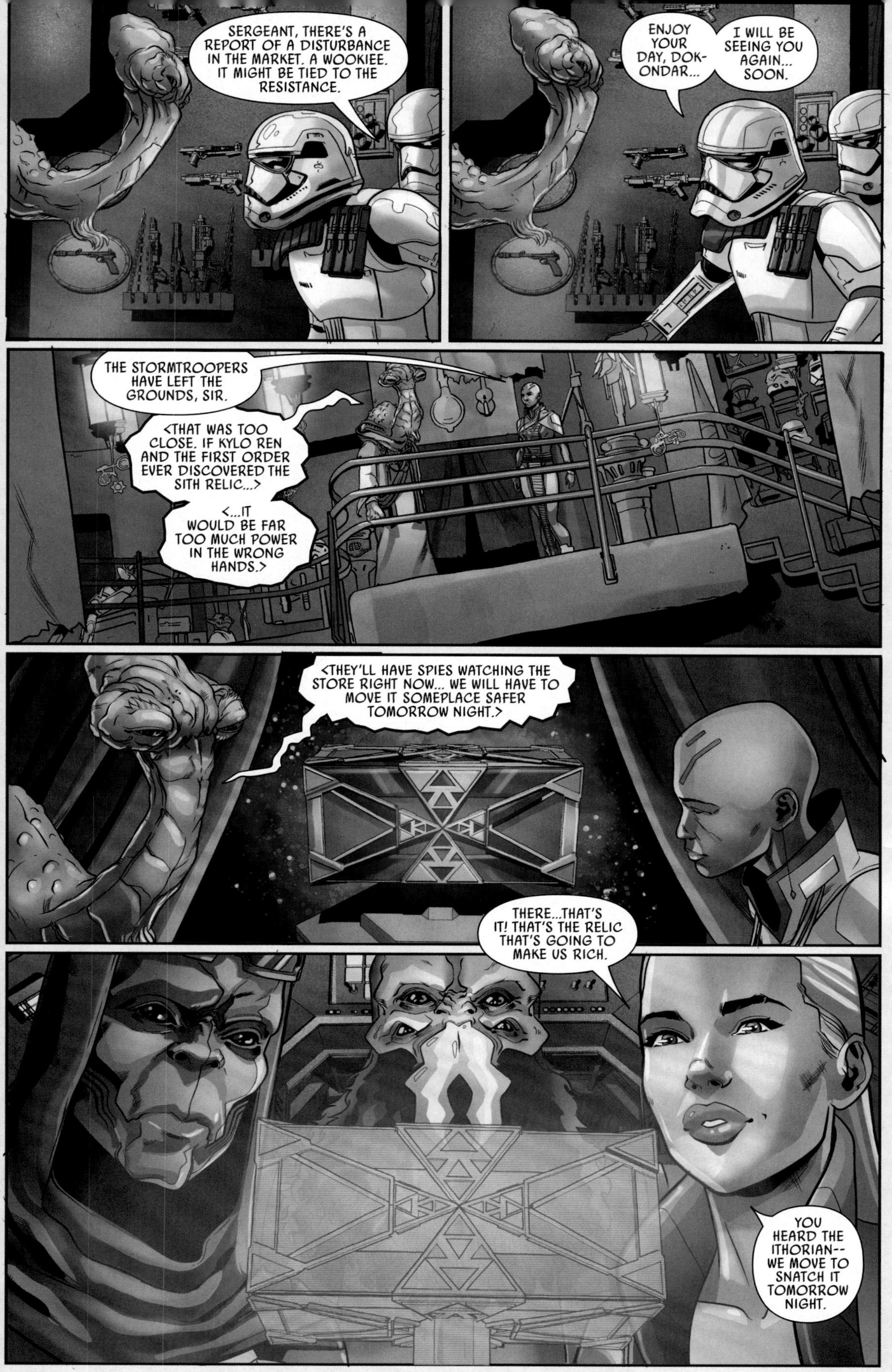
SERGEANT, THERE'S A REPORT OF A DISTURBANCE IN THE MARKET. A WOOKIEE. IT MIGHT BE TIED TO THE RESISTANCE.
ENJOY YOUR DAY, DOK-ONDAR...
I WILL BE SEEING YOU AGAIN... SOON.
THE STORMTROOPERS HAVE LEFT THE GROUNDS, SIR.
<THAT WAS TOO CLOSE. IF KYLO REN AND THE FIRST ORDER EVER DISCOVERED THE SITH RELIC...>
<...IT WOULD BE FAR TOO MUCH POWER IN THE WRONG HANDS.>
<THEY'LL HAVE SPIES WATCHING THE STORE RIGHT NOW... WE WILL HAVE TO MOVE IT SOMEPLACE SAFER TOMORROW NIGHT.>
THERE...THAT'S IT! THAT'S THE RELIC THAT'S GOING TO MAKE US RICH.
YOU HEARD THE ITHORIAN-- WE MOVE TO SNATCH IT TOMORROW NIGHT.

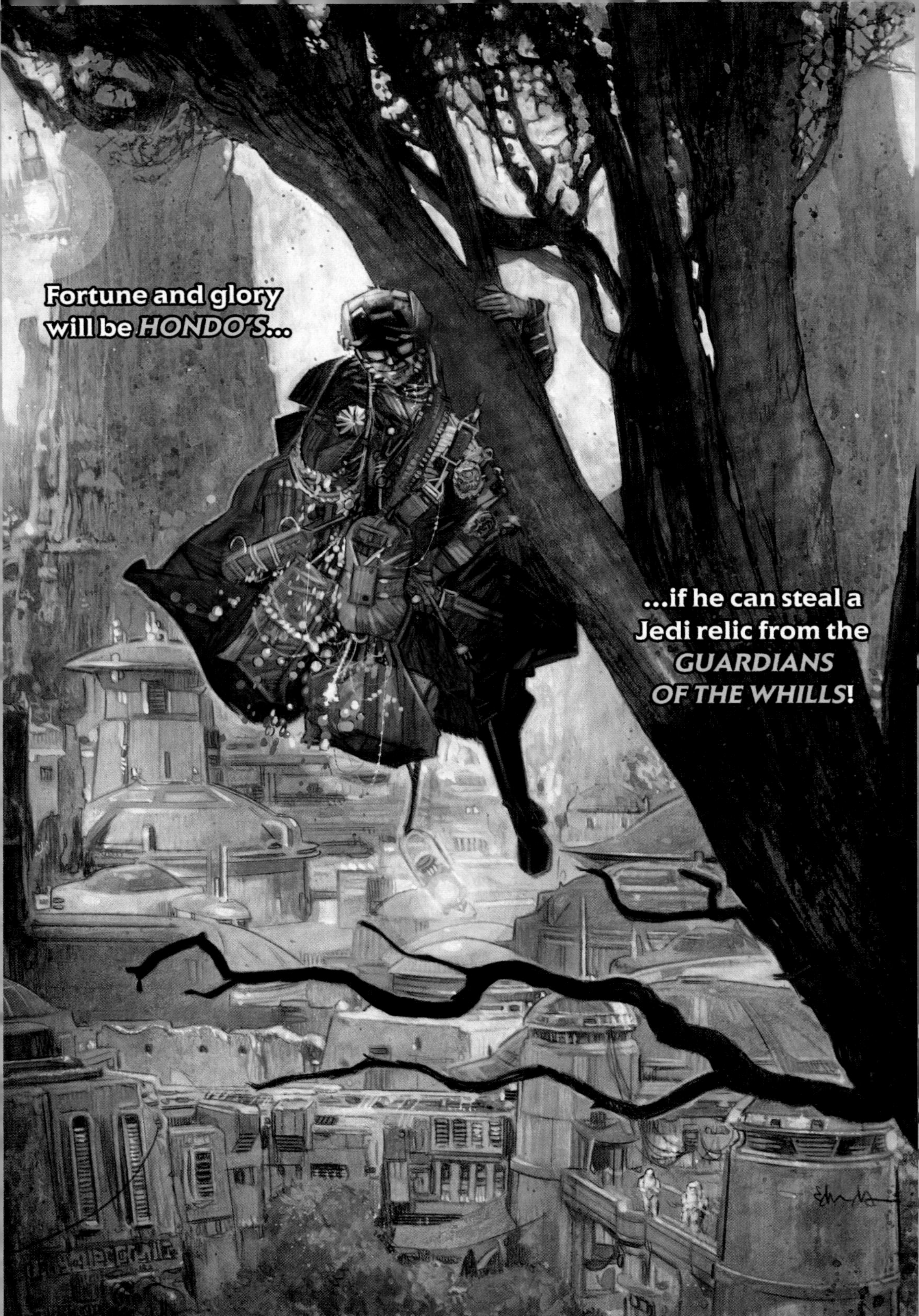
Fortune and glory will be HONDO'S...
...if he can steal a Jedi relic from the GUARDIANS OF THE WHILLS!

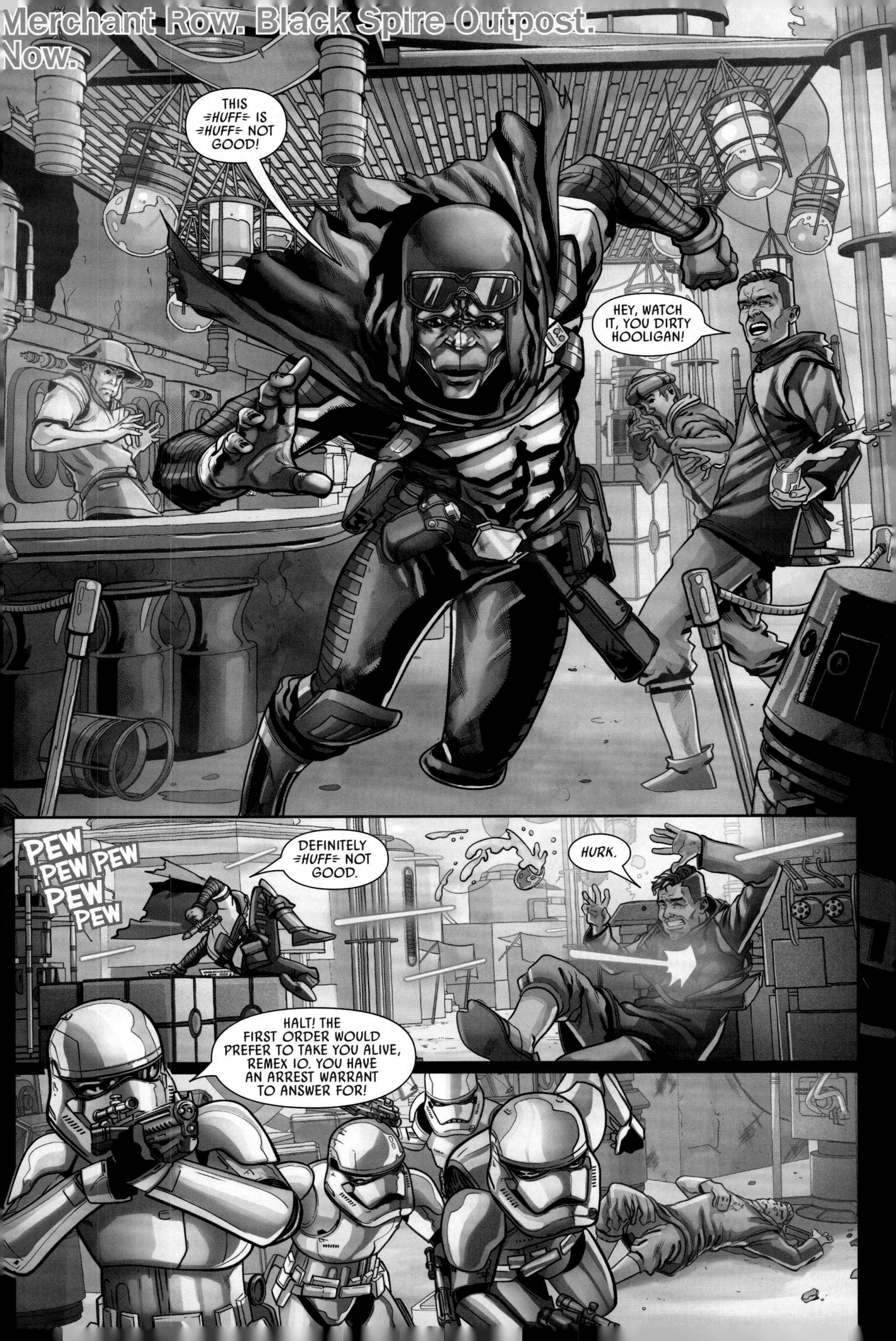
Merchant Row. Black Spire Outpost. Now.
THIS =HUFF= IS =HUFF= NOT GOOD!
HEY, WATCH IT, YOU DIRTY HOOLIGAN!
PEW PEW PEW PEW PEW
DEFINITELY =HUFF= NOT GOOD.
HURK.
HALT! THE FIRST ORDER WOULD PREFER TO TAKE YOU ALIVE, REMEX IO. YOU HAVE AN ARREST WARRANT TO ANSWER FOR!

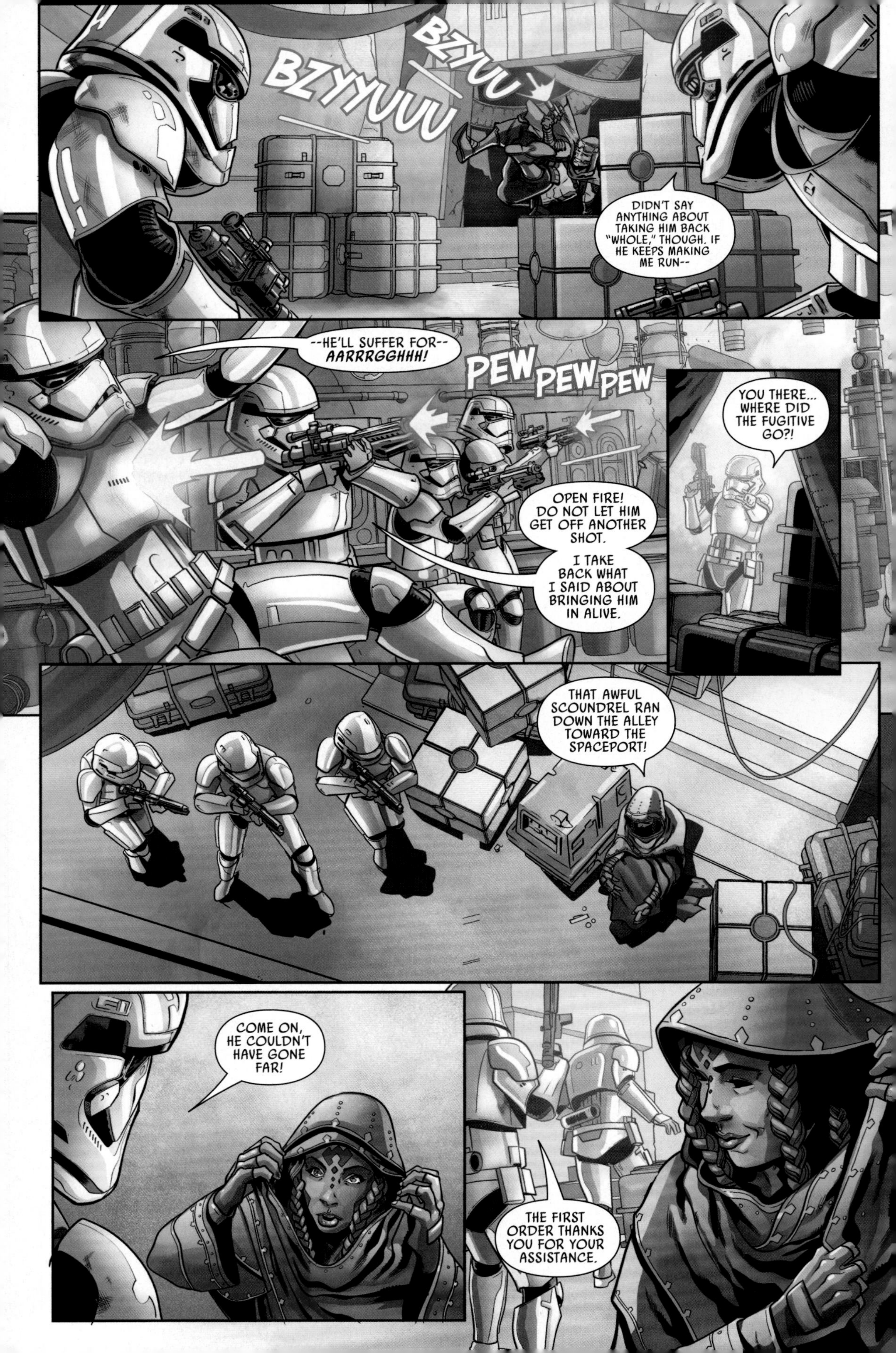
BZYYUUU
BZYUU
DIDN'T SAY ANYTHING ABOUT TAKING HIM BACK "WHOLE," THOUGH. IF HE KEEPS MAKING ME RUN--
--HE'LL SUFFER FOR-- AARRRGGHHH!
PEW PEW PEW
OPEN FIRE! DO NOT LET HIM GET OFF ANOTHER SHOT.
I TAKE BACK WHAT I SAID ABOUT BRINGING HIM IN ALIVE.
YOU THERE... WHERE DID THE FUGITIVE GO?!
THAT AWFUL SCOUNDREL RAN DOWN THE ALLEY TOWARD THE SPACEPORT!
COME ON, HE COULDN'T HAVE GONE FAR!
THE FIRST ORDER THANKS YOU FOR YOUR ASSISTANCE.

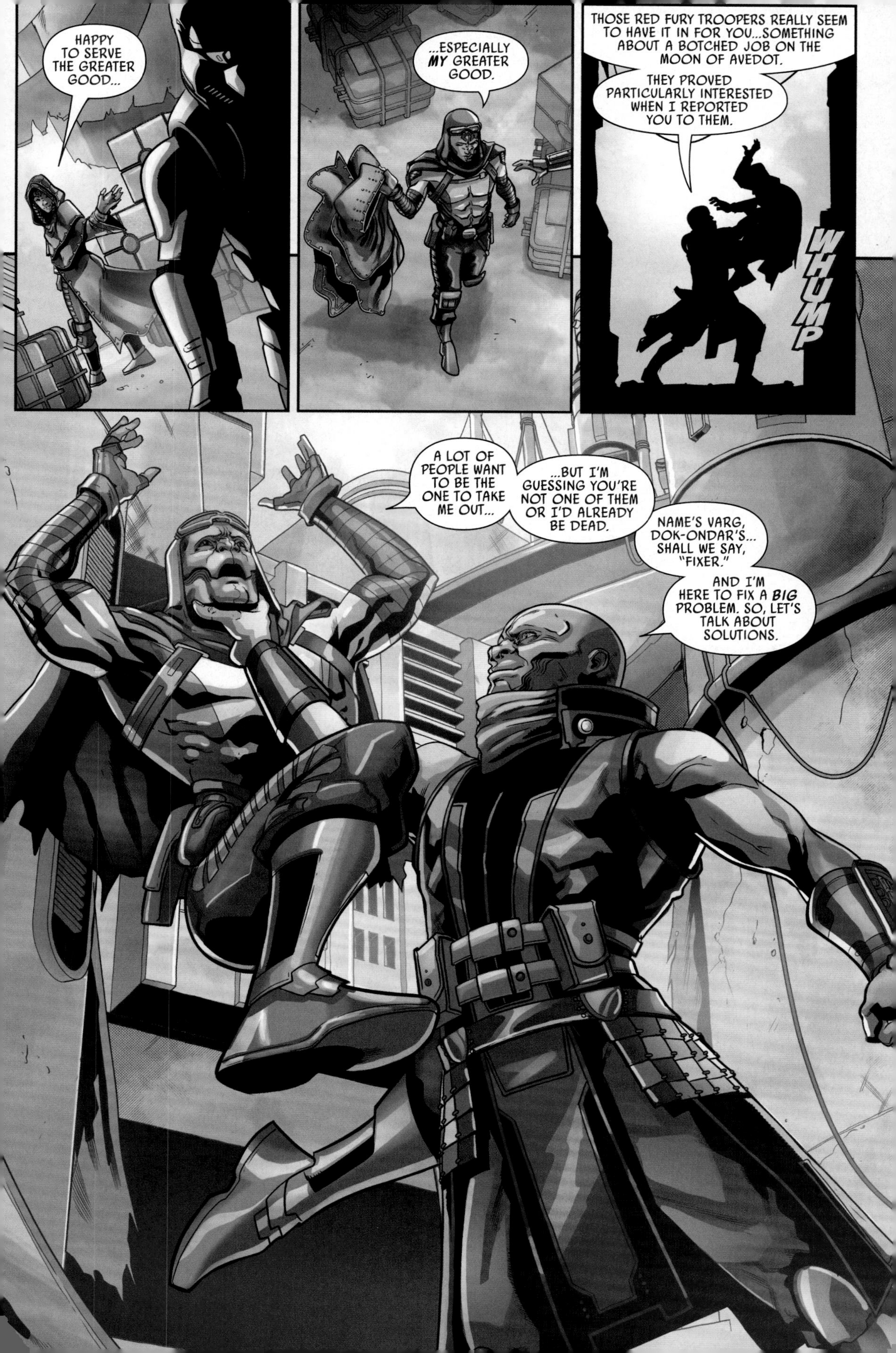

HAPPY TO SERVE THE GREATER GOOD...
...ESPECIALLY *MY* GREATER GOOD.
THOSE RED FURY TROOPERS REALLY SEEM TO HAVE IT IN FOR YOU...SOMETHING ABOUT A BOTCHED JOB ON THE MOON OF AVEDOT.
THEY PROVED PARTICULARLY INTERESTED WHEN I REPORTED YOU TO THEM.
WHUMP
A LOT OF PEOPLE WANT TO BE THE ONE TO TAKE ME OUT...
...BUT I'M GUESSING YOU'RE NOT ONE OF THEM OR I'D ALREADY BE DEAD.
NAME'S VARG, DOK-ONDAR'S... SHALL WE SAY, "FIXER."
AND I'M HERE TO FIX A *BIG* PROBLEM. SO, LET'S TALK ABOUT SOLUTIONS.

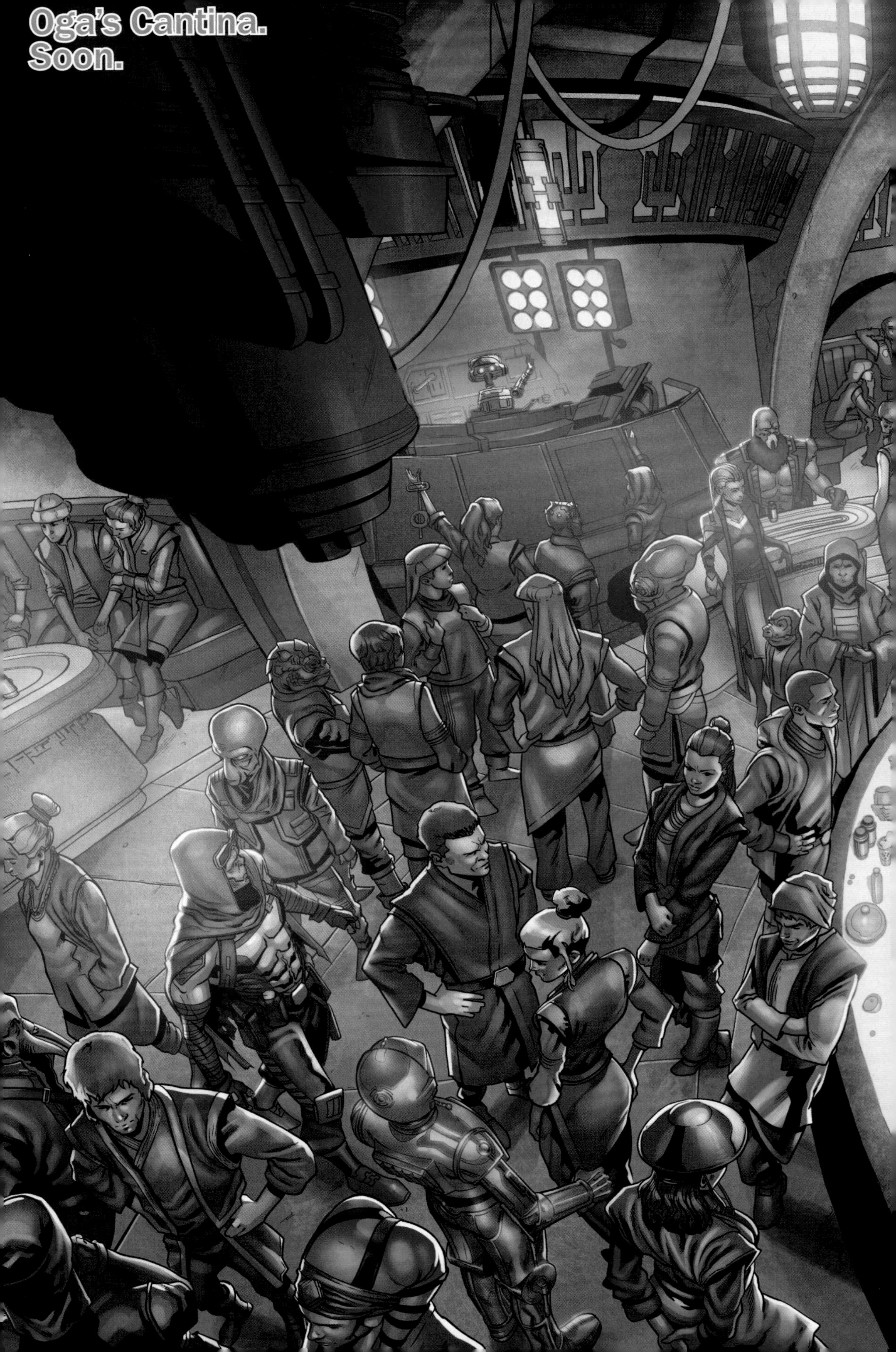
Oga's Cantina.
Soon.

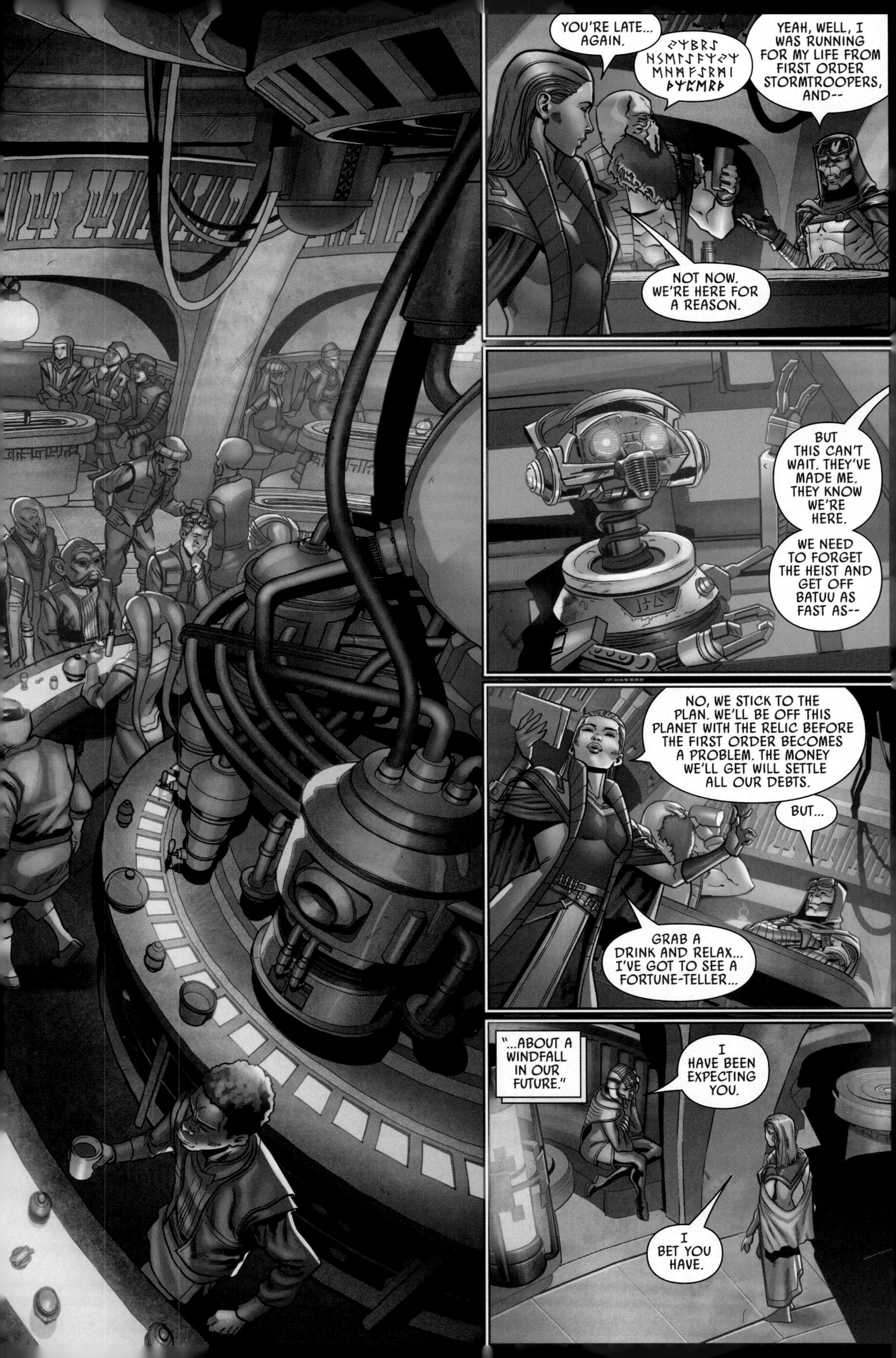
YOU'RE LATE... AGAIN.
YEAH, WELL, I WAS RUNNING FOR MY LIFE FROM FIRST ORDER STORMTROOPERS, AND--
NOT NOW. WE'RE HERE FOR A REASON.
BUT THIS CAN'T WAIT. THEY'VE MADE ME. THEY KNOW WE'RE HERE.
WE NEED TO FORGET THE HEIST AND GET OFF BATUU AS FAST AS--
NO, WE STICK TO THE PLAN. WE'LL BE OFF THIS PLANET WITH THE RELIC BEFORE THE FIRST ORDER BECOMES A PROBLEM. THE MONEY WE'LL GET WILL SETTLE ALL OUR DEBTS.
BUT...
GRAB A DRINK AND RELAX... I'VE GOT TO SEE A FORTUNE-TELLER...
"...ABOUT A WINDFALL IN OUR FUTURE."
I HAVE BEEN EXPECTING YOU.
I BET YOU HAVE.

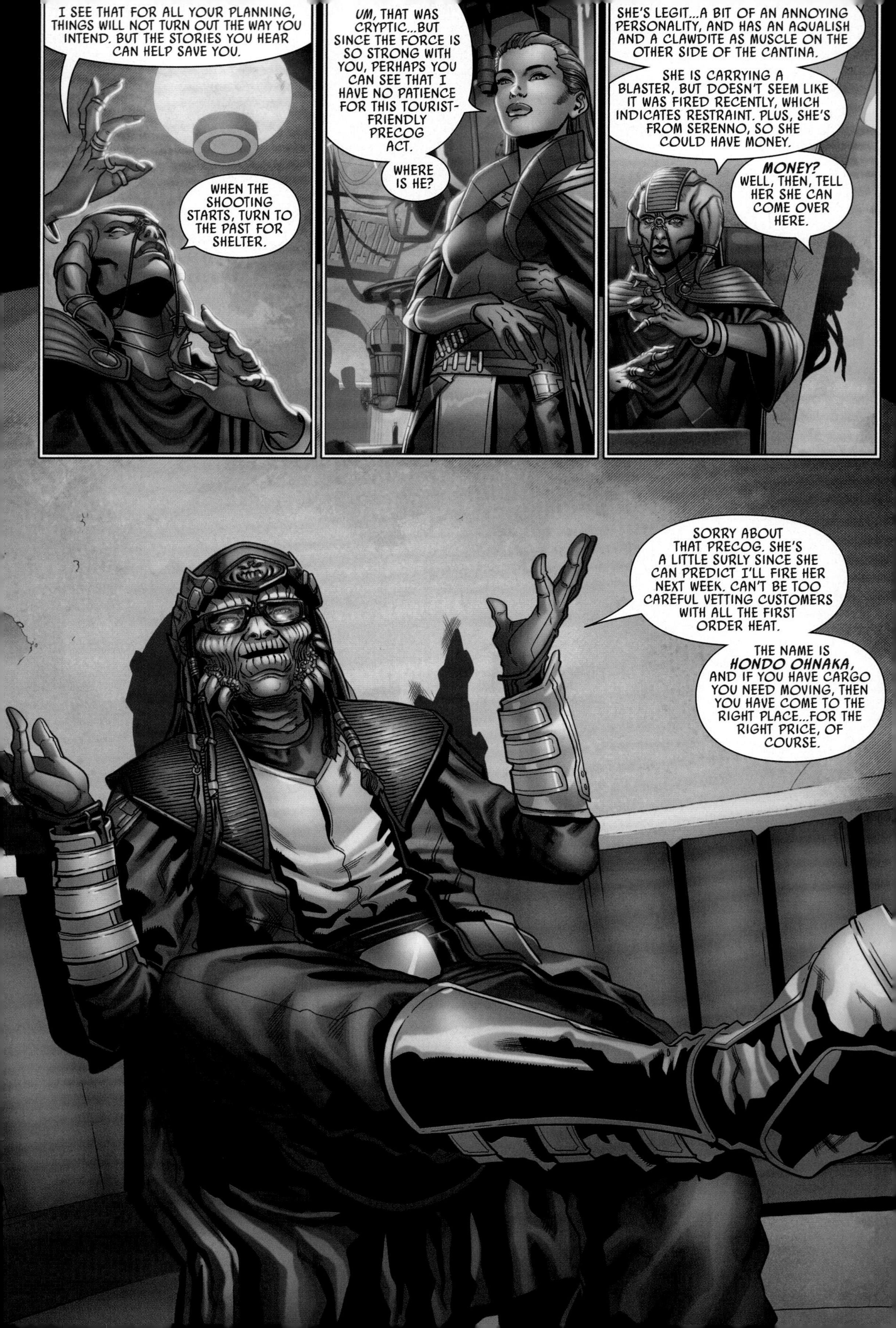

I SEE THAT FOR ALL YOUR PLANNING, THINGS WILL NOT TURN OUT THE WAY YOU INTEND. BUT THE STORIES YOU HEAR CAN HELP SAVE YOU.
WHEN THE SHOOTING STARTS, TURN TO THE PAST FOR SHELTER.
UM, THAT WAS CRYPTIC...BUT SINCE THE FORCE IS SO STRONG WITH YOU, PERHAPS YOU CAN SEE THAT I HAVE NO PATIENCE FOR THIS TOURIST-FRIENDLY PRECOG ACT.
WHERE IS HE?
SHE'S LEGIT...A BIT OF AN ANNOYING PERSONALITY, AND HAS AN AQUALISH AND A CLAWDITE AS MUSCLE ON THE OTHER SIDE OF THE CANTINA.
SHE IS CARRYING A BLASTER, BUT DOESN'T SEEM LIKE IT WAS FIRED RECENTLY, WHICH INDICATES RESTRAINT. PLUS, SHE'S FROM SERENNO, SO SHE COULD HAVE MONEY.
MONEY? WELL, THEN, TELL HER SHE CAN COME OVER HERE.
SORRY ABOUT THAT PRECOG. SHE'S A LITTLE SURLY SINCE SHE CAN PREDICT I'LL FIRE HER NEXT WEEK. CAN'T BE TOO CAREFUL VETTING CUSTOMERS WITH ALL THE FIRST ORDER HEAT.
THE NAME IS ***HONDO OHNAKA***, AND IF YOU HAVE CARGO YOU NEED MOVING, THEN YOU HAVE COME TO THE RIGHT PLACE...FOR THE RIGHT PRICE, OF COURSE.

PRICE IS NOT A PROBLEM... BUT I NEED A PILOT WHO CAN MAKE A RUN THROUGH THE FIRST ORDER BLOCKADE.

YOU CERTAINLY HAVE THE RIGHT REPUTATION AS A PIRATE.

DON'T SAY THAT TOO LOUDLY. SOMEONE MIGHT GET THE WRONG IDEA.

I'M A LEGITIMATE BUSINESSMAN.

CAN YOU GET US PAST IT OR NOT?

WHY DOES KENDOH NEED TO HIRE A PILOT? SHE'S GOT A DAMN GOOD ONE RIGHT HERE.

ᚨᚠᚨᛈᛏᛒᛊᚱᛒ ᛗᚠᛒᚺᚾᛊᛗ ᚨᛈᚾᚦᛒᛘᚺᛗ ᚨᚺᛗᚨ ᚠᛗᚠ

WHAT DO YOU MEAN "IT'S ALL JUST A PLOY"?

ᚨᛈᛒᚱᚨᚺᛊᛗᛈᛊ ᚠᛈᚨᛈᛒᛗᚾᛗᚠᛊᚱᛗᛁ ᚦᛈᛈᛗᚱᚦᛈᛘᛏᚱᛒ

UH, OF COURSE... I REMEMBER HEARING THE PLAN. JUST BEEN A BAD DAY.

CAN *I* DO IT? YOU WOUND ME. YOU'RE LOOKING AT THE PIRA--*BUSINESSMAN* WHO ONCE ESCAPED THE GUARDIANS OF THE WHILLS AND RAN THROUGH AN IMPERIAL BLOCKADE.

I WAS TAUGHT THAT THE GUARDIANS WERE NOBLE PROTECTORS OF THE TEMPLE OF KYBER. BACK WHEN THERE *WAS* A TEMPLE OF THE KYBER.

SURE, THEY'RE ALL NOBLE-SOUNDING IN THE PAST TENSE, BUT BELIEVE ME--UP CLOSE AND PERSONAL, THEY'RE A DANGEROUS BUNCH. THEY *WERE* A DANGEROUS BUNCH. I MEAN, MY PAL DOK-ONDAR USED TO SAY...

I MEAN, MY PAL DOK-ONDAR USED TO SAY...

<CAREFUL! WHAT KIND OF CRINKING SPY NAME-CHECKS THE PERSON HE'S SPYING FOR? THIS IS NOT PART OF THE PLAN! JUST PUMP HER FOR DETAILS ABOUT *HER PLANS*.>*

*TRANSLATED FROM ITHORIAN.

UH...I JUST MEANT... HAVE SOME FAITH, MY FRIEND.

FAITH IN WHAT? AND WE'RE NOT EXACTLY FRIENDS.

ER, HAVE SOME FAITH IN THE PILOT YOU JUST HIRED, MY... POTENTIAL CLIENT. NOW, LET ME TELL YOU--

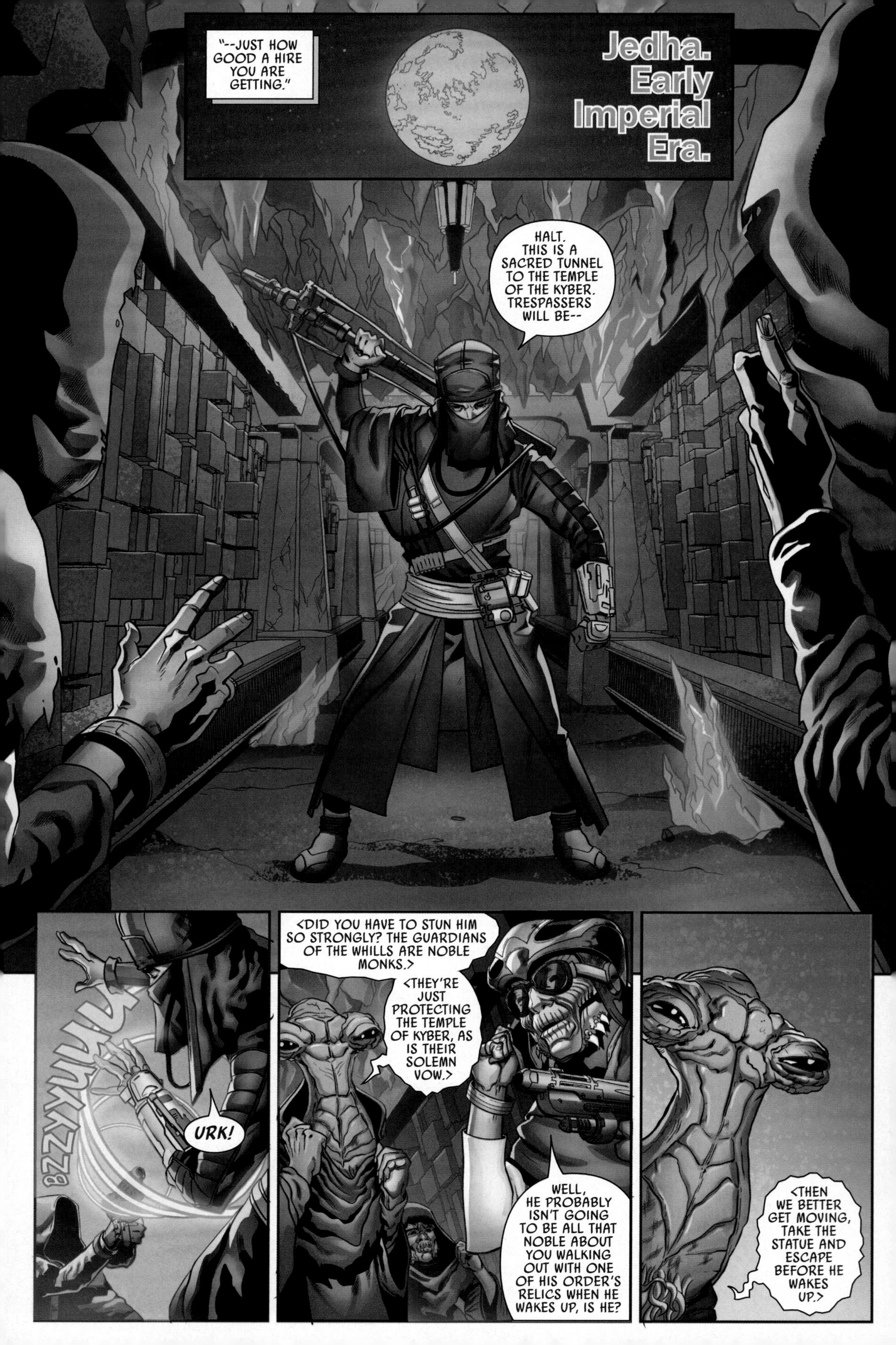

"--JUST HOW GOOD A HIRE YOU ARE GETTING."
Jedha. Early Imperial Era.
HALT. THIS IS A SACRED TUNNEL TO THE TEMPLE OF THE KYBER. TRESPASSERS WILL BE--
BZZKKZHHNK
URK!
<DID YOU HAVE TO STUN HIM SO STRONGLY? THE GUARDIANS OF THE WHILLS ARE NOBLE MONKS.>
<THEY'RE JUST PROTECTING THE TEMPLE OF KYBER, AS IS THEIR SOLEMN VOW.>
WELL, HE PROBABLY ISN'T GOING TO BE ALL THAT NOBLE ABOUT YOU WALKING OUT WITH ONE OF HIS ORDER'S RELICS WHEN HE WAKES UP, IS HE?
<THEN WE BETTER GET MOVING, TAKE THE STATUE AND ESCAPE BEFORE HE WAKES UP.>

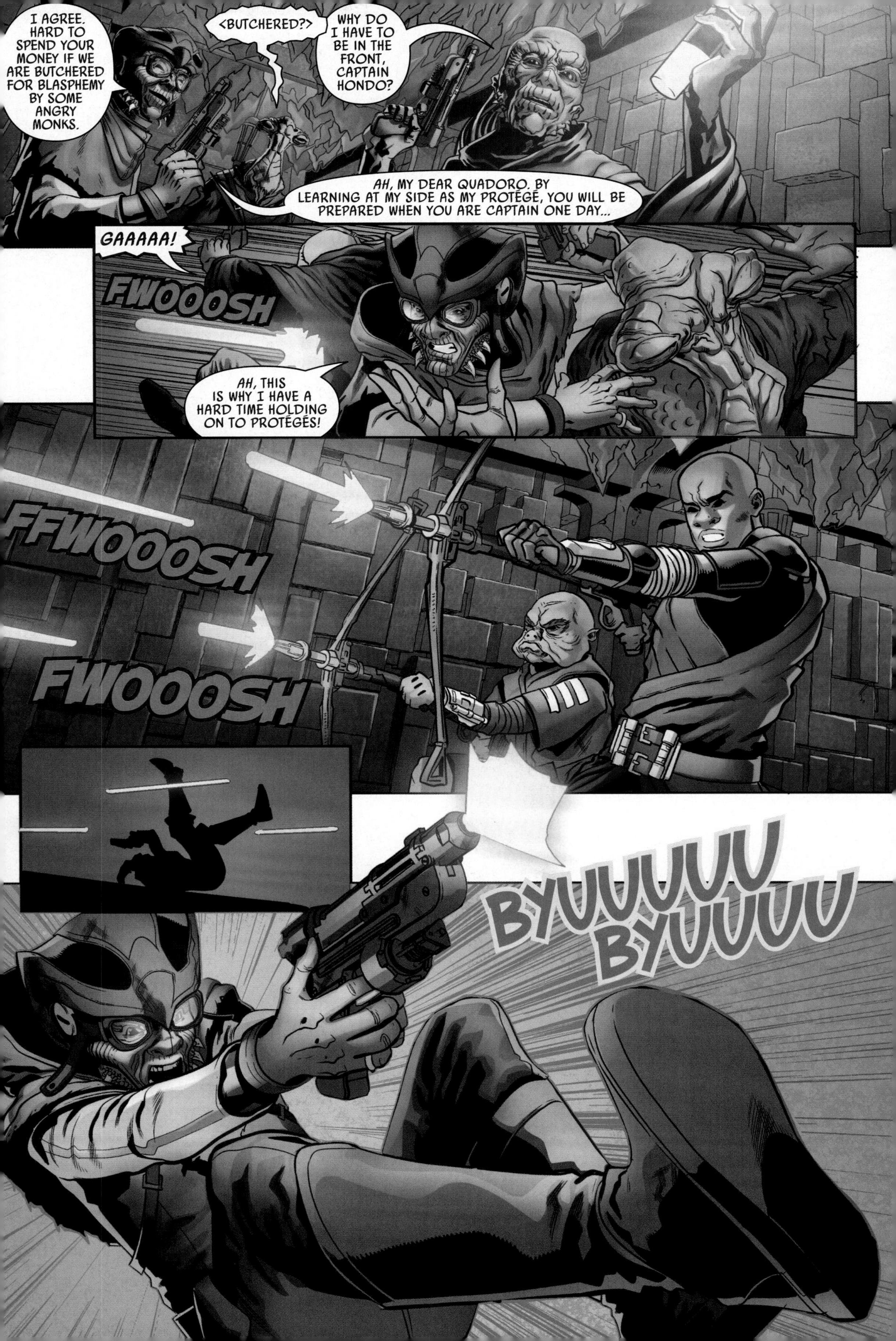
I AGREE. HARD TO SPEND YOUR MONEY IF WE ARE BUTCHERED FOR BLASPHEMY BY SOME ANGRY MONKS.
<BUTCHERED?>
WHY DO I HAVE TO BE IN THE FRONT, CAPTAIN HONDO?
AH, MY DEAR QUADORO. BY LEARNING AT MY SIDE AS MY PROTÉGÉ, YOU WILL BE PREPARED WHEN YOU ARE CAPTAIN ONE DAY...
GAAAAA!
FWOOOSH
AH, THIS IS WHY I HAVE A HARD TIME HOLDING ON TO PROTÉGÉS!
FFWOOOSH
FWOOOSH
BYUUUUU
BYUUUUU

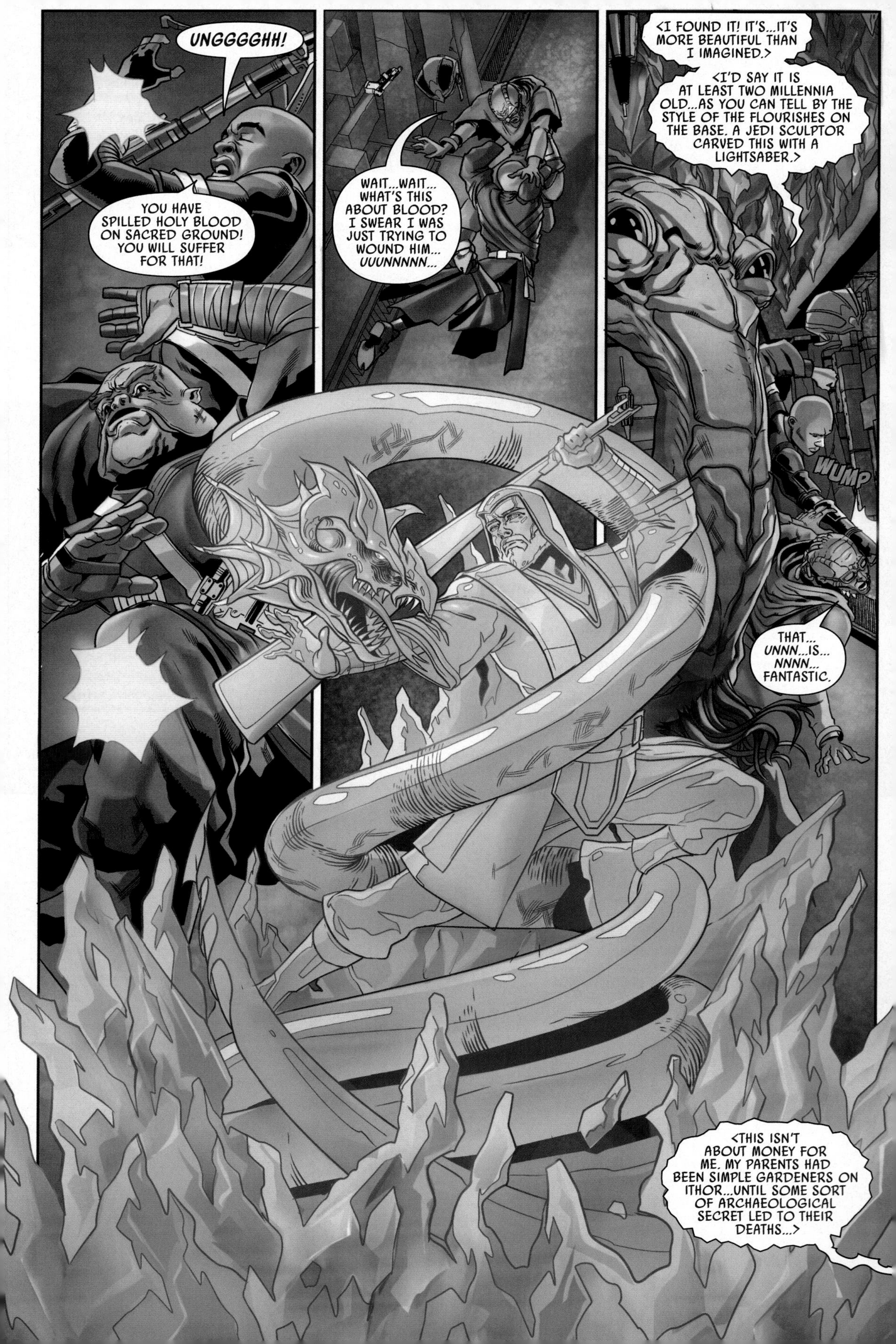
UNGGGGHH!
YOU HAVE SPILLED HOLY BLOOD ON SACRED GROUND! YOU WILL SUFFER FOR THAT!
WAIT...WAIT... WHAT'S THIS ABOUT BLOOD? I SWEAR I WAS JUST TRYING TO WOUND HIM... UUUNNNNN...
<I FOUND IT! IT'S...IT'S MORE BEAUTIFUL THAN I IMAGINED.>
<I'D SAY IT IS AT LEAST TWO MILLENNIA OLD...AS YOU CAN TELL BY THE STYLE OF THE FLOURISHES ON THE BASE. A JEDI SCULPTOR CARVED THIS WITH A LIGHTSABER.>
WUMP
THAT... UNNN...IS... NNNN... FANTASTIC.
<THIS ISN'T ABOUT MONEY FOR ME. MY PARENTS HAD BEEN SIMPLE GARDENERS ON ITHOR...UNTIL SOME SORT OF ARCHAEOLOGICAL SECRET LED TO THEIR DEATHS...>

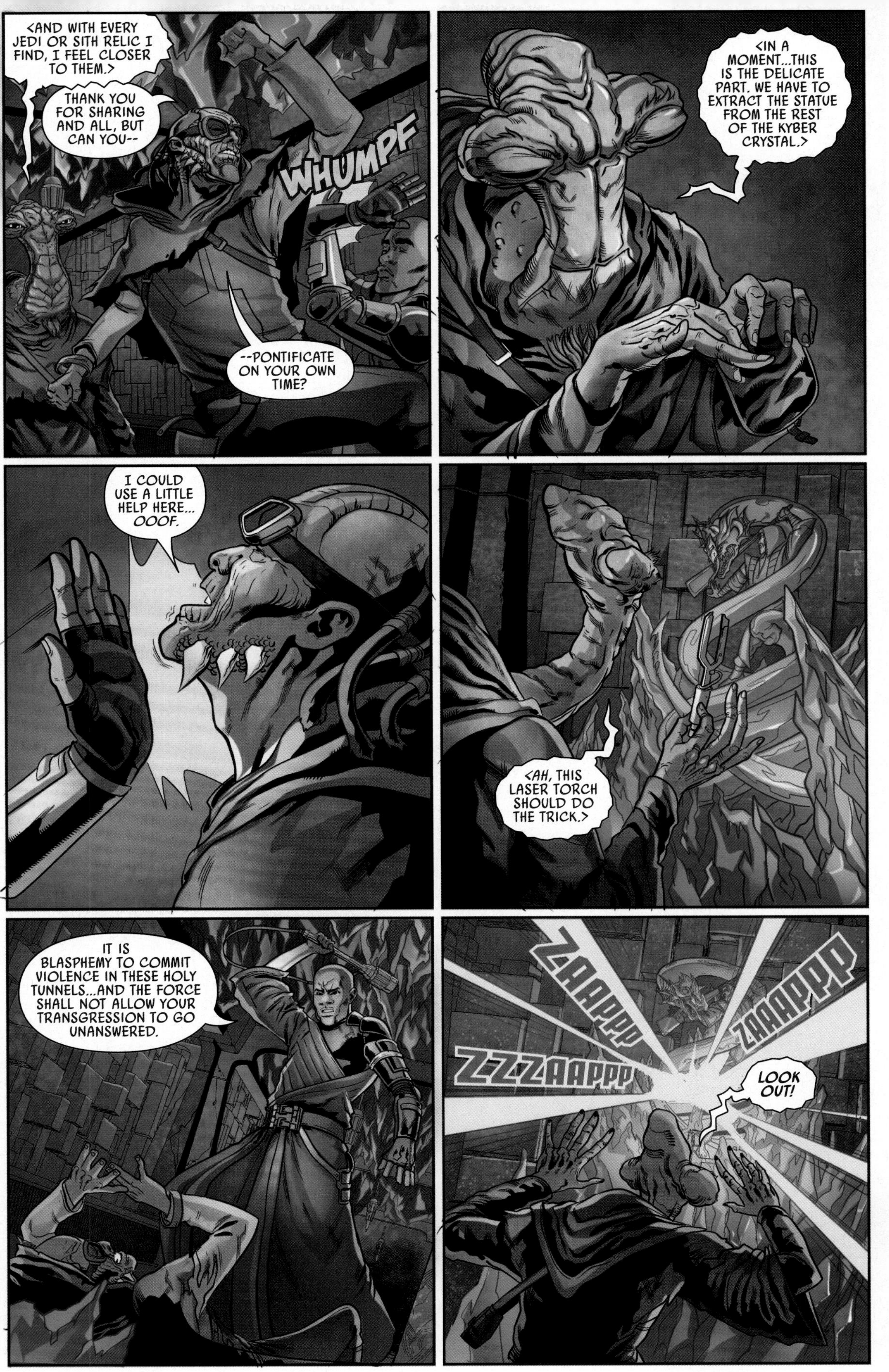
<AND WITH EVERY JEDI OR SITH RELIC I FIND, I FEEL CLOSER TO THEM.>
THANK YOU FOR SHARING AND ALL, BUT CAN YOU--
WHUMPF
--PONTIFICATE ON YOUR OWN TIME?
<IN A MOMENT...THIS IS THE DELICATE PART. WE HAVE TO EXTRACT THE STATUE FROM THE REST OF THE KYBER CRYSTAL.>
I COULD USE A LITTLE HELP HERE... OOOF.
<AH, THIS LASER TORCH SHOULD DO THE TRICK.>
IT IS BLASPHEMY TO COMMIT VIOLENCE IN THESE HOLY TUNNELS...AND THE FORCE SHALL NOT ALLOW YOUR TRANSGRESSION TO GO UNANSWERED.
ZAAPPP
ZAAAPPP
ZZZAAPPP
LOOK OUT!

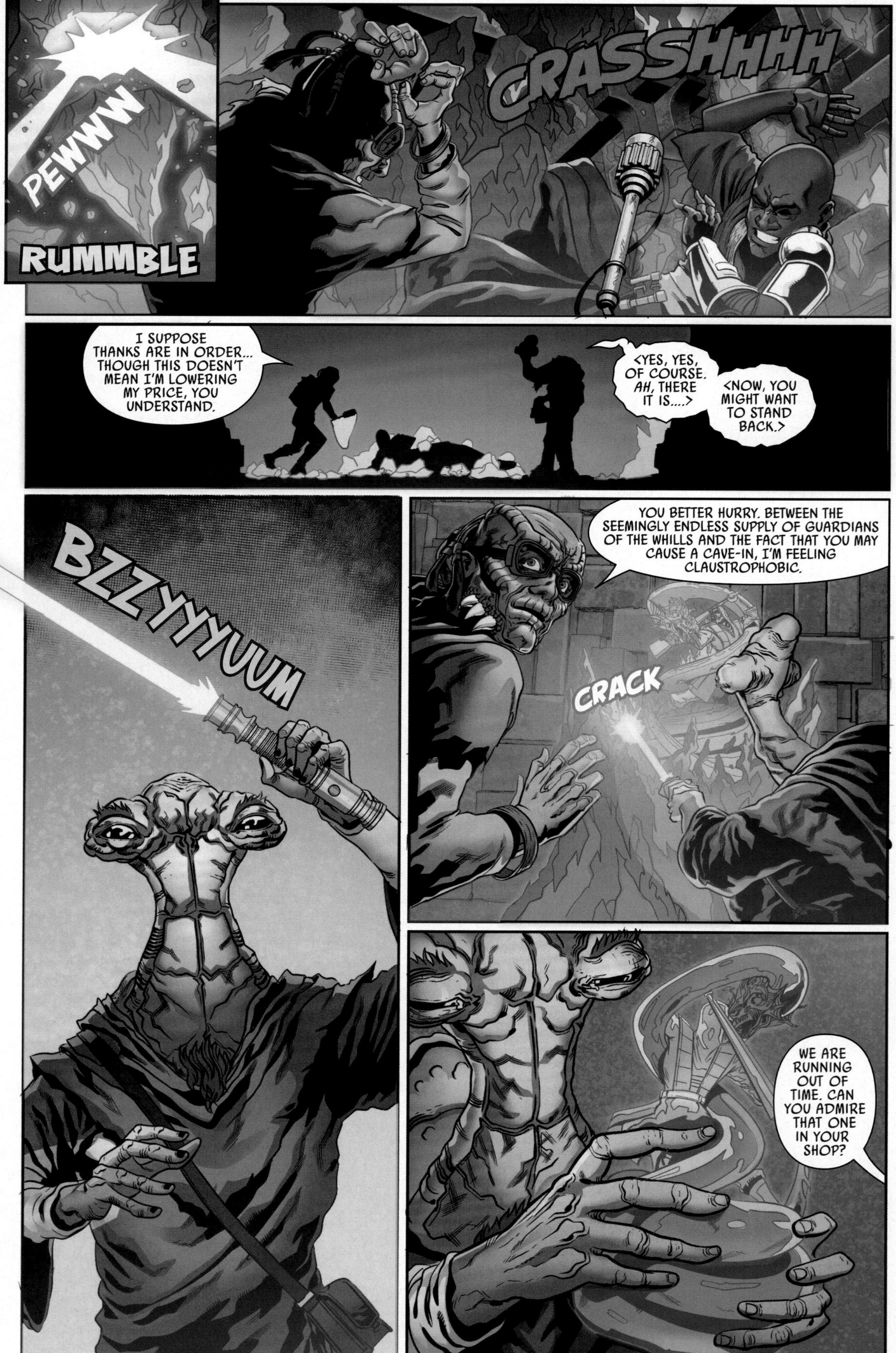
PEWWW
RUMMBLE
CRASSHHHH
I SUPPOSE THANKS ARE IN ORDER... THOUGH THIS DOESN'T MEAN I'M LOWERING MY PRICE, YOU UNDERSTAND.
<YES, YES, OF COURSE. AH, THERE IT IS....>
<NOW, YOU MIGHT WANT TO STAND BACK.>
BZZYYYUUM
YOU BETTER HURRY. BETWEEN THE SEEMINGLY ENDLESS SUPPLY OF GUARDIANS OF THE WHILLS AND THE FACT THAT YOU MAY CAUSE A CAVE-IN, I'M FEELING CLAUSTROPHOBIC.
CRACK
WE ARE RUNNING OUT OF TIME. CAN YOU ADMIRE THAT ONE IN YOUR SHOP?

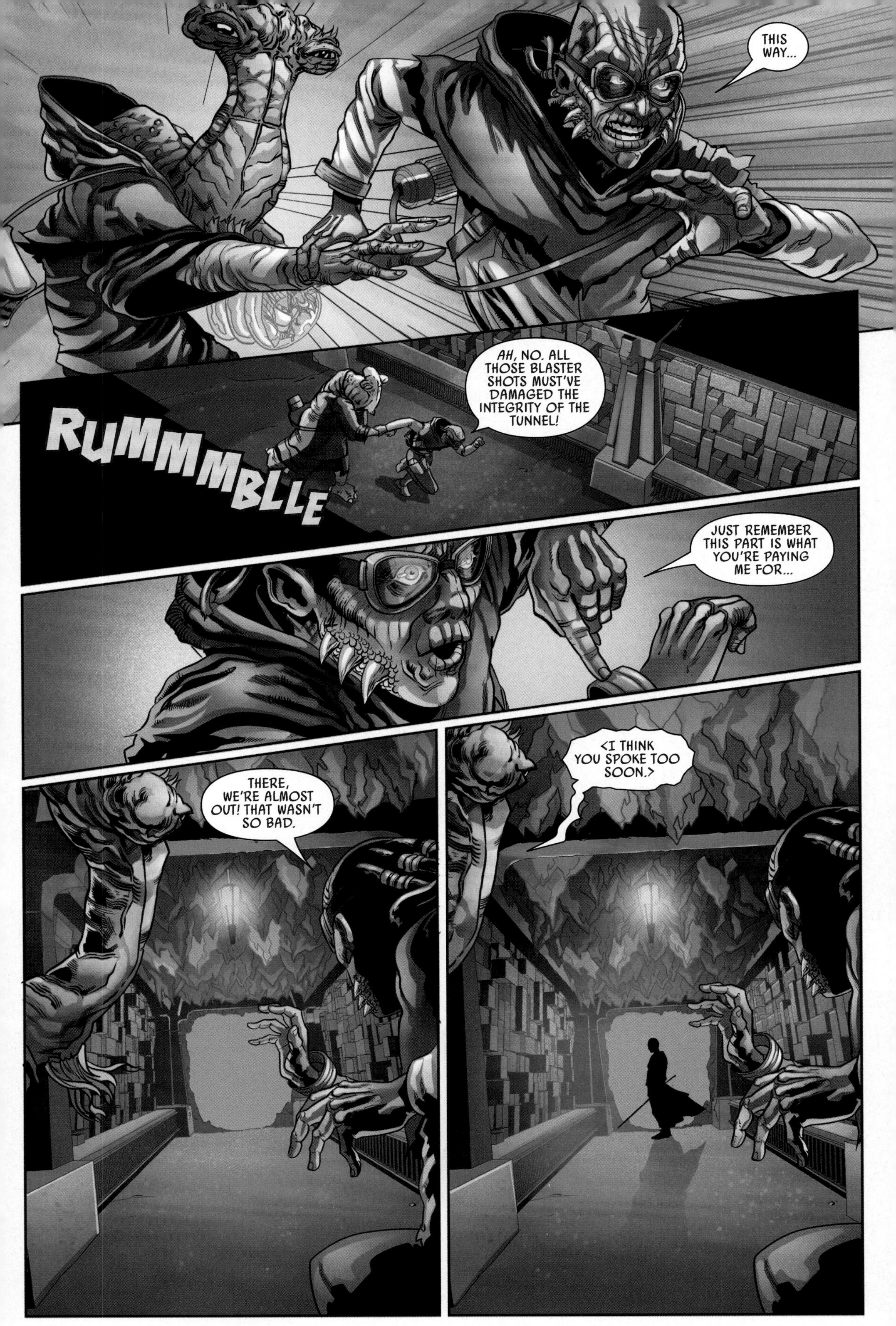
THIS WAY...
AH, NO. ALL THOSE BLASTER SHOTS MUST'VE DAMAGED THE INTEGRITY OF THE TUNNEL!
RUMMMBLLE
JUST REMEMBER THIS PART IS WHAT YOU'RE PAYING ME FOR...
THERE, WE'RE ALMOST OUT! THAT WASN'T SO BAD.
<I THINK YOU SPOKE TOO SOON.>

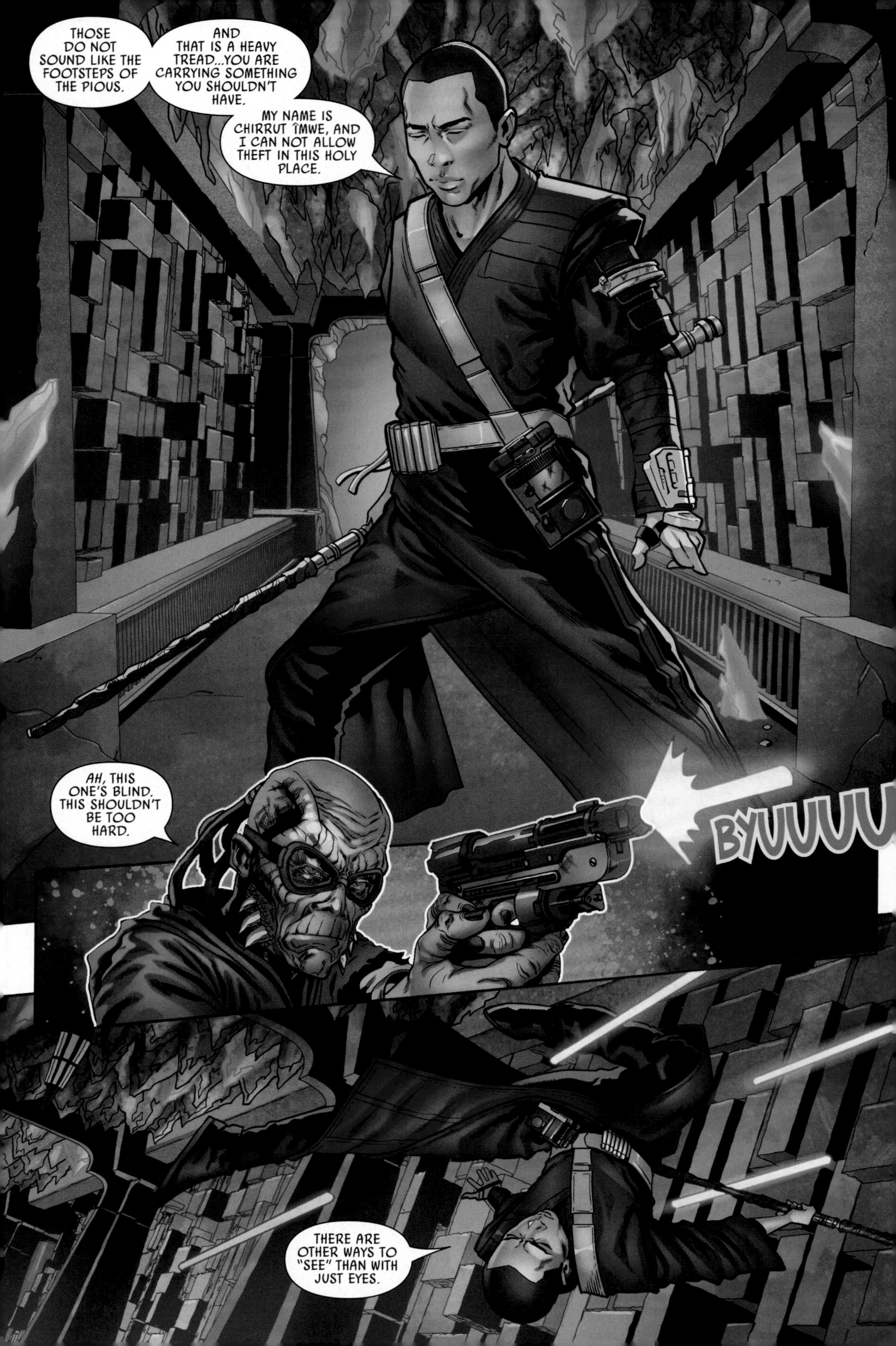
THOSE DO NOT SOUND LIKE THE FOOTSTEPS OF THE PIOUS.
AND THAT IS A HEAVY TREAD...YOU ARE CARRYING SOMETHING YOU SHOULDN'T HAVE.
MY NAME IS CHIRRUT ÎMWE, AND I CAN NOT ALLOW THEFT IN THIS HOLY PLACE.
AH, THIS ONE'S BLIND. THIS SHOULDN'T BE TOO HARD.
BYUUUU
THERE ARE OTHER WAYS TO "SEE" THAN WITH JUST EYES.

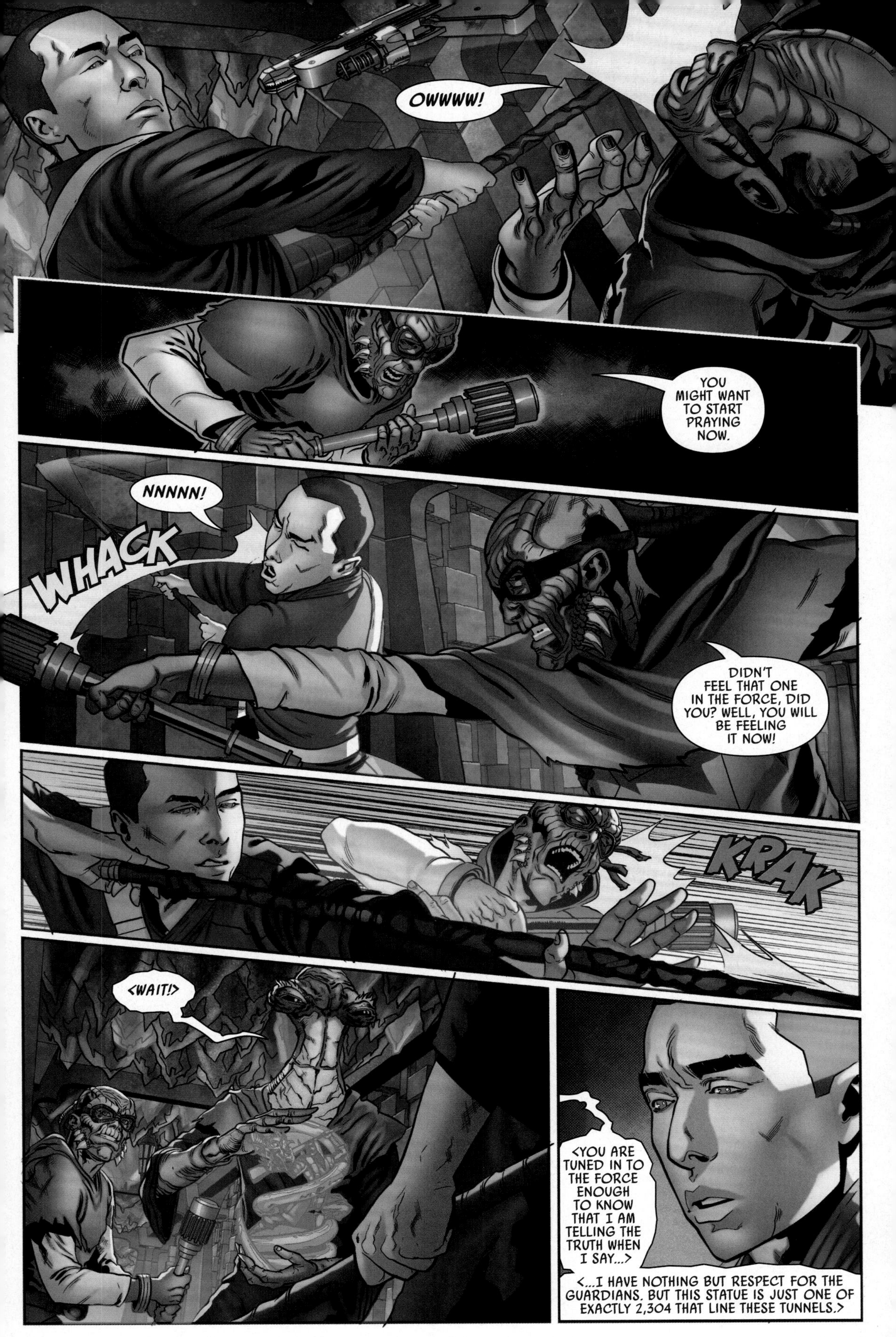
OWWWW!
YOU MIGHT WANT TO START PRAYING NOW.
NNNNN!
WHACK
DIDN'T FEEL THAT ONE IN THE FORCE, DID YOU? WELL, YOU WILL BE FEELING IT NOW!
KRAK
<WAIT!>
<YOU ARE TUNED IN TO THE FORCE ENOUGH TO KNOW THAT I AM TELLING THE TRUTH WHEN I SAY...>
<...I HAVE NOTHING BUT RESPECT FOR THE GUARDIANS. BUT THIS STATUE IS JUST ONE OF EXACTLY 2,304 THAT LINE THESE TUNNELS.>

<I'M NOT A PIRATE...>

THERE'S NOTHING WRONG WITH SUCH A NOBLE PROFESSION.

<...THIS STATUE IS PRICELESS TO ME. I'VE BEEN ACROSS THE GALAXY AND ONLY SEEN ONE LIKE IT--->

<--IN A BOX BELONGING TO MY PARENTS DELIVERED TO ME AFTER THEIR DEATHS.>

<PLEASE...LET ME USE THIS CLUE TO MOVE CLOSER TO SOLVING THEIR MURDERS.>

<LET ME TAKE THE STATUE OUT OF THE DARK AND INTO THE LIGHT WHERE IT BELONGS.>

...GO.

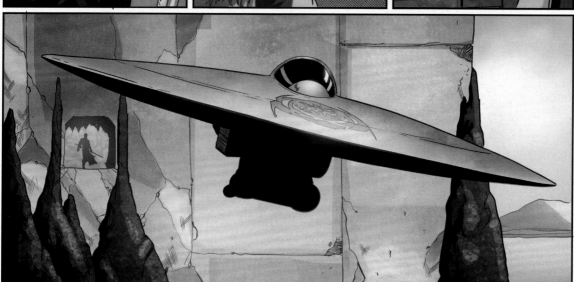

DID YOU MEAN WHAT YOU SAID?

<MOST OF IT.>

YOU KNOW I WOULD HAVE BEEN ABLE TO WIN THAT FIGHT IF YOU HADN'T GOTTEN INVOLVED, RIGHT?

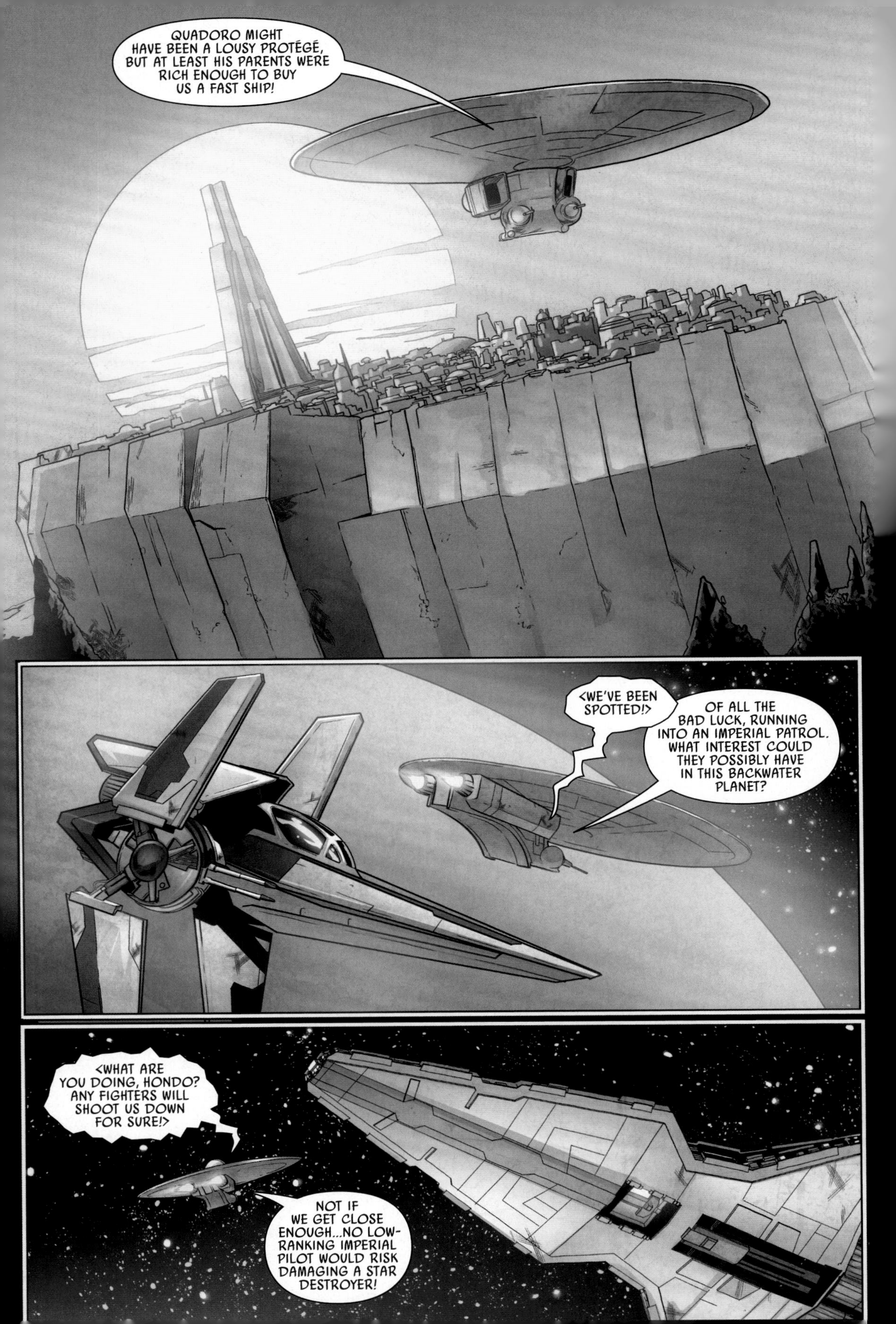
QUADORO MIGHT HAVE BEEN A LOUSY PROTÉGÉ, BUT AT LEAST HIS PARENTS WERE RICH ENOUGH TO BUY US A FAST SHIP!
<WE'VE BEEN SPOTTED!>
OF ALL THE BAD LUCK, RUNNING INTO AN IMPERIAL PATROL. WHAT INTEREST COULD THEY POSSIBLY HAVE IN THIS BACKWATER PLANET?
<WHAT ARE YOU DOING, HONDO? ANY FIGHTERS WILL SHOOT US DOWN FOR SURE!>
NOT IF WE GET CLOSE ENOUGH...NO LOW-RANKING IMPERIAL PILOT WOULD RISK DAMAGING A STAR DESTROYER!

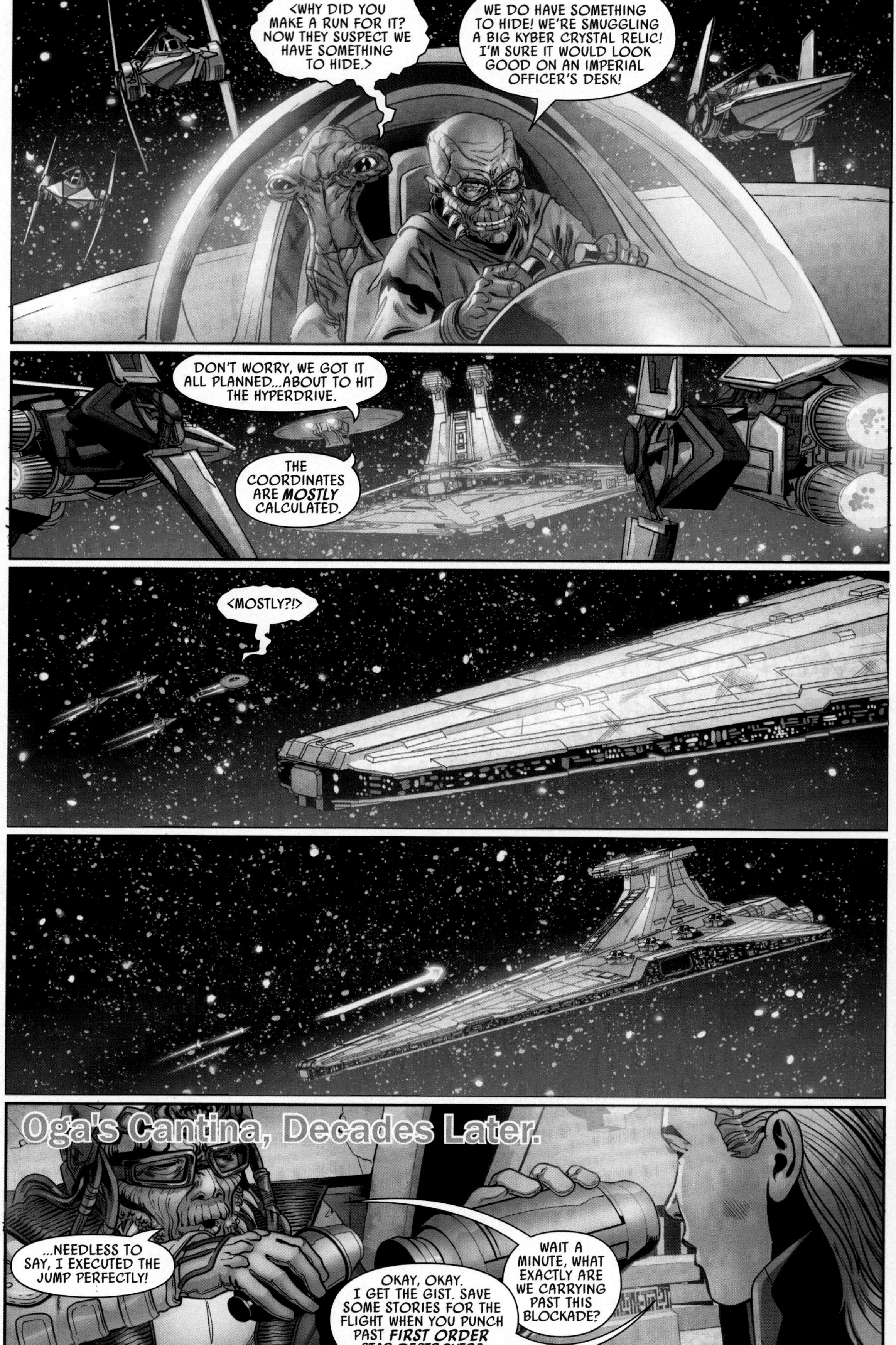
<WHY DID YOU MAKE A RUN FOR IT? NOW THEY SUSPECT WE HAVE SOMETHING TO HIDE.>
WE DO HAVE SOMETHING TO HIDE! WE'RE SMUGGLING A BIG KYBER CRYSTAL RELIC! I'M SURE IT WOULD LOOK GOOD ON AN IMPERIAL OFFICER'S DESK!
DON'T WORRY, WE GOT IT ALL PLANNED...ABOUT TO HIT THE HYPERDRIVE.
THE COORDINATES ARE *MOSTLY* CALCULATED.
<MOSTLY?!>
Oga's Cantina, Decades Later.
...NEEDLESS TO SAY, I EXECUTED THE JUMP PERFECTLY!
OKAY, OKAY. I GET THE GIST. SAVE SOME STORIES FOR THE FLIGHT WHEN YOU PUNCH PAST *FIRST ORDER* STAR DESTROYERS.
WAIT A MINUTE, WHAT EXACTLY ARE WE CARRYING PAST THIS BLOCKADE?

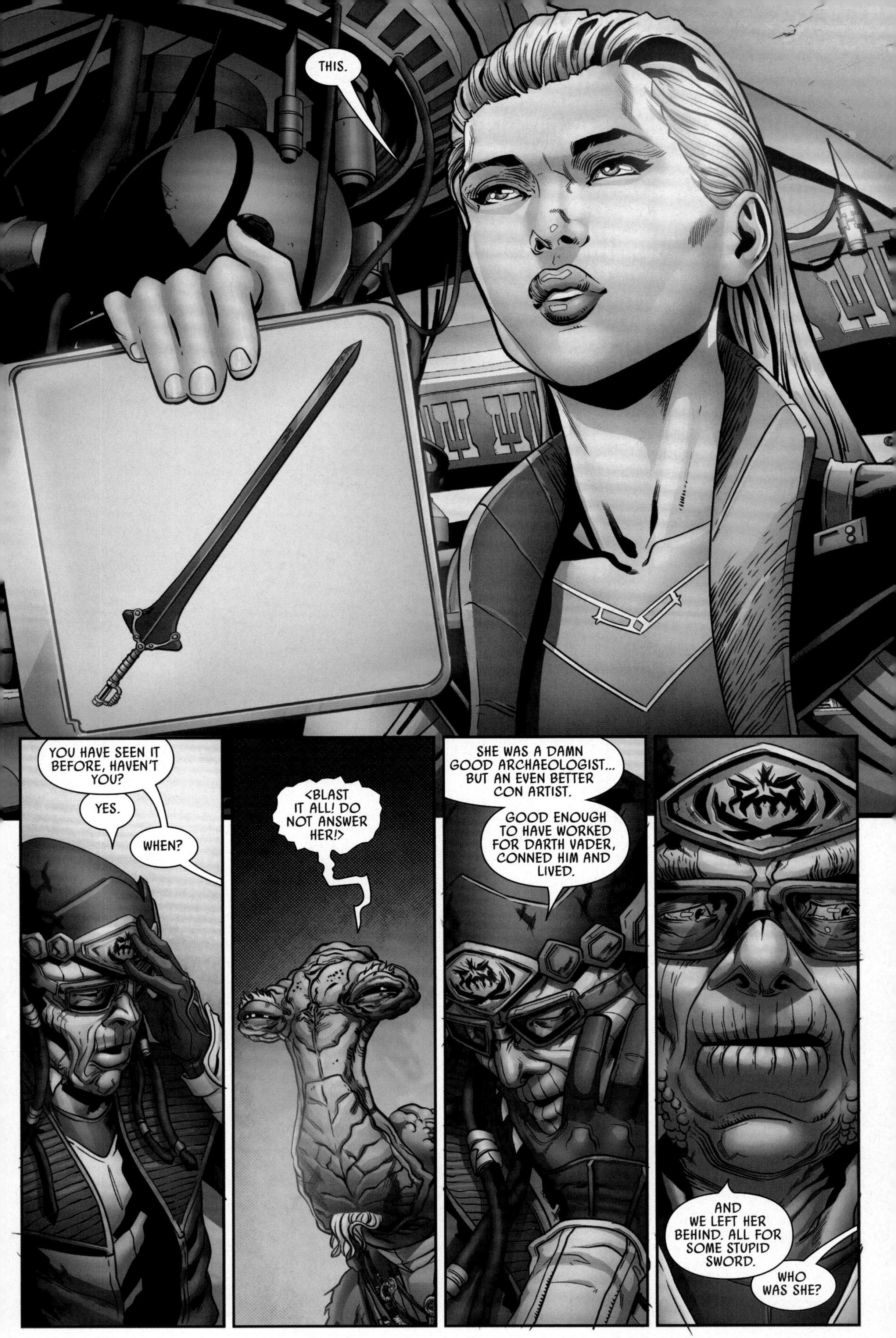
THIS.
YOU HAVE SEEN IT BEFORE, HAVEN'T YOU?
YES.
WHEN?
<BLAST IT ALL! DO NOT ANSWER HER!>
SHE WAS A DAMN GOOD ARCHAEOLOGIST... BUT AN EVEN BETTER CON ARTIST.
GOOD ENOUGH TO HAVE WORKED FOR DARTH VADER, CONNED HIM AND LIVED.
AND WE LEFT HER BEHIND. ALL FOR SOME STUPID SWORD.
WHO WAS SHE?

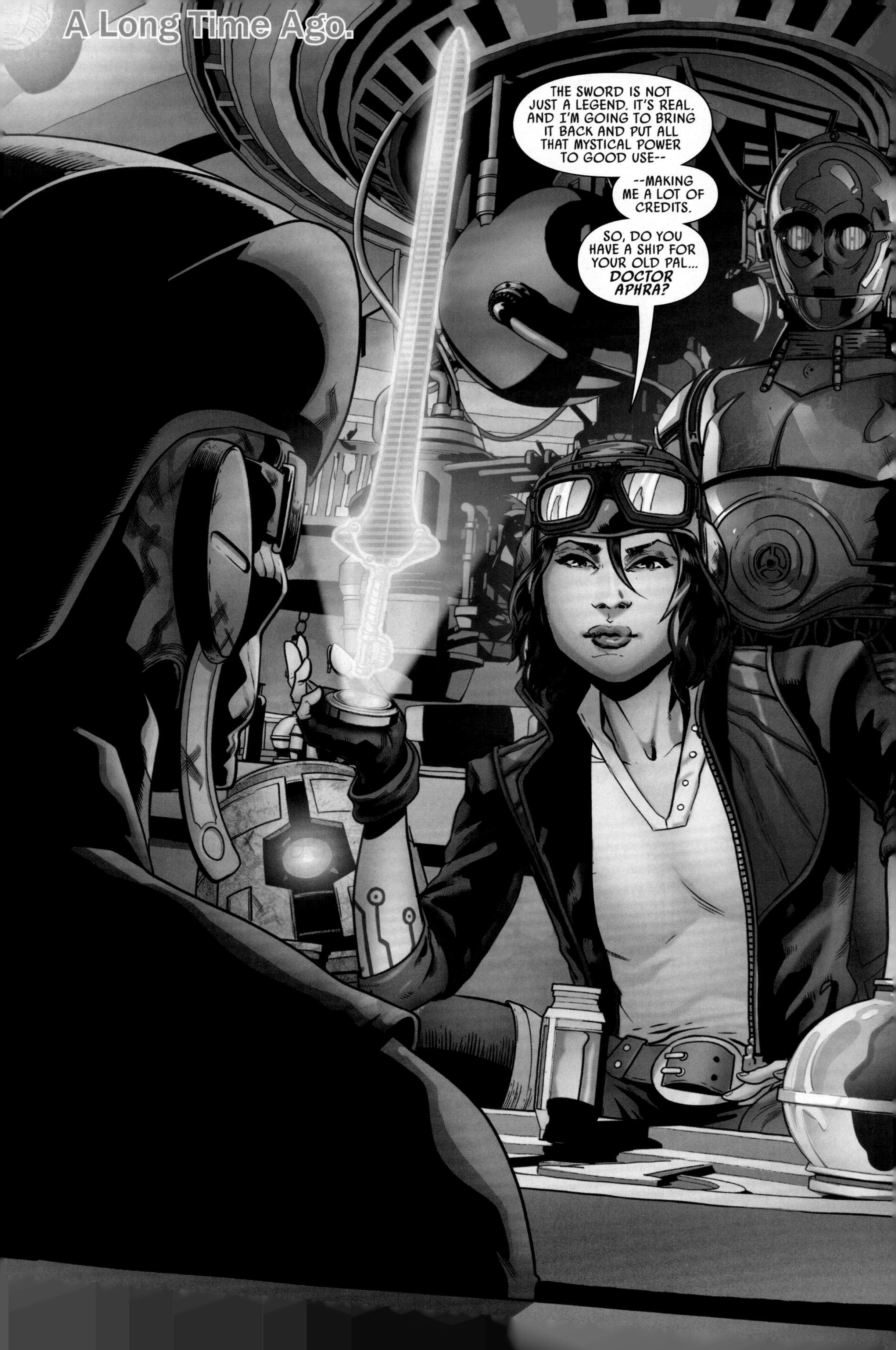
A Long Time Ago.
THE SWORD IS NOT JUST A LEGEND. IT'S REAL. AND I'M GOING TO BRING IT BACK AND PUT ALL THAT MYSTICAL POWER TO GOOD USE--
--MAKING ME A LOT OF CREDITS.
SO, DO YOU HAVE A SHIP FOR YOUR OLD PAL... DOCTOR APHRA?

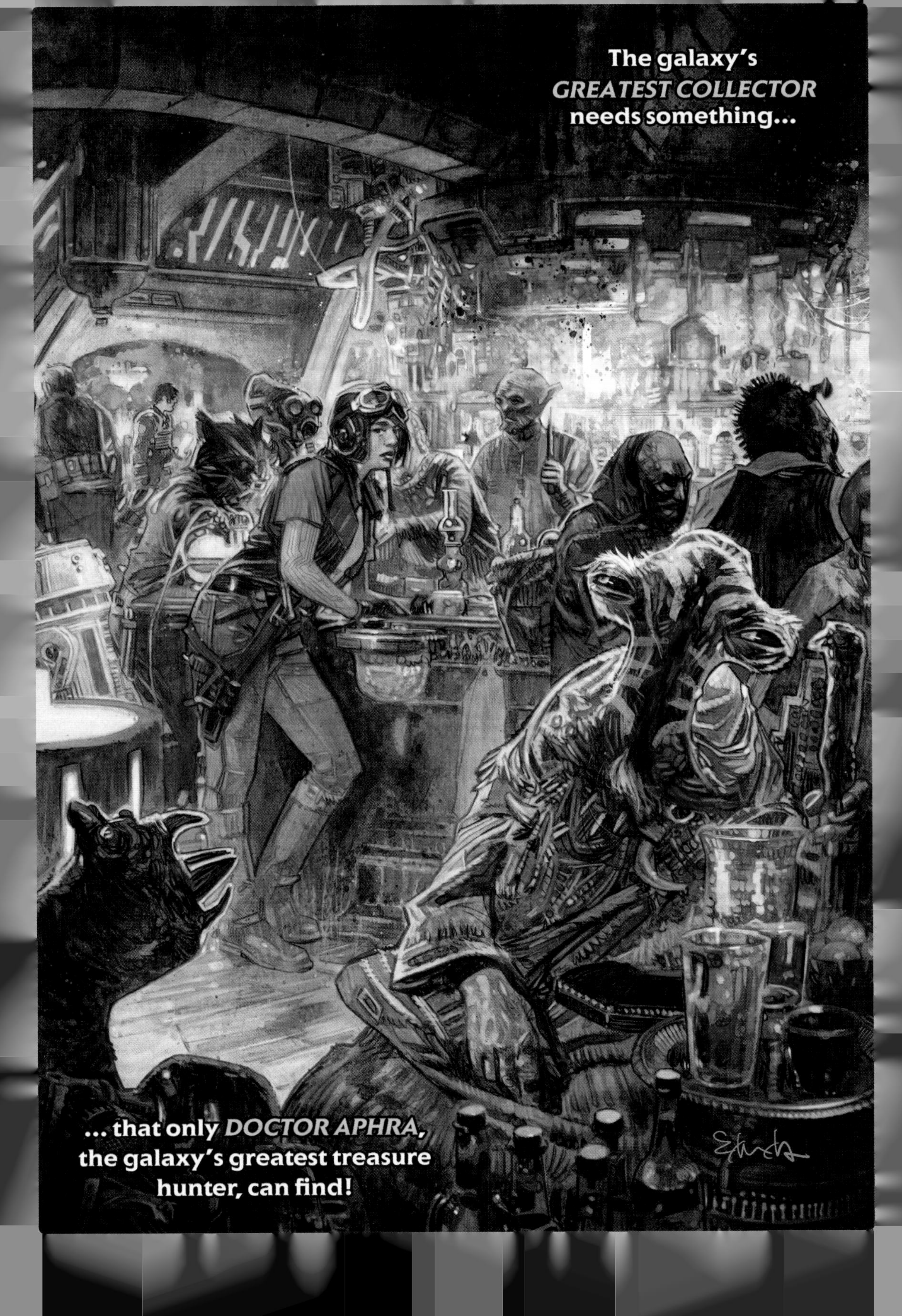
The galaxy's *GREATEST COLLECTOR* needs something...
... that only *DOCTOR APHRA*, the galaxy's greatest treasure hunter, can find!

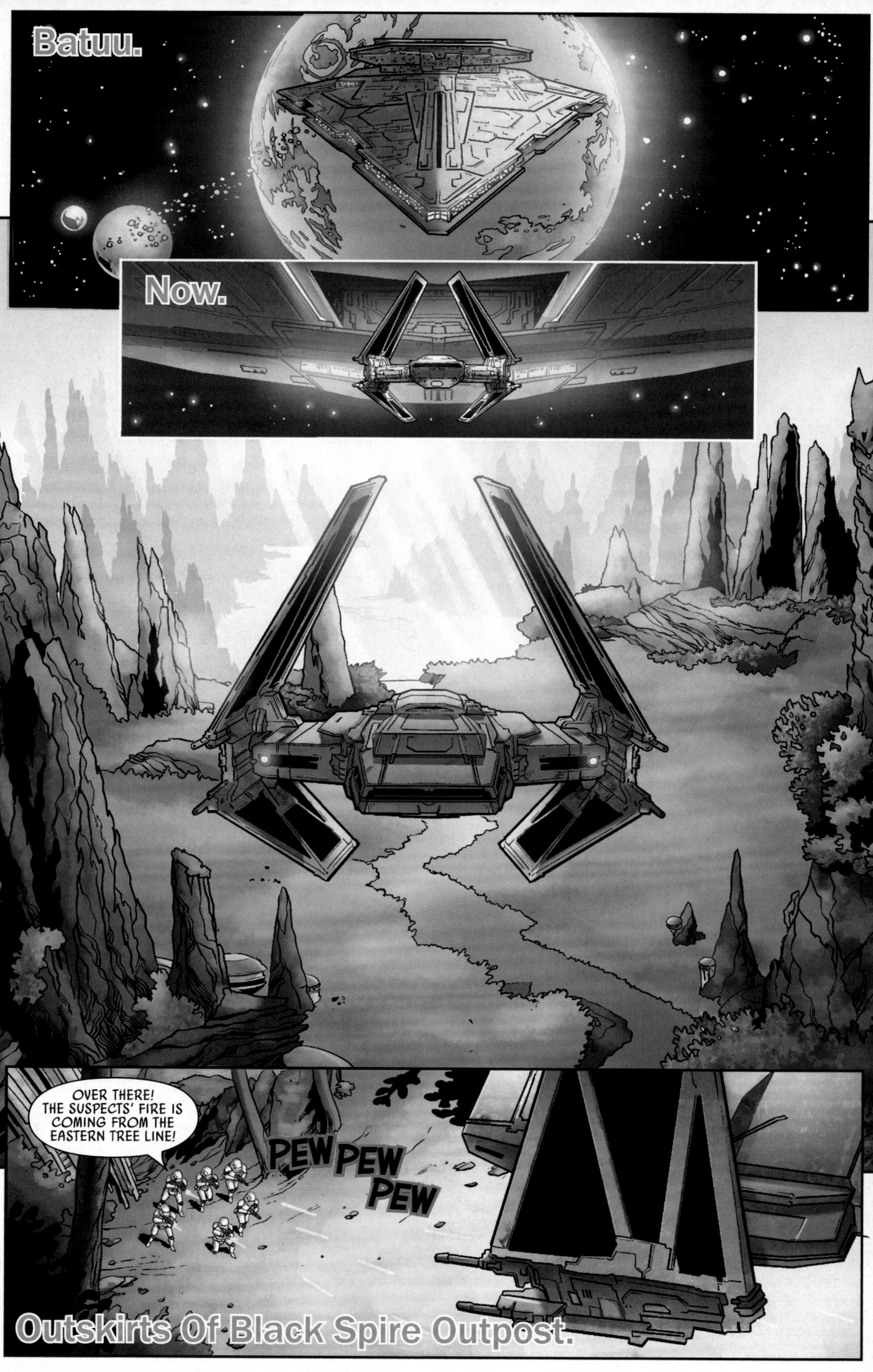
Batuu.
Now.
OVER THERE! THE SUSPECTS' FIRE IS COMING FROM THE EASTERN TREE LINE!
PEW PEW PEW
Outskirts Of Black Spire Outpost.

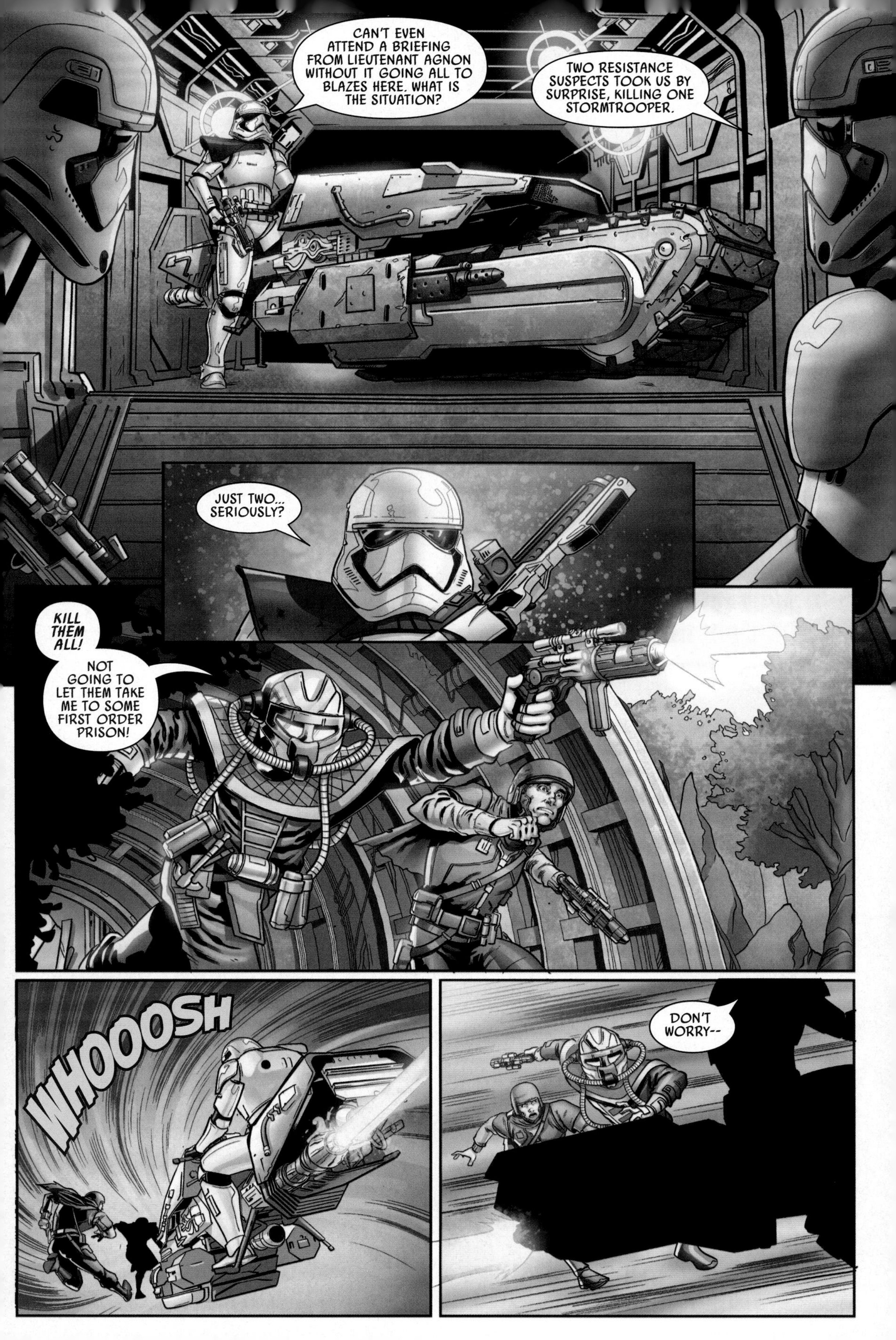
CAN'T EVEN ATTEND A BRIEFING FROM LIEUTENANT AGNON WITHOUT IT GOING ALL TO BLAZES HERE. WHAT IS THE SITUATION?
TWO RESISTANCE SUSPECTS TOOK US BY SURPRISE, KILLING ONE STORMTROOPER.
JUST TWO... SERIOUSLY?
KILL THEM ALL!
NOT GOING TO LET THEM TAKE ME TO SOME FIRST ORDER PRISON!
WHOOOSH
DON'T WORRY--

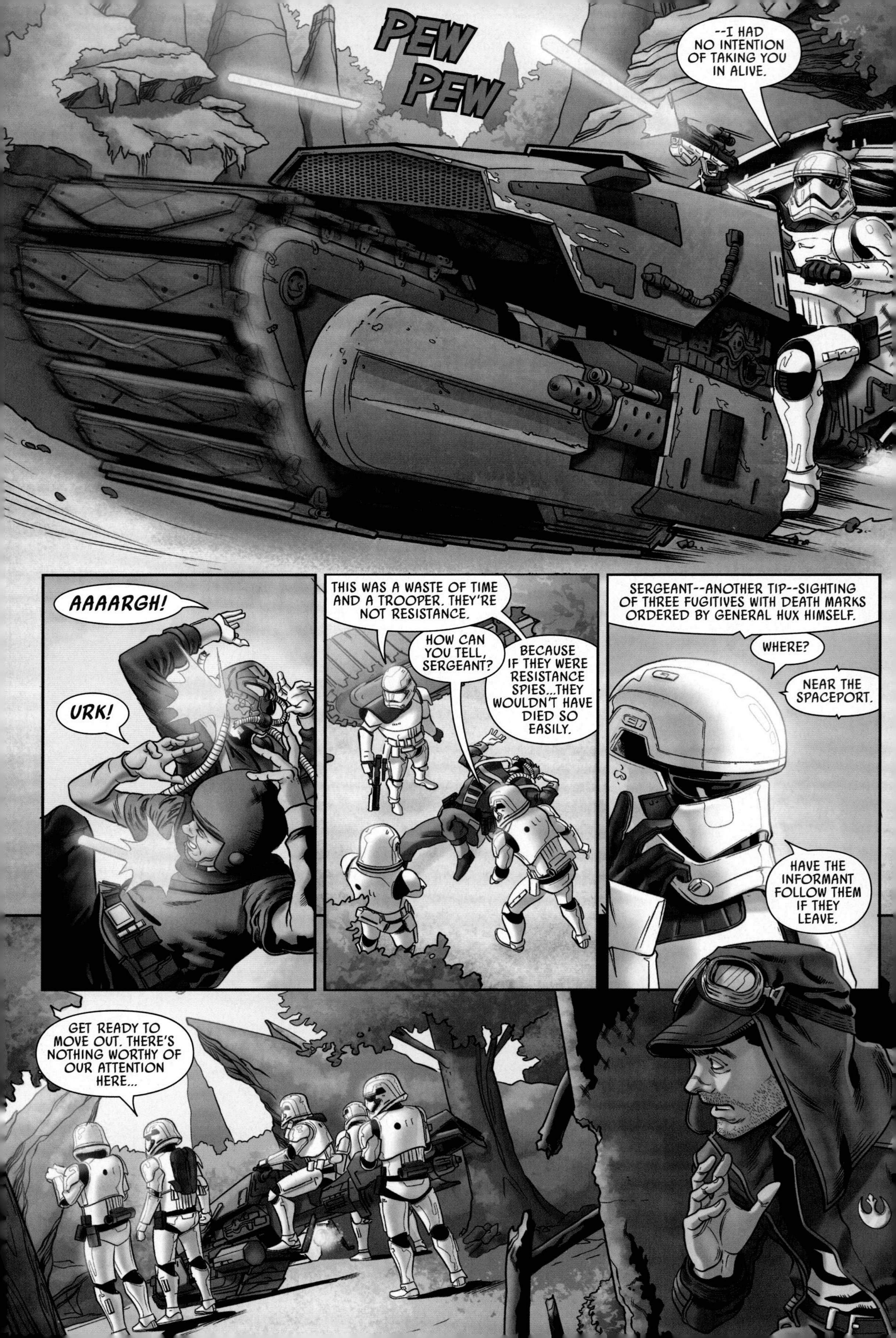
PEW
PEW
--I HAD NO INTENTION OF TAKING YOU IN ALIVE.
AAAARGH!
URK!
THIS WAS A WASTE OF TIME AND A TROOPER. THEY'RE NOT RESISTANCE.
HOW CAN YOU TELL, SERGEANT?
BECAUSE IF THEY WERE RESISTANCE SPIES...THEY WOULDN'T HAVE DIED SO EASILY.
SERGEANT--ANOTHER TIP--SIGHTING OF THREE FUGITIVES WITH DEATH MARKS ORDERED BY GENERAL HUX HIMSELF.
WHERE?
NEAR THE SPACEPORT.
HAVE THE INFORMANT FOLLOW THEM IF THEY LEAVE.
GET READY TO MOVE OUT. THERE'S NOTHING WORTHY OF OUR ATTENTION HERE...

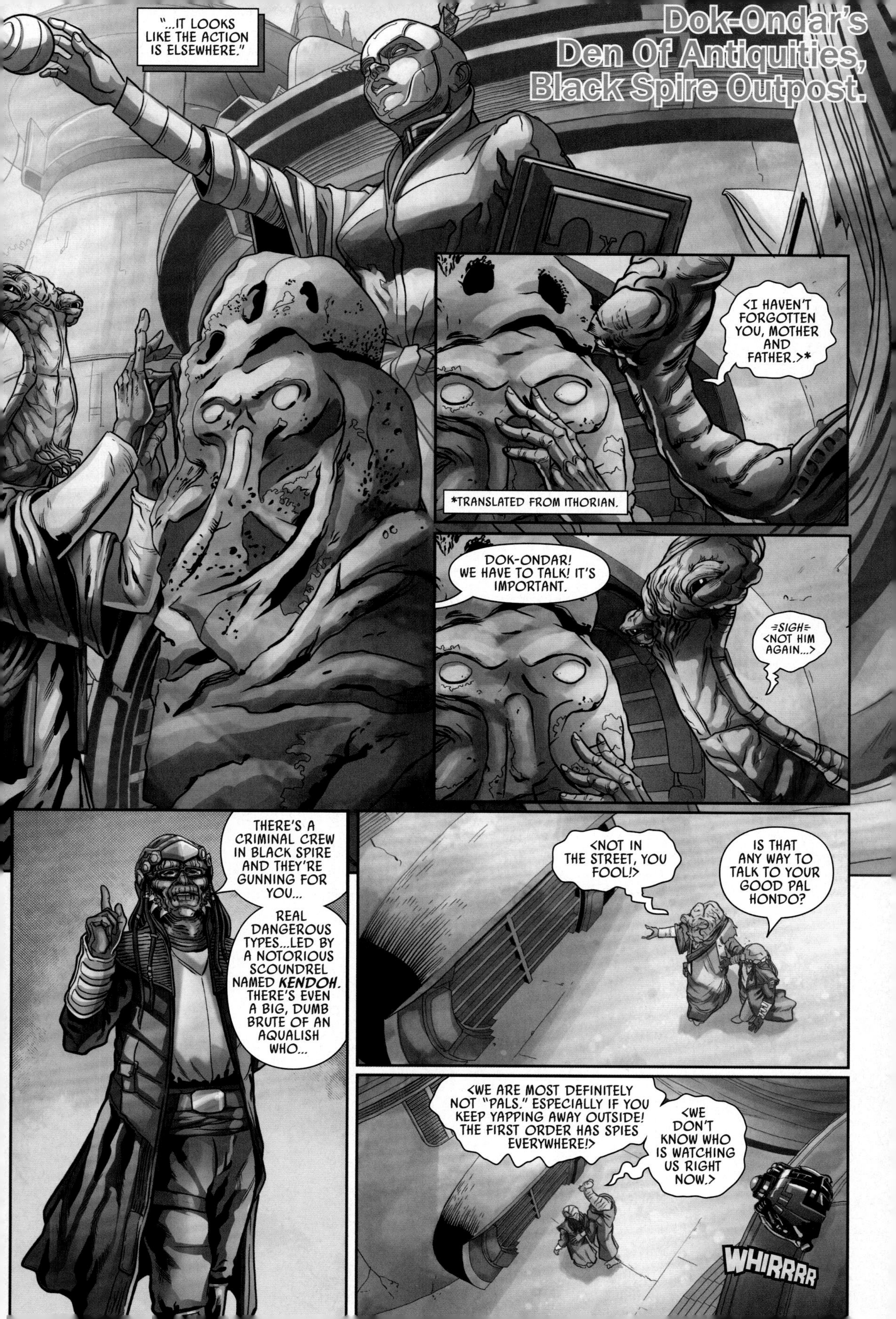
"...IT LOOKS LIKE THE ACTION IS ELSEWHERE."
Dok-Ondar's Den Of Antiquities, Black Spire Outpost.
<I HAVEN'T FORGOTTEN YOU, MOTHER AND FATHER.>*
*TRANSLATED FROM ITHORIAN.
DOK-ONDAR! WE HAVE TO TALK! IT'S IMPORTANT.
=SIGH= <NOT HIM AGAIN...>
THERE'S A CRIMINAL CREW IN BLACK SPIRE AND THEY'RE GUNNING FOR YOU...
REAL DANGEROUS TYPES...LED BY A NOTORIOUS SCOUNDREL NAMED KENDOH. THERE'S EVEN A BIG, DUMB BRUTE OF AN AQUALISH WHO...
<NOT IN THE STREET, YOU FOOL!>
IS THAT ANY WAY TO TALK TO YOUR GOOD PAL HONDO?
<WE ARE MOST DEFINITELY NOT "PALS." ESPECIALLY IF YOU KEEP YAPPING AWAY OUTSIDE! THE FIRST ORDER HAS SPIES EVERYWHERE!>
<WE DON'T KNOW WHO IS WATCHING US RIGHT NOW.>
WHIRRRR

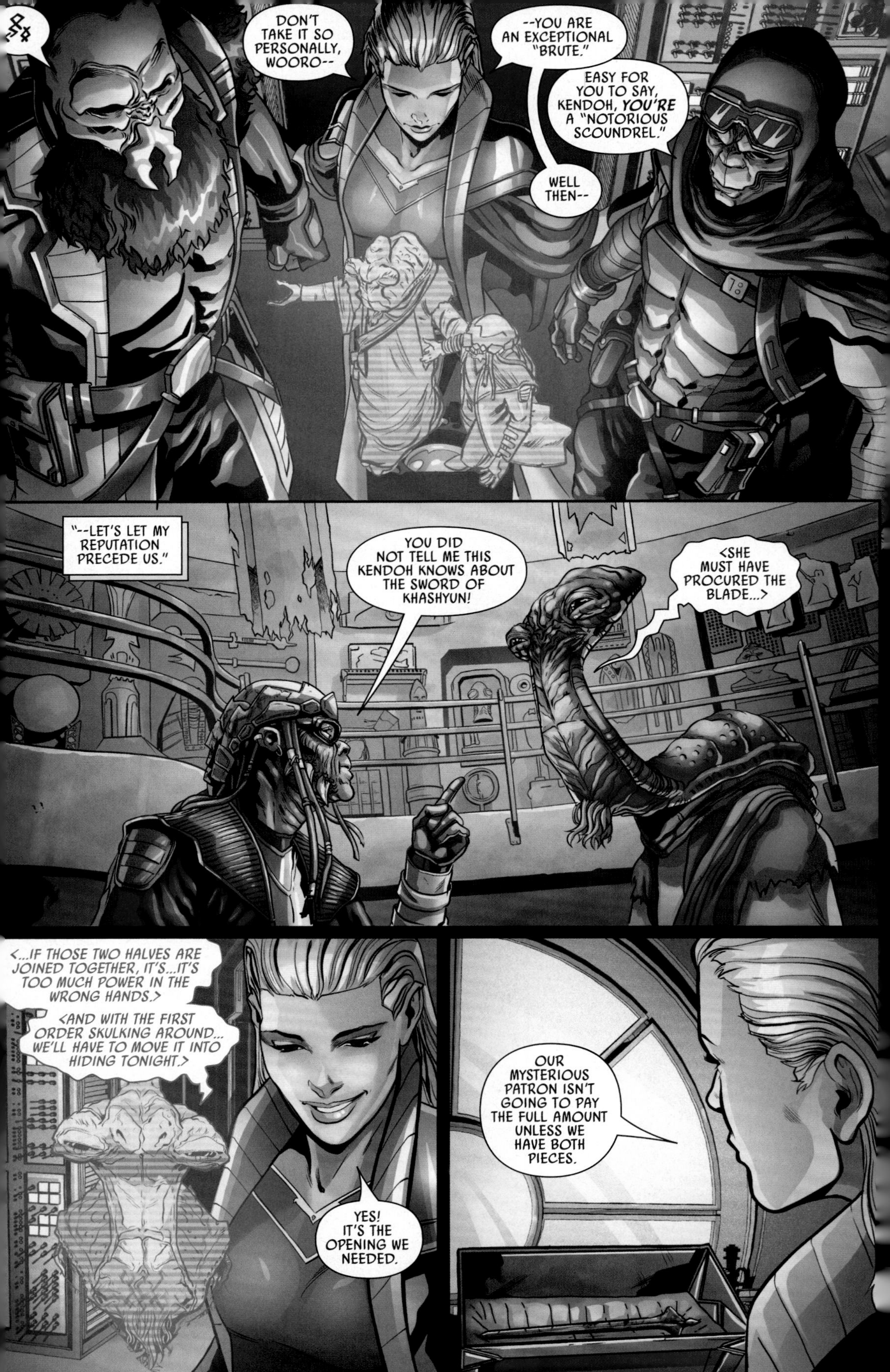
DON'T TAKE IT SO PERSONALLY, WOORO--
--YOU ARE AN EXCEPTIONAL "BRUTE."
EASY FOR YOU TO SAY, KENDOH, *YOU'RE* A "NOTORIOUS SCOUNDREL."
WELL THEN--
"--LET'S LET MY REPUTATION PRECEDE US."
YOU DID NOT TELL ME THIS KENDOH KNOWS ABOUT THE SWORD OF KHASHYUN!
<SHE MUST HAVE PROCURED THE BLADE...>
<...IF THOSE TWO HALVES ARE JOINED TOGETHER, IT'S...IT'S TOO MUCH POWER IN THE WRONG HANDS.>
<AND WITH THE FIRST ORDER SKULKING AROUND... WE'LL HAVE TO MOVE IT INTO HIDING TONIGHT.>
YES! IT'S THE OPENING WE NEEDED.
OUR MYSTERIOUS PATRON ISN'T GOING TO PAY THE FULL AMOUNT UNLESS WE HAVE BOTH PIECES.

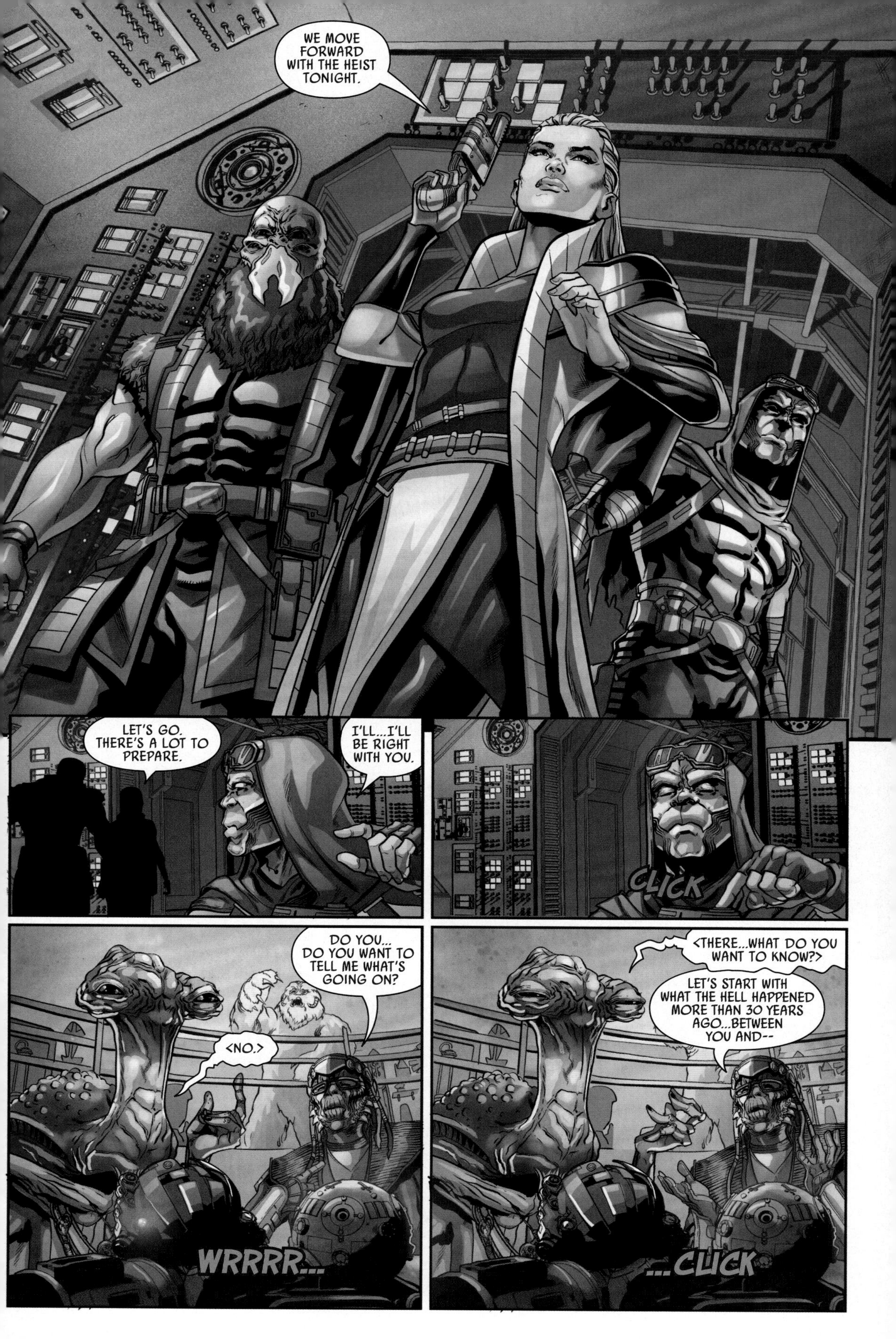
WE MOVE FORWARD WITH THE HEIST TONIGHT.
LET'S GO. THERE'S A LOT TO PREPARE.
I'LL...I'LL BE RIGHT WITH YOU.
CLICK
DO YOU... DO YOU WANT TO TELL ME WHAT'S GOING ON?
<NO.>
WRRRR...
<THERE...WHAT DO YOU WANT TO KNOW?>
LET'S START WITH WHAT THE HELL HAPPENED MORE THAN 30 YEARS AGO...BETWEEN YOU AND--
...CLICK

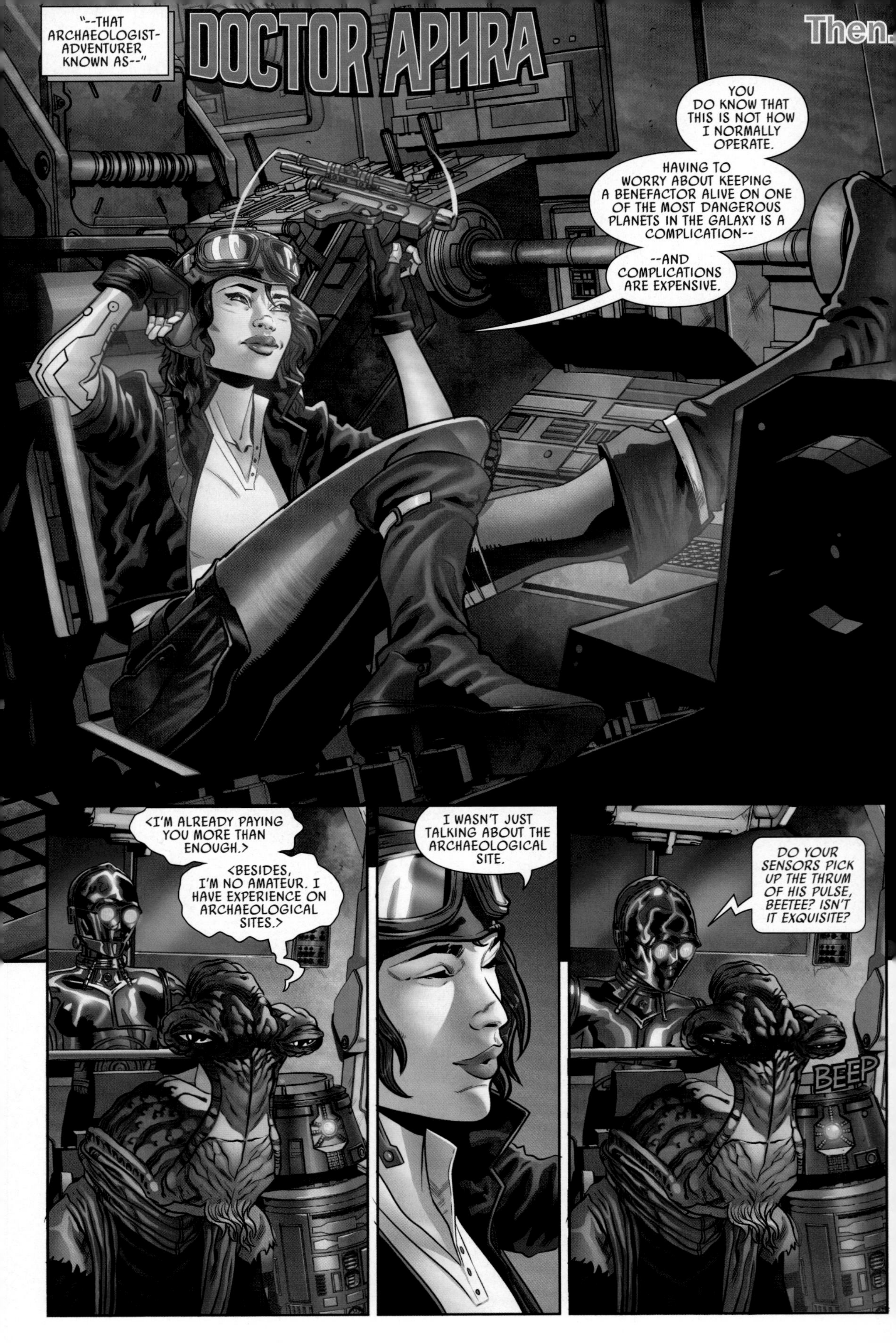

"--THAT ARCHAEOLOGIST-ADVENTURER KNOWN AS--"
DOCTOR APHRA
Then...
YOU DO KNOW THAT THIS IS NOT HOW I NORMALLY OPERATE.
HAVING TO WORRY ABOUT KEEPING A BENEFACTOR ALIVE ON ONE OF THE MOST DANGEROUS PLANETS IN THE GALAXY IS A COMPLICATION--
--AND COMPLICATIONS ARE EXPENSIVE.
<I'M ALREADY PAYING YOU MORE THAN ENOUGH.>
<BESIDES, I'M NO AMATEUR. I HAVE EXPERIENCE ON ARCHAEOLOGICAL SITES.>
I WASN'T JUST TALKING ABOUT THE ARCHAEOLOGICAL SITE.
DO YOUR SENSORS PICK UP THE THRUM OF HIS PULSE, BEETEE? ISN'T IT EXQUISITE?
BEEP

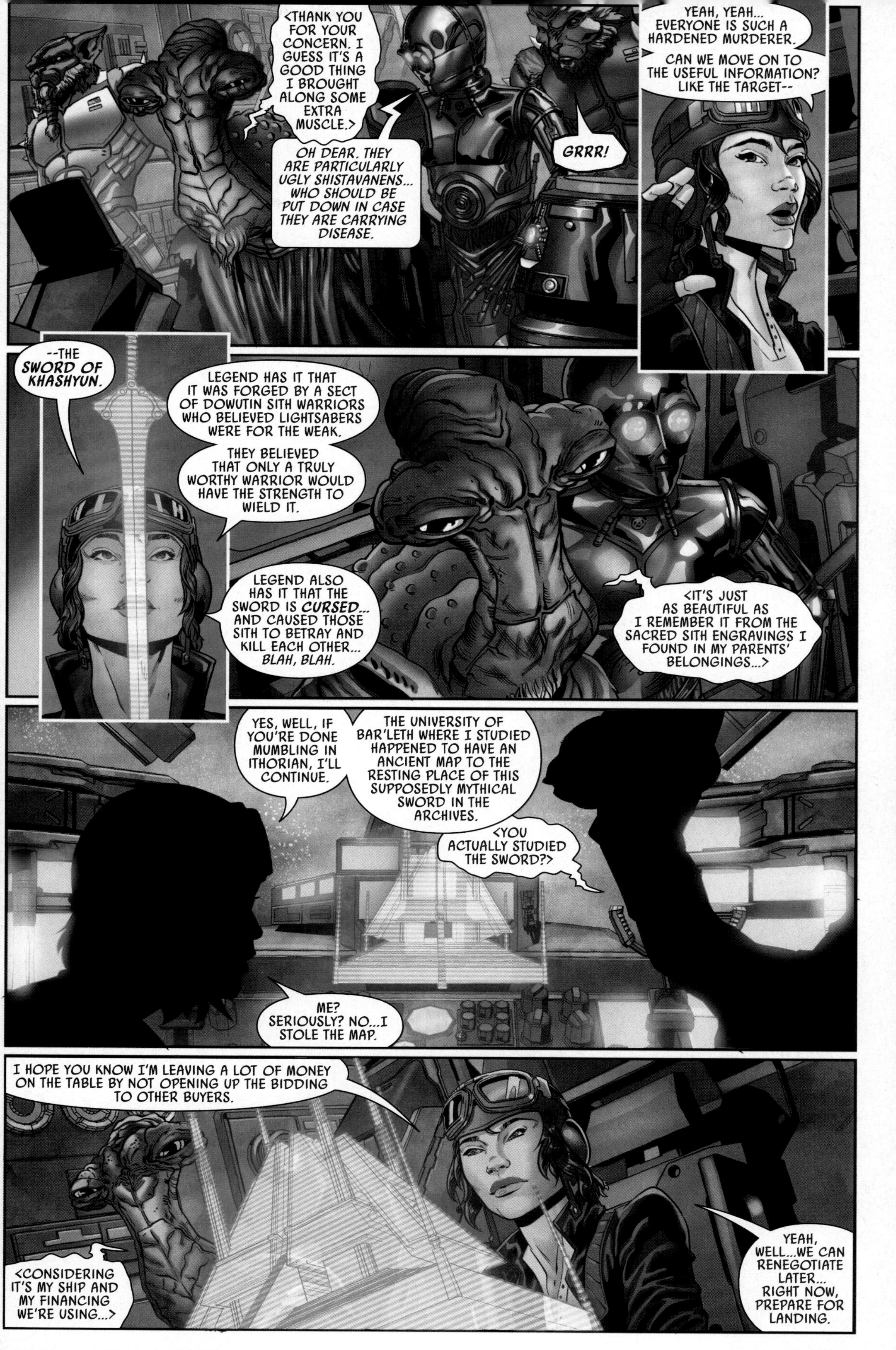
<THANK YOU FOR YOUR CONCERN. I GUESS IT'S A GOOD THING I BROUGHT ALONG SOME EXTRA MUSCLE.>
OH DEAR. THEY ARE PARTICULARLY UGLY SHISTAVANENS... WHO SHOULD BE PUT DOWN IN CASE THEY ARE CARRYING DISEASE.
GRRR!
YEAH, YEAH... EVERYONE IS SUCH A HARDENED MURDERER.
CAN WE MOVE ON TO THE USEFUL INFORMATION? LIKE THE TARGET--
--THE SWORD OF KHASHYUN.
LEGEND HAS IT THAT IT WAS FORGED BY A SECT OF DOWUTIN SITH WARRIORS WHO BELIEVED LIGHTSABERS WERE FOR THE WEAK.
THEY BELIEVED THAT ONLY A TRULY WORTHY WARRIOR WOULD HAVE THE STRENGTH TO WIELD IT.
LEGEND ALSO HAS IT THAT THE SWORD IS CURSED... AND CAUSED THOSE SITH TO BETRAY AND KILL EACH OTHER... BLAH, BLAH.
<IT'S JUST AS BEAUTIFUL AS I REMEMBER IT FROM THE SACRED SITH ENGRAVINGS I FOUND IN MY PARENTS' BELONGINGS...>
YES, WELL, IF YOU'RE DONE MUMBLING IN ITHORIAN, I'LL CONTINUE.
THE UNIVERSITY OF BAR'LETH WHERE I STUDIED HAPPENED TO HAVE AN ANCIENT MAP TO THE RESTING PLACE OF THIS SUPPOSEDLY MYTHICAL SWORD IN THE ARCHIVES.
<YOU ACTUALLY STUDIED THE SWORD?>
ME? SERIOUSLY? NO...I STOLE THE MAP.
I HOPE YOU KNOW I'M LEAVING A LOT OF MONEY ON THE TABLE BY NOT OPENING UP THE BIDDING TO OTHER BUYERS.
<CONSIDERING IT'S MY SHIP AND MY FINANCING WE'RE USING...>
YEAH, WELL...WE CAN RENEGOTIATE LATER... RIGHT NOW, PREPARE FOR LANDING.

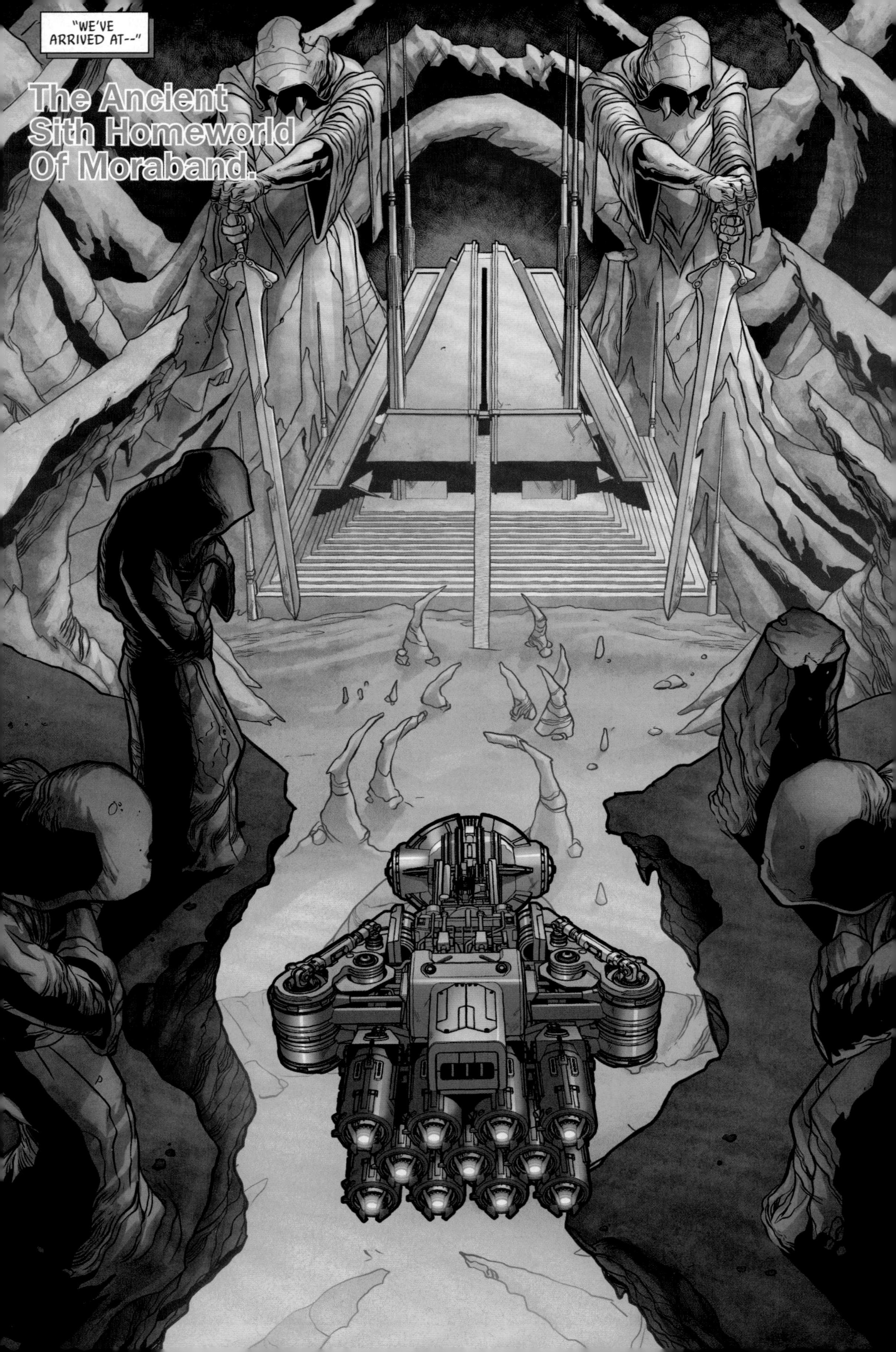
"WE'VE ARRIVED AT--"
The Ancient Sith Homeworld Of Moraband.

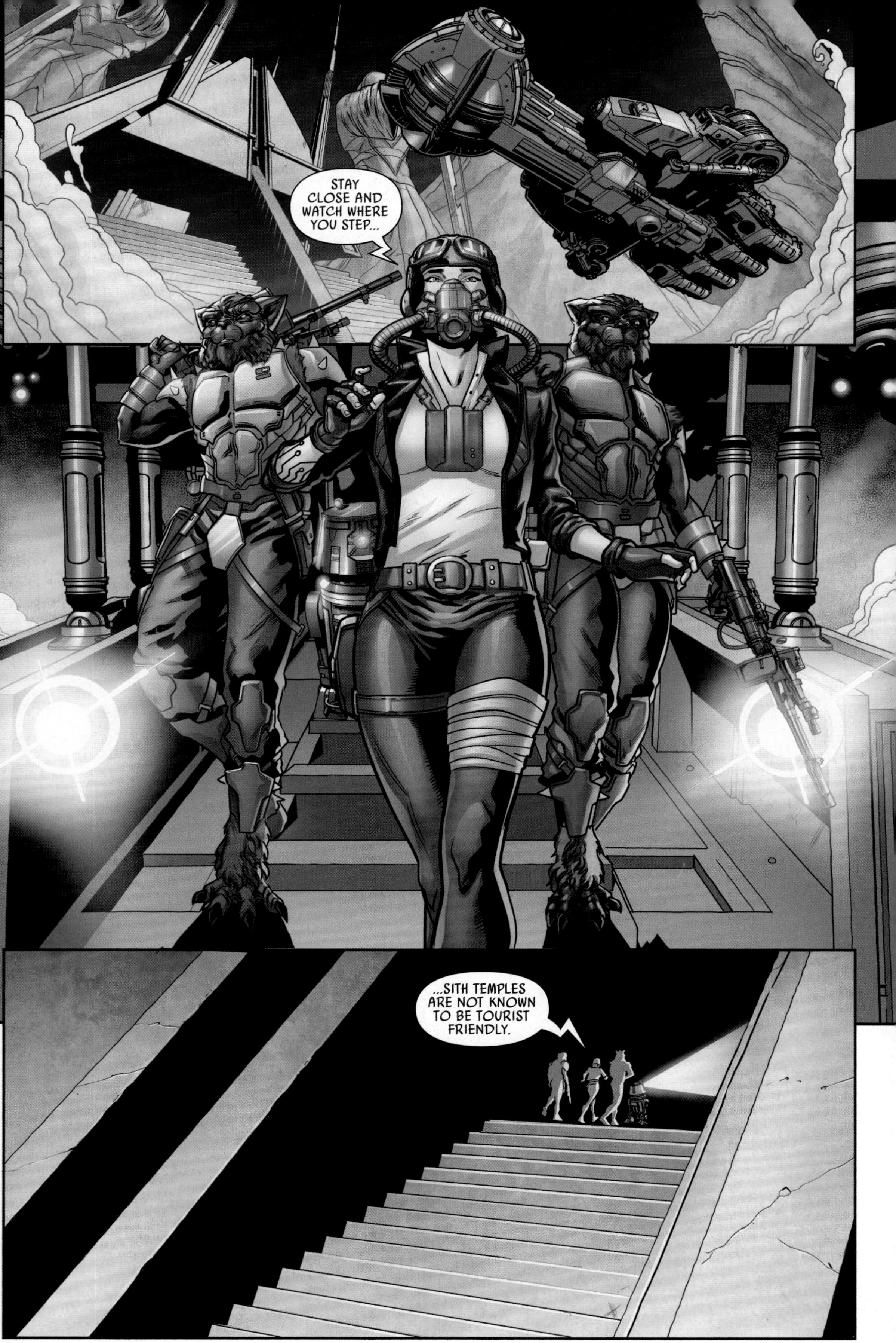
STAY CLOSE AND WATCH WHERE YOU STEP...
...SITH TEMPLES ARE NOT KNOWN TO BE TOURIST FRIENDLY.

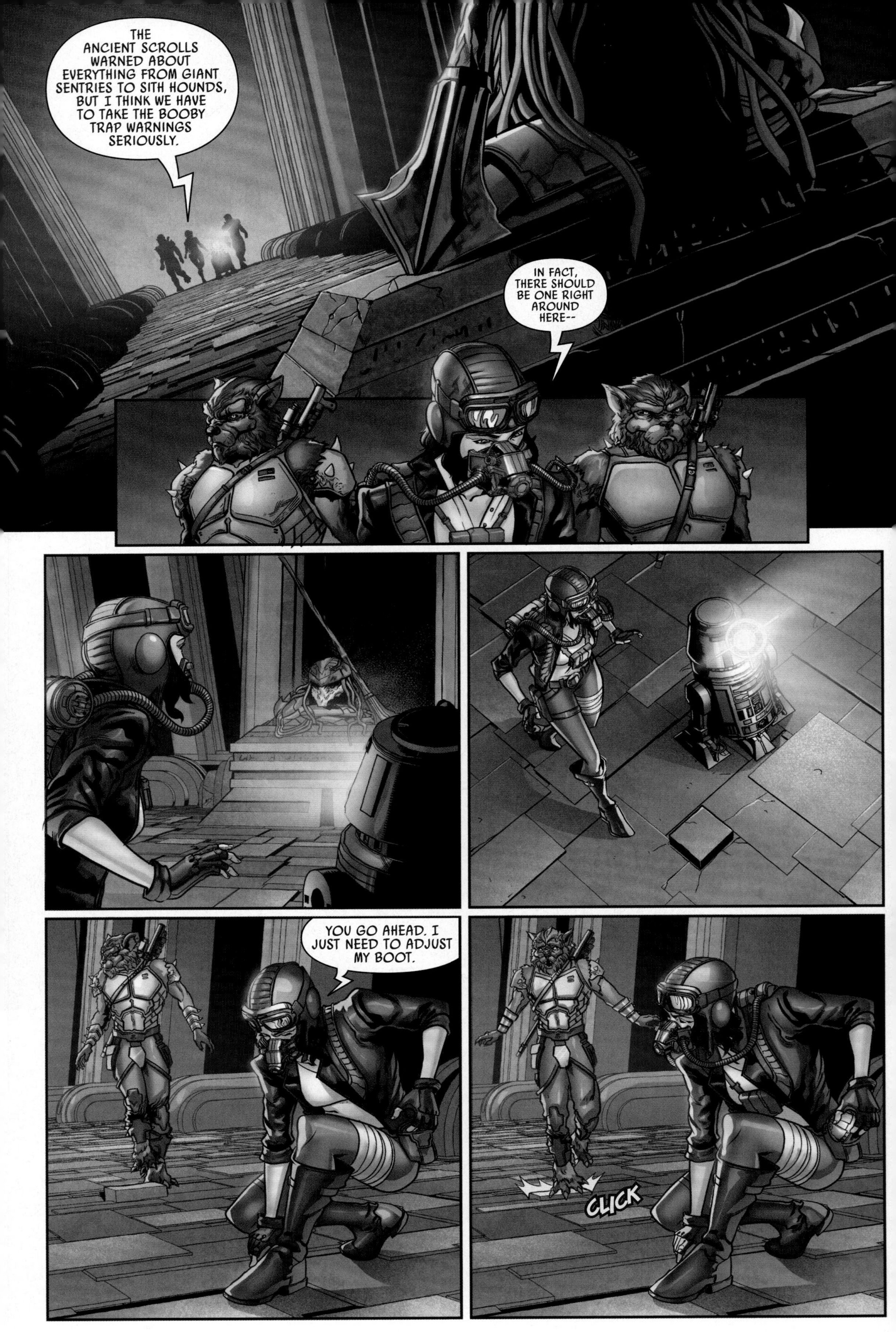
THE ANCIENT SCROLLS WARNED ABOUT EVERYTHING FROM GIANT SENTRIES TO SITH HOUNDS, BUT I THINK WE HAVE TO TAKE THE BOOBY TRAP WARNINGS SERIOUSLY.
IN FACT, THERE SHOULD BE ONE RIGHT AROUND HERE--
YOU GO AHEAD. I JUST NEED TO ADJUST MY BOOT.
CLICK

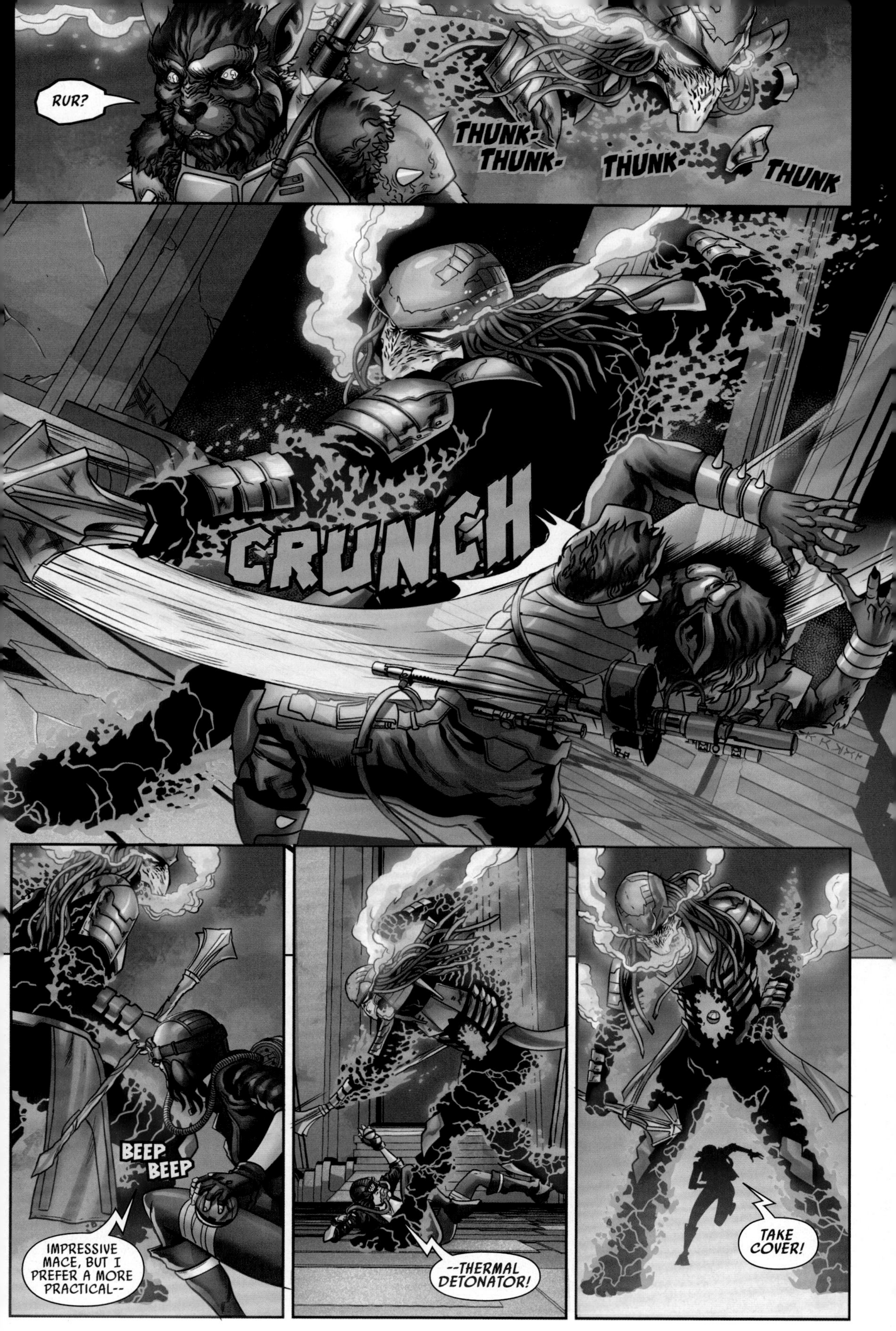

RUR?
THUNK-
THUNK-
THUNK-
THUNK
CRUNCH
BEEP BEEP
IMPRESSIVE MACE, BUT I PREFER A MORE PRACTICAL--
--THERMAL DETONATOR!
TAKE COVER!

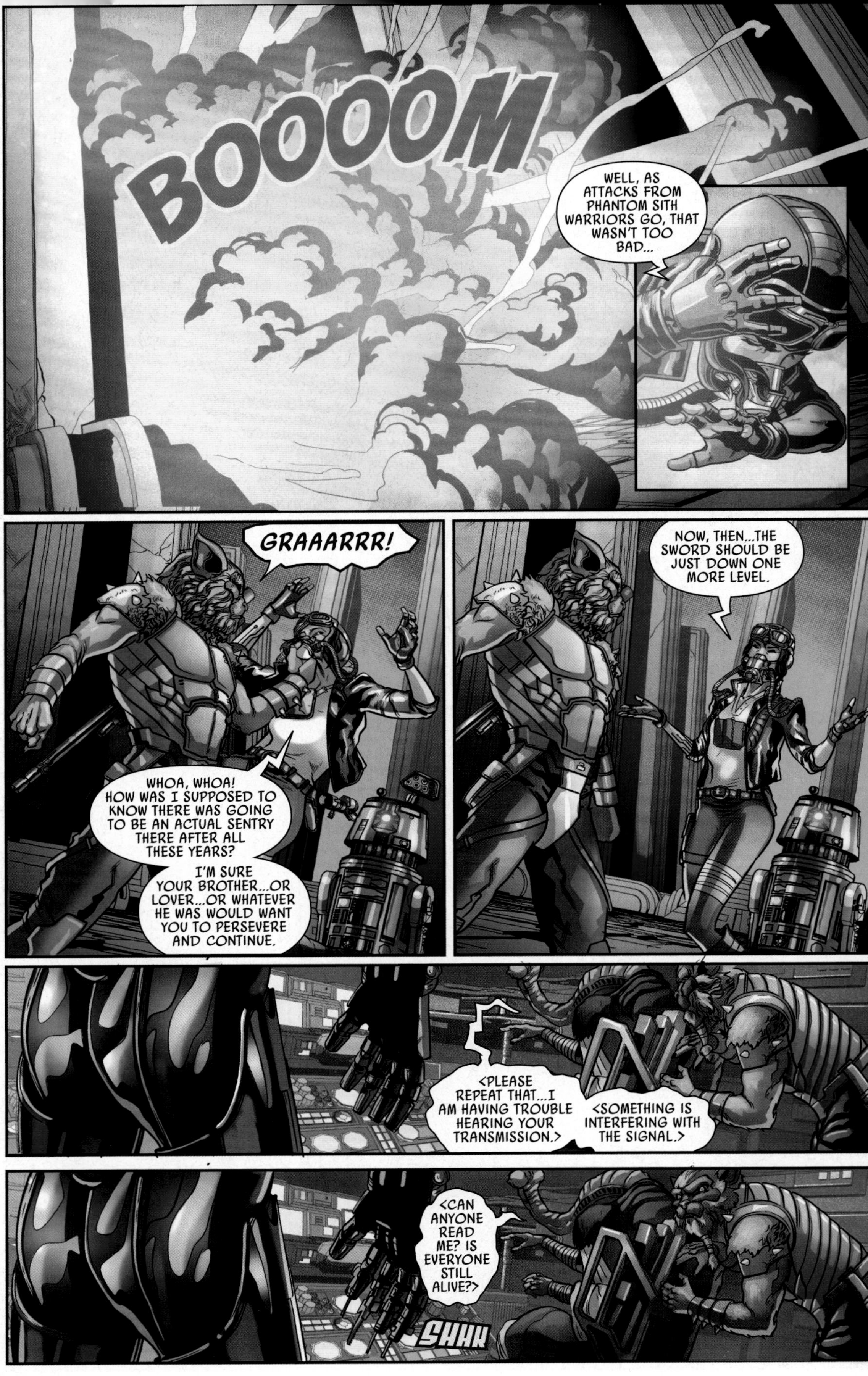
BOOOOOM
WELL, AS ATTACKS FROM PHANTOM SITH WARRIORS GO, THAT WASN'T TOO BAD...
GRAAARRR!
WHOA, WHOA! HOW WAS I SUPPOSED TO KNOW THERE WAS GOING TO BE AN ACTUAL SENTRY THERE AFTER ALL THESE YEARS?
I'M SURE YOUR BROTHER...OR LOVER...OR WHATEVER HE WAS WOULD WANT YOU TO PERSEVERE AND CONTINUE.
NOW, THEN...THE SWORD SHOULD BE JUST DOWN ONE MORE LEVEL.
<PLEASE REPEAT THAT...I AM HAVING TROUBLE HEARING YOUR TRANSMISSION.>
<SOMETHING IS INTERFERING WITH THE SIGNAL.>
<CAN ANYONE READ ME? IS EVERYONE STILL ALIVE?>
SHHH

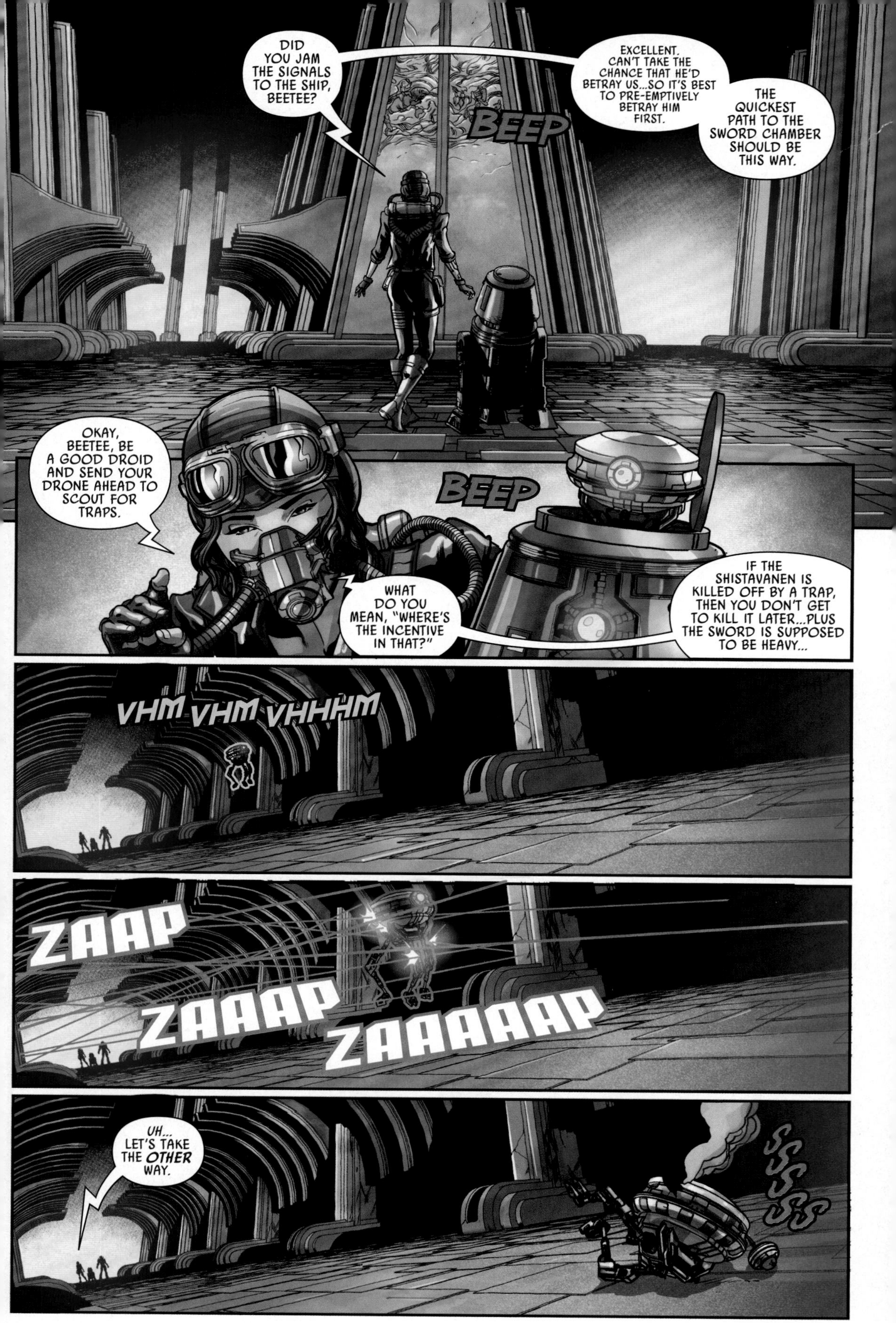
DID YOU JAM THE SIGNALS TO THE SHIP, BEETEE?
BEEP
EXCELLENT. CAN'T TAKE THE CHANCE THAT HE'D BETRAY US...SO IT'S BEST TO PRE-EMPTIVELY BETRAY HIM FIRST.
THE QUICKEST PATH TO THE SWORD CHAMBER SHOULD BE THIS WAY.
OKAY, BEETEE, BE A GOOD DROID AND SEND YOUR DRONE AHEAD TO SCOUT FOR TRAPS.
BEEP
WHAT DO YOU MEAN, "WHERE'S THE INCENTIVE IN THAT?"
IF THE SHISTAVANEN IS KILLED OFF BY A TRAP, THEN YOU DON'T GET TO KILL IT LATER...PLUS THE SWORD IS SUPPOSED TO BE HEAVY...
VHM VHM VHHHM
ZAAP
ZAAAP
ZAAAAAP
UH... LET'S TAKE THE OTHER WAY.
SSSSS

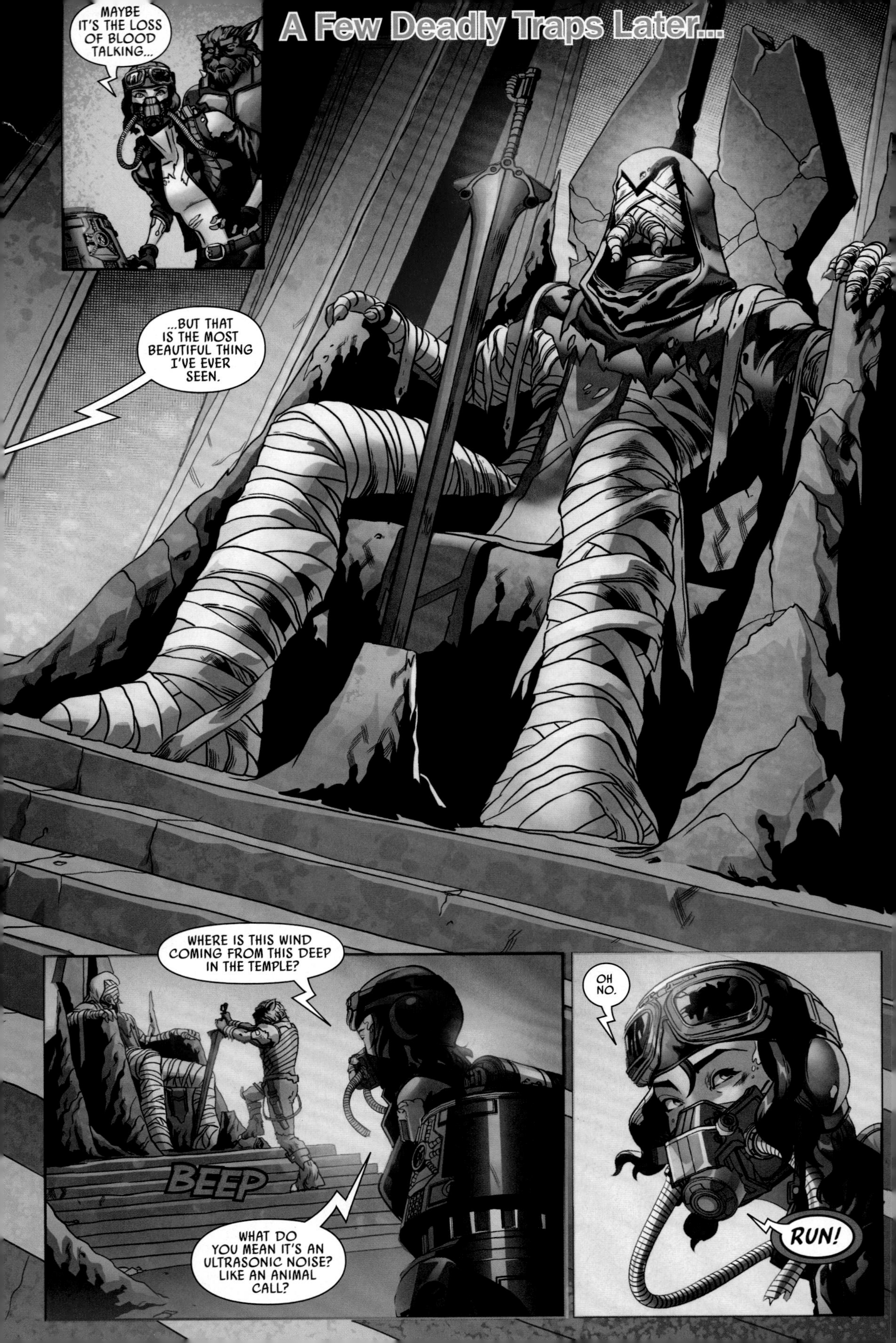
A Few Deadly Traps Later...
MAYBE IT'S THE LOSS OF BLOOD TALKING...
...BUT THAT IS THE MOST BEAUTIFUL THING I'VE EVER SEEN.
WHERE IS THIS WIND COMING FROM THIS DEEP IN THE TEMPLE?
BEEP
WHAT DO YOU MEAN IT'S AN ULTRASONIC NOISE? LIKE AN ANIMAL CALL?
OH NO.
RUN!

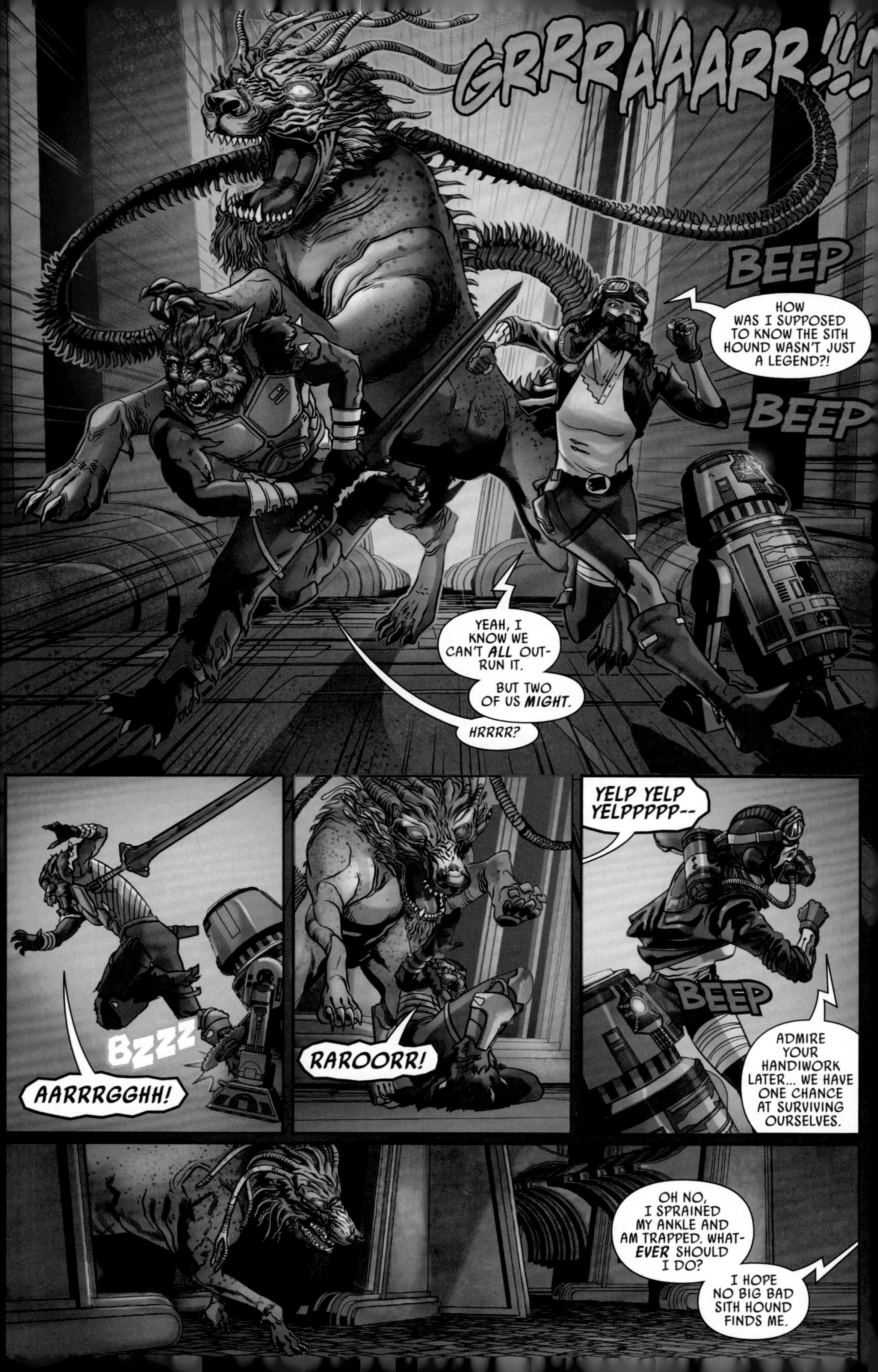
GRRRAAARR!!!
BEEP
HOW WAS I SUPPOSED TO KNOW THE SITH HOUND WASN'T JUST A LEGEND?!
BEEP
YEAH, I KNOW WE CAN'T **ALL** OUT-RUN IT.
BUT TWO OF US **MIGHT**.
HRRRR?
BZZZ
AARRRGGHH!
RAROORR!
YELP YELP YELPPPPP--
BEEP
ADMIRE YOUR HANDIWORK LATER... WE HAVE ONE CHANCE AT SURVIVING OURSELVES.
OH NO, I SPRAINED MY ANKLE AND AM TRAPPED. WHAT-**EVER** SHOULD I DO?
I HOPE NO BIG BAD SITH HOUND FINDS ME.

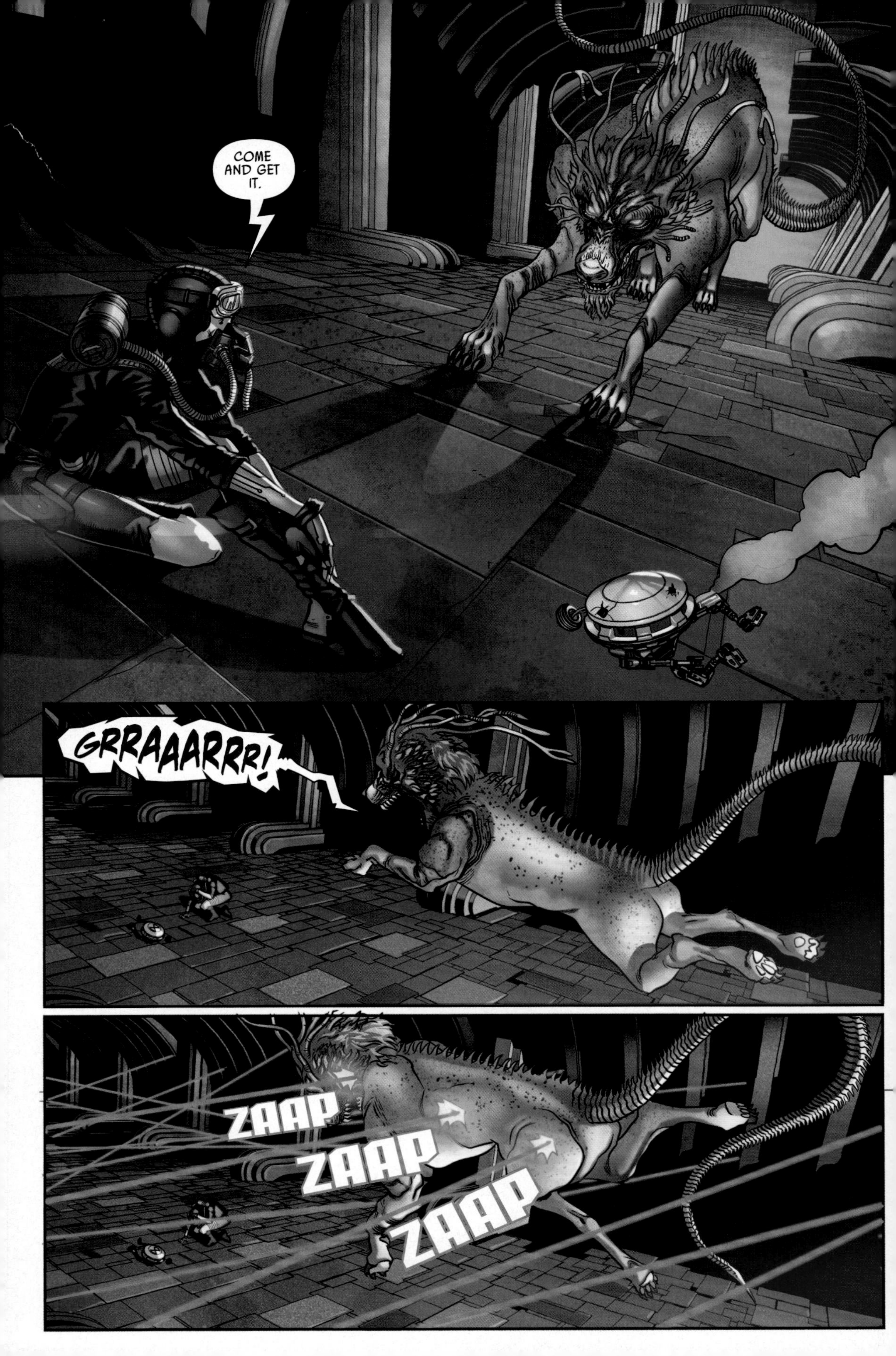
COME AND GET IT.
GRRAAARRR!
ZAAP
ZAAP
ZAAP

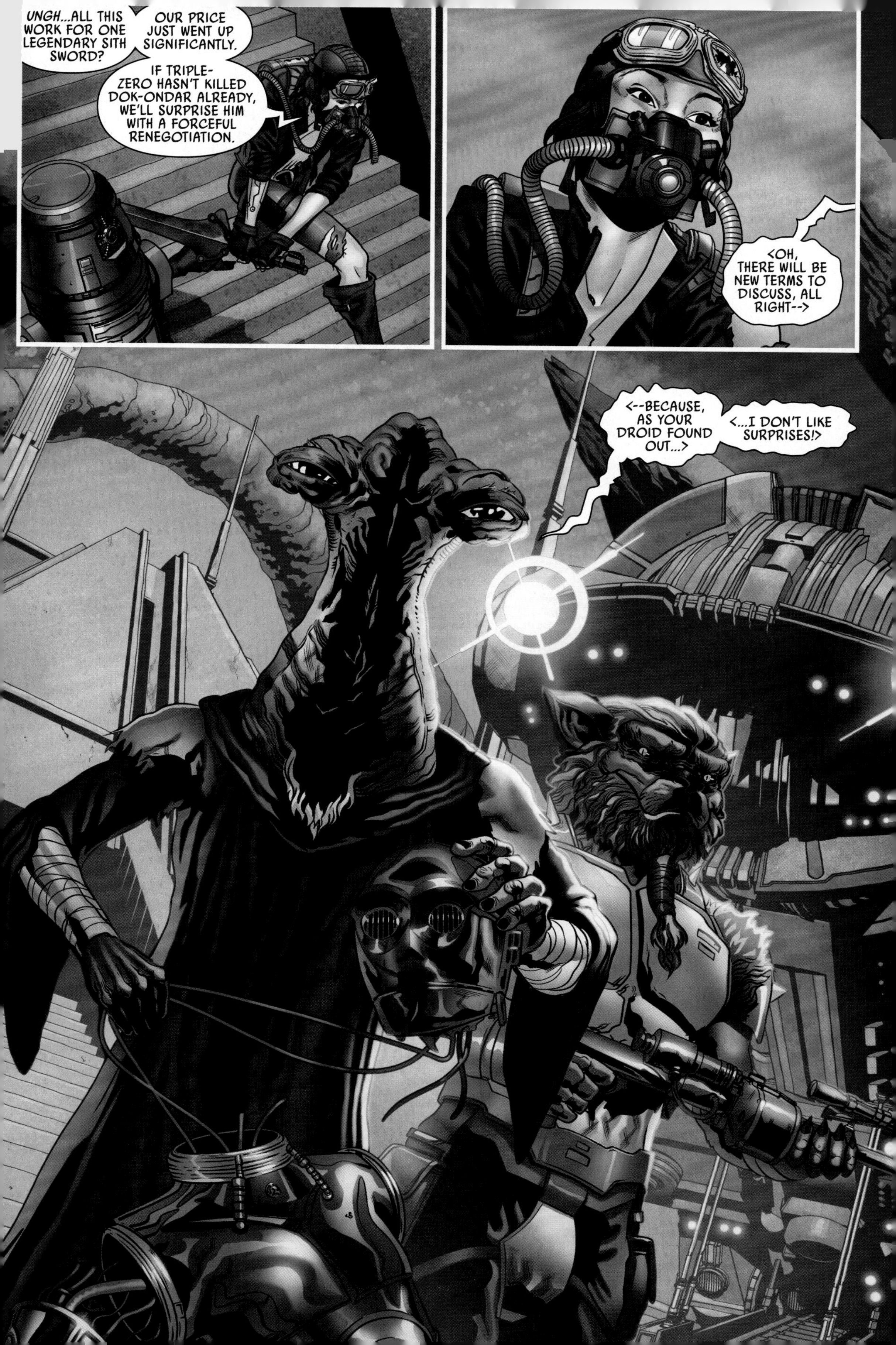
UNGH...ALL THIS WORK FOR ONE LEGENDARY SITH SWORD?
OUR PRICE JUST WENT UP SIGNIFICANTLY.
IF TRIPLE-ZERO HASN'T KILLED DOK-ONDAR ALREADY, WE'LL SURPRISE HIM WITH A FORCEFUL RENEGOTIATION.
<OH, THERE WILL BE NEW TERMS TO DISCUSS, ALL RIGHT-->
<--BECAUSE, AS YOUR DROID FOUND OUT...>
<...I DON'T LIKE SURPRISES!>

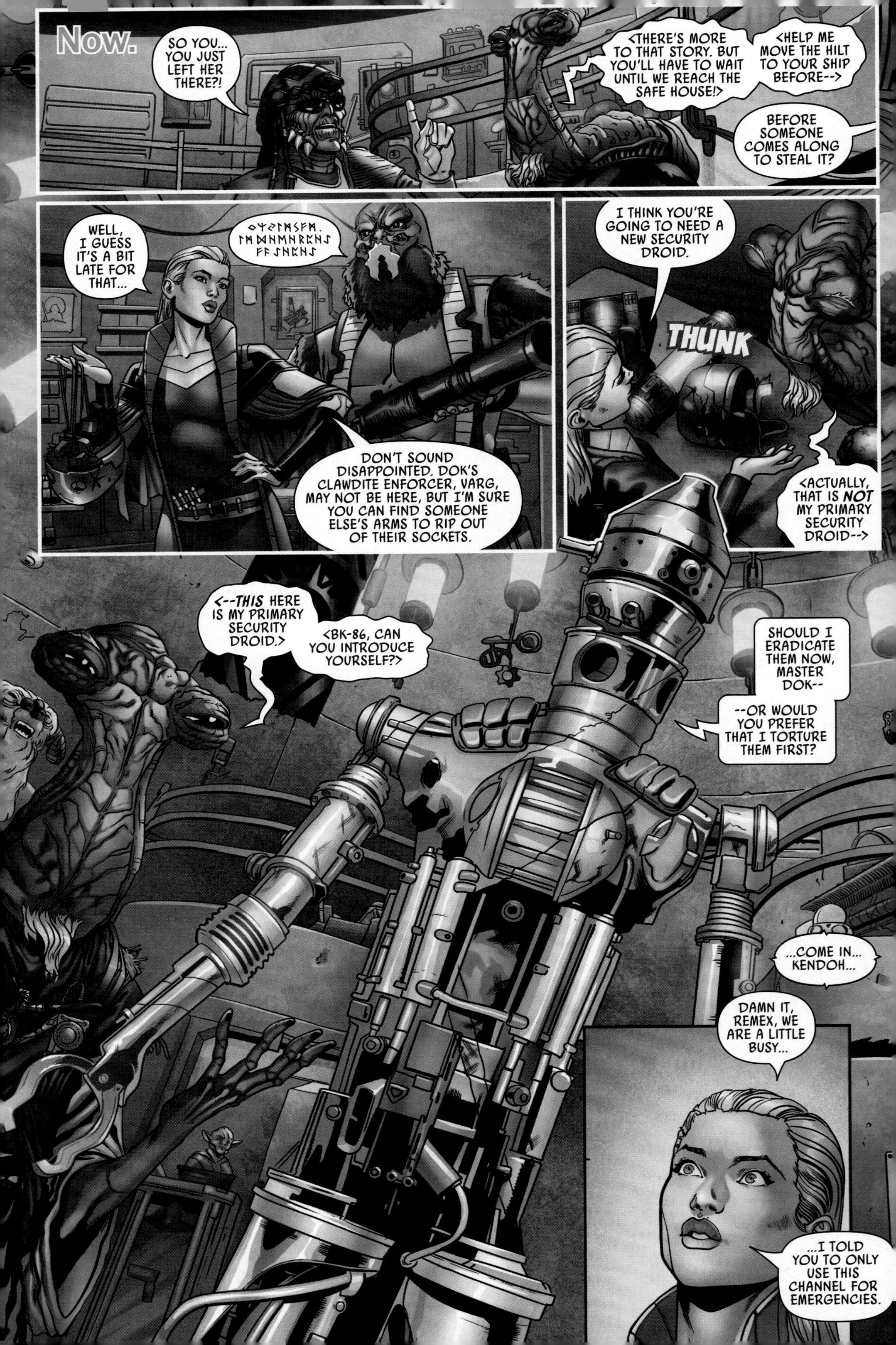
Now.
SO YOU... YOU JUST LEFT HER THERE?!
<THERE'S MORE TO THAT STORY. BUT YOU'LL HAVE TO WAIT UNTIL WE REACH THE SAFE HOUSE!>
<HELP ME MOVE THE HILT TO YOUR SHIP BEFORE-->
BEFORE SOMEONE COMES ALONG TO STEAL IT?
WELL, I GUESS IT'S A BIT LATE FOR THAT...
DON'T SOUND DISAPPOINTED. DOK'S CLAWDITE ENFORCER, VARG, MAY NOT BE HERE, BUT I'M SURE YOU CAN FIND SOMEONE ELSE'S ARMS TO RIP OUT OF THEIR SOCKETS.
I THINK YOU'RE GOING TO NEED A NEW SECURITY DROID.
THUNK
<ACTUALLY, THAT IS NOT MY PRIMARY SECURITY DROID-->
<--THIS HERE IS MY PRIMARY SECURITY DROID.>
<BK-86, CAN YOU INTRODUCE YOURSELF?>
SHOULD I ERADICATE THEM NOW, MASTER DOK--
--OR WOULD YOU PREFER THAT I TORTURE THEM FIRST?
...COME IN... KENDOH...
DAMN IT, REMEX, WE ARE A LITTLE BUSY...
...I TOLD YOU TO ONLY USE THIS CHANNEL FOR EMERGENCIES.

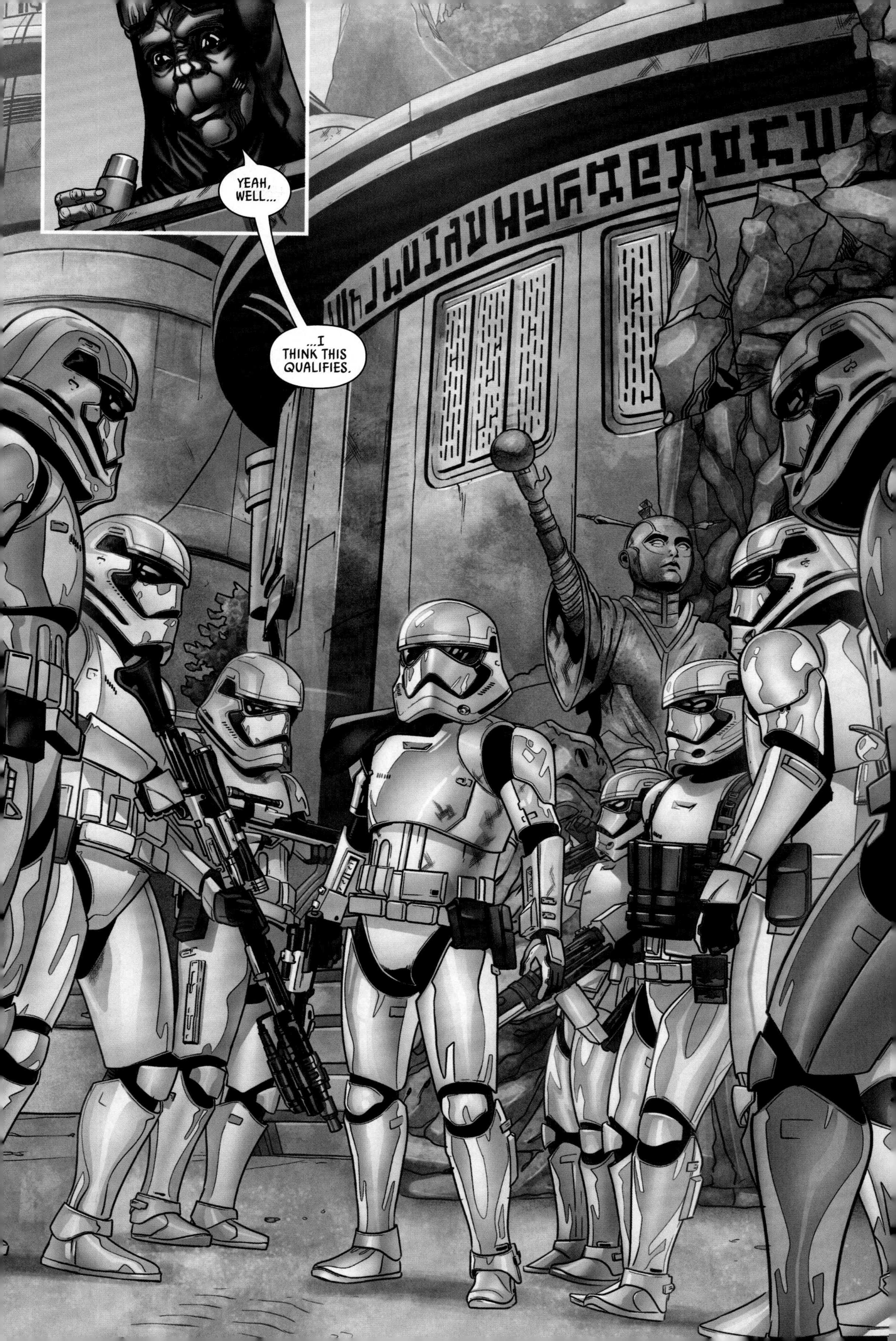
YEAH, WELL...
...I THINK THIS QUALIFIES.

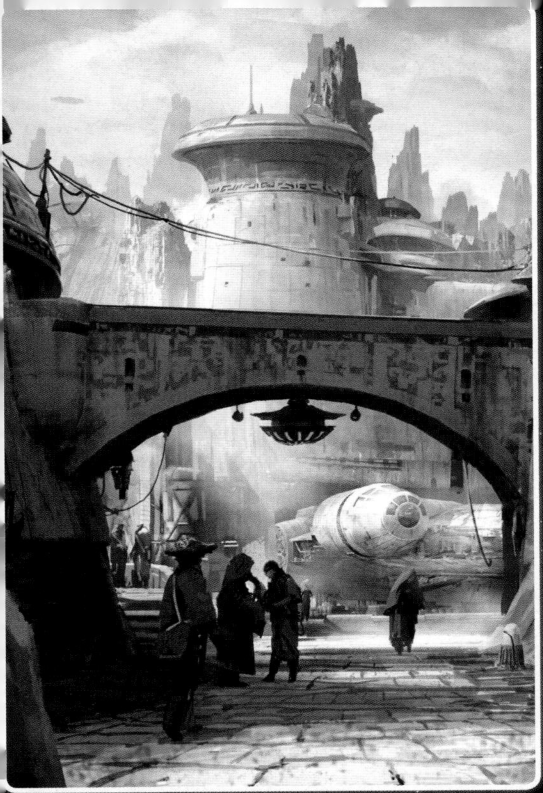

STAR WARS: GALAXY'S EDGE 1
Attraction Variant by **RICHARD LIM**

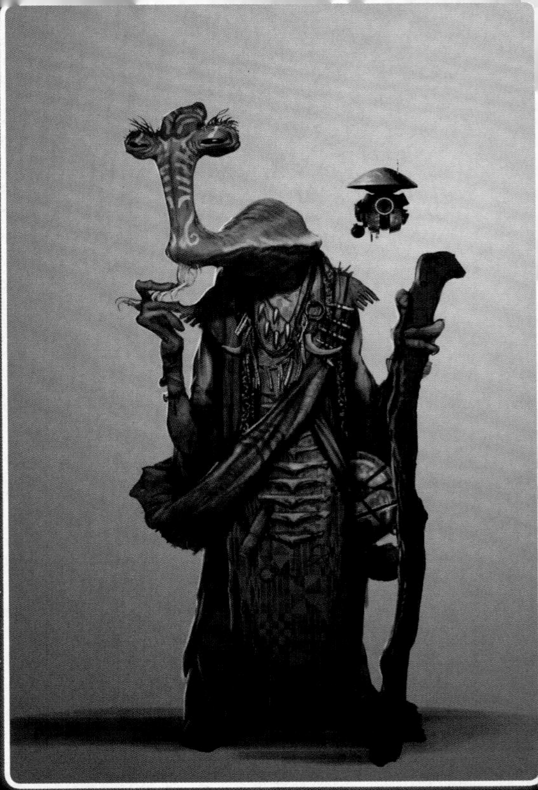

STAR WARS: GALAXY'S EDGE 1
Concept Art Variant by
KARL LINDBERG & IAIN McCAIG

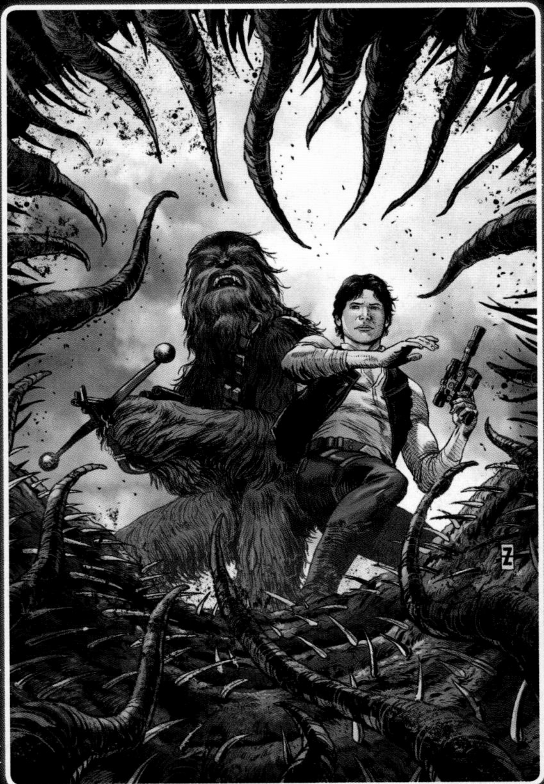

STAR WARS: GALAXY'S EDGE 1 Variant by
PATCH ZIRCHER & FEDERICO BLEE

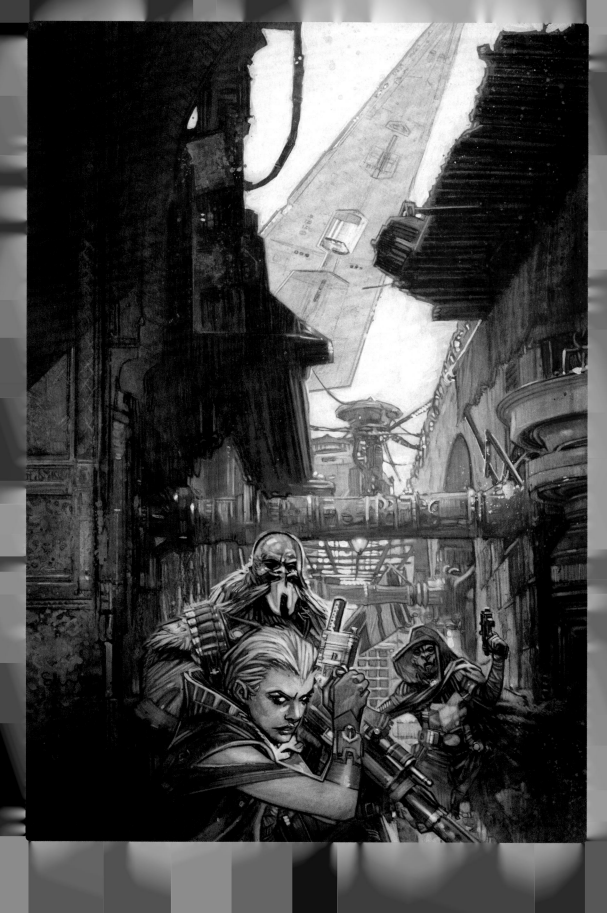

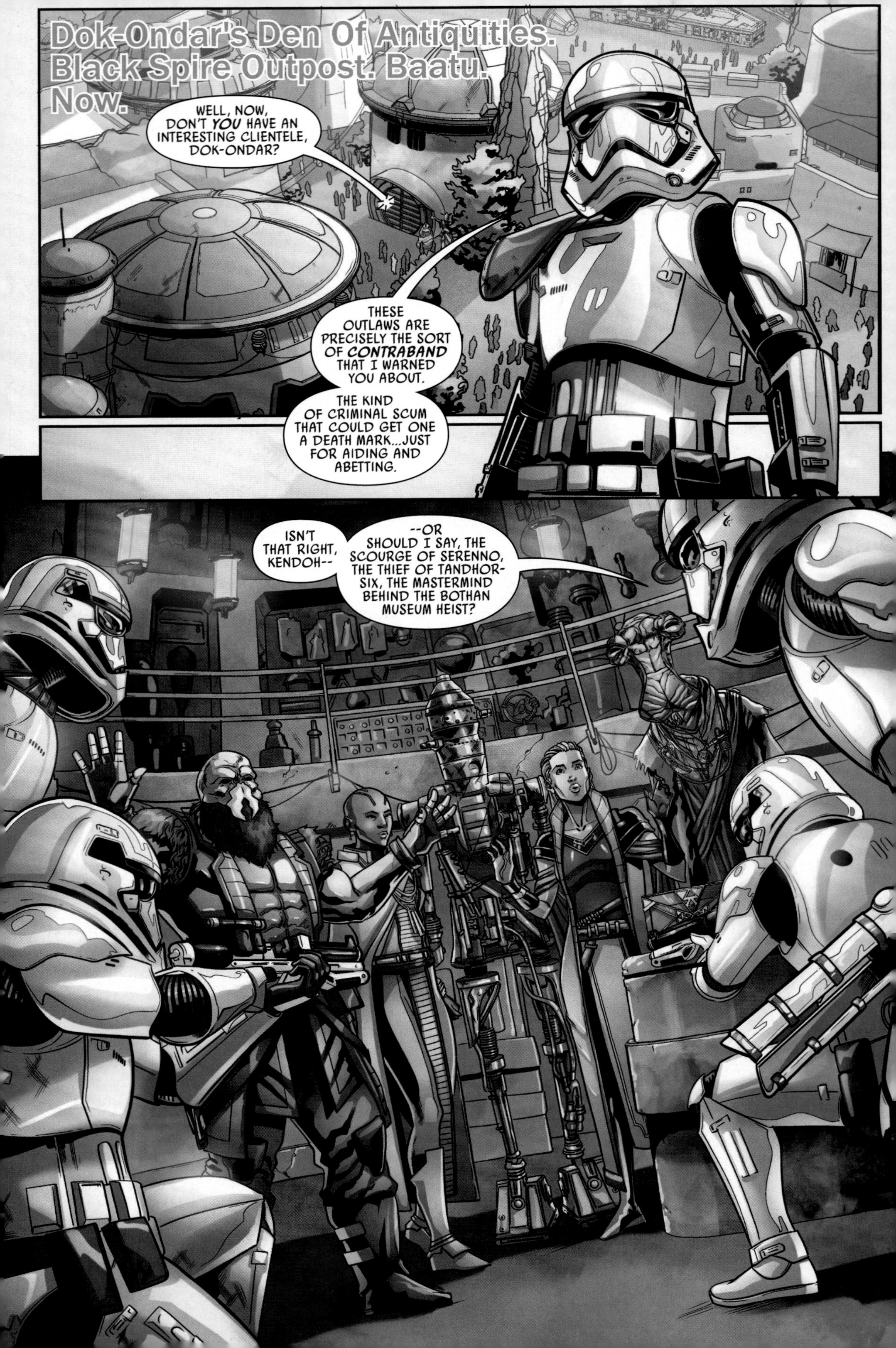
Dok-Ondar's Den Of Antiquities. Black Spire Outpost. Baatu. Now.
WELL, NOW, DON'T YOU HAVE AN INTERESTING CLIENTELE, DOK-ONDAR?
THESE OUTLAWS ARE PRECISELY THE SORT OF CONTRABAND THAT I WARNED YOU ABOUT.
THE KIND OF CRIMINAL SCUM THAT COULD GET ONE A DEATH MARK...JUST FOR AIDING AND ABETTING.
ISN'T THAT RIGHT, KENDOH--
--OR SHOULD I SAY, THE SCOURGE OF SERENNO, THE THIEF OF TANDHOR-SIX, THE MASTERMIND BEHIND THE BOTHAN MUSEUM HEIST?

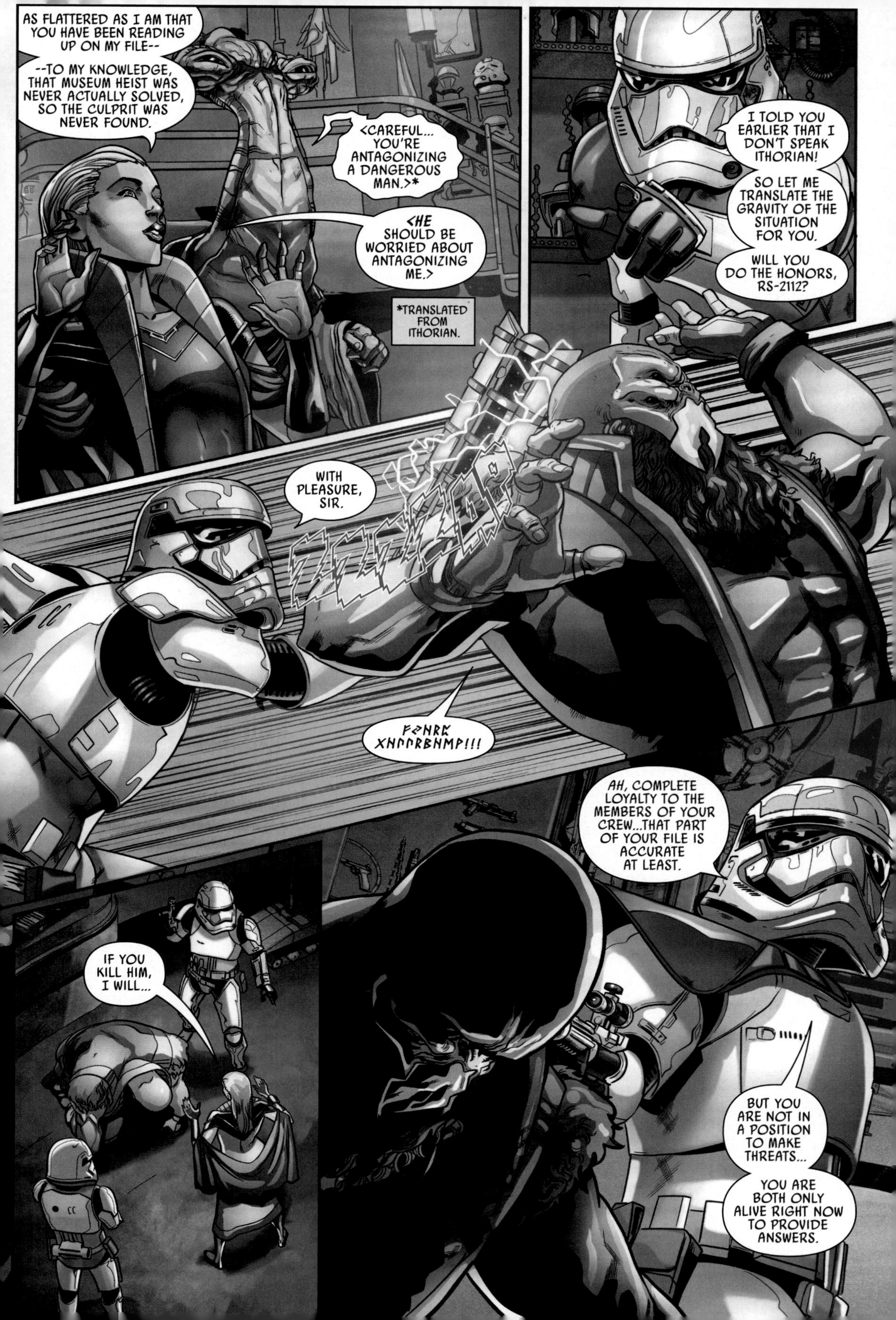
AS FLATTERED AS I AM THAT YOU HAVE BEEN READING UP ON MY FILE--
--TO MY KNOWLEDGE, THAT MUSEUM HEIST WAS NEVER ACTUALLY SOLVED, SO THE CULPRIT WAS NEVER FOUND.
<CAREFUL... YOU'RE ANTAGONIZING A DANGEROUS MAN.>*
<HE SHOULD BE WORRIED ABOUT ANTAGONIZING ME.>
*TRANSLATED FROM ITHORIAN.
I TOLD YOU EARLIER THAT I DON'T SPEAK ITHORIAN!
SO LET ME TRANSLATE THE GRAVITY OF THE SITUATION FOR YOU.
WILL YOU DO THE HONORS, RS-2112?
WITH PLEASURE, SIR.
AH, COMPLETE LOYALTY TO THE MEMBERS OF YOUR CREW...THAT PART OF YOUR FILE IS ACCURATE AT LEAST.
IF YOU KILL HIM, I WILL...
BUT YOU ARE NOT IN A POSITION TO MAKE THREATS...
YOU ARE BOTH ONLY ALIVE RIGHT NOW TO PROVIDE ANSWERS.

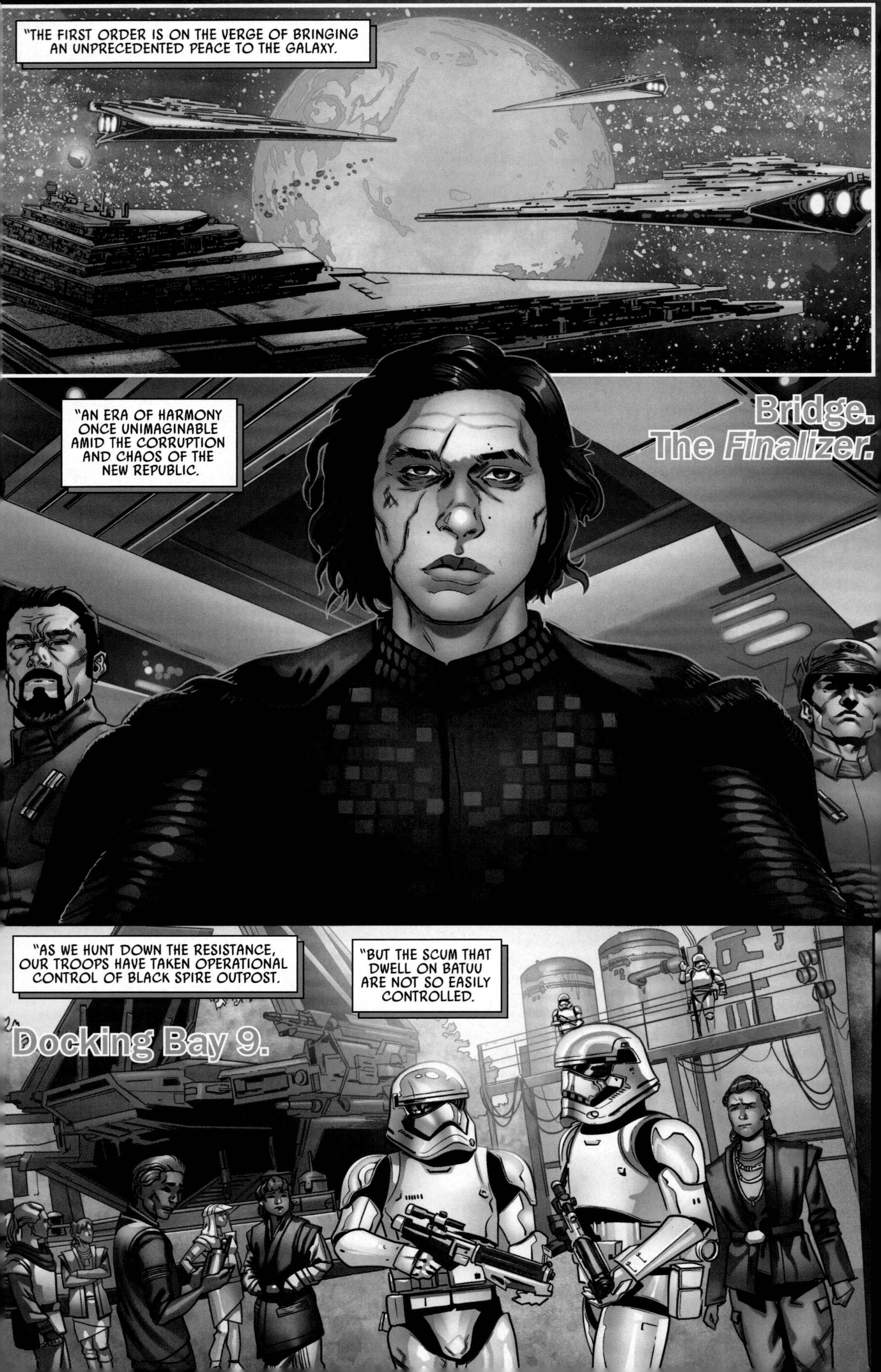
"THE FIRST ORDER IS ON THE VERGE OF BRINGING AN UNPRECEDENTED PEACE TO THE GALAXY.
Bridge. The *Finalizer.*
"AN ERA OF HARMONY ONCE UNIMAGINABLE AMID THE CORRUPTION AND CHAOS OF THE NEW REPUBLIC.
"AS WE HUNT DOWN THE RESISTANCE, OUR TROOPS HAVE TAKEN OPERATIONAL CONTROL OF BLACK SPIRE OUTPOST.
"BUT THE SCUM THAT DWELL ON BATUU ARE NOT SO EASILY CONTROLLED.
Docking Bay 9.

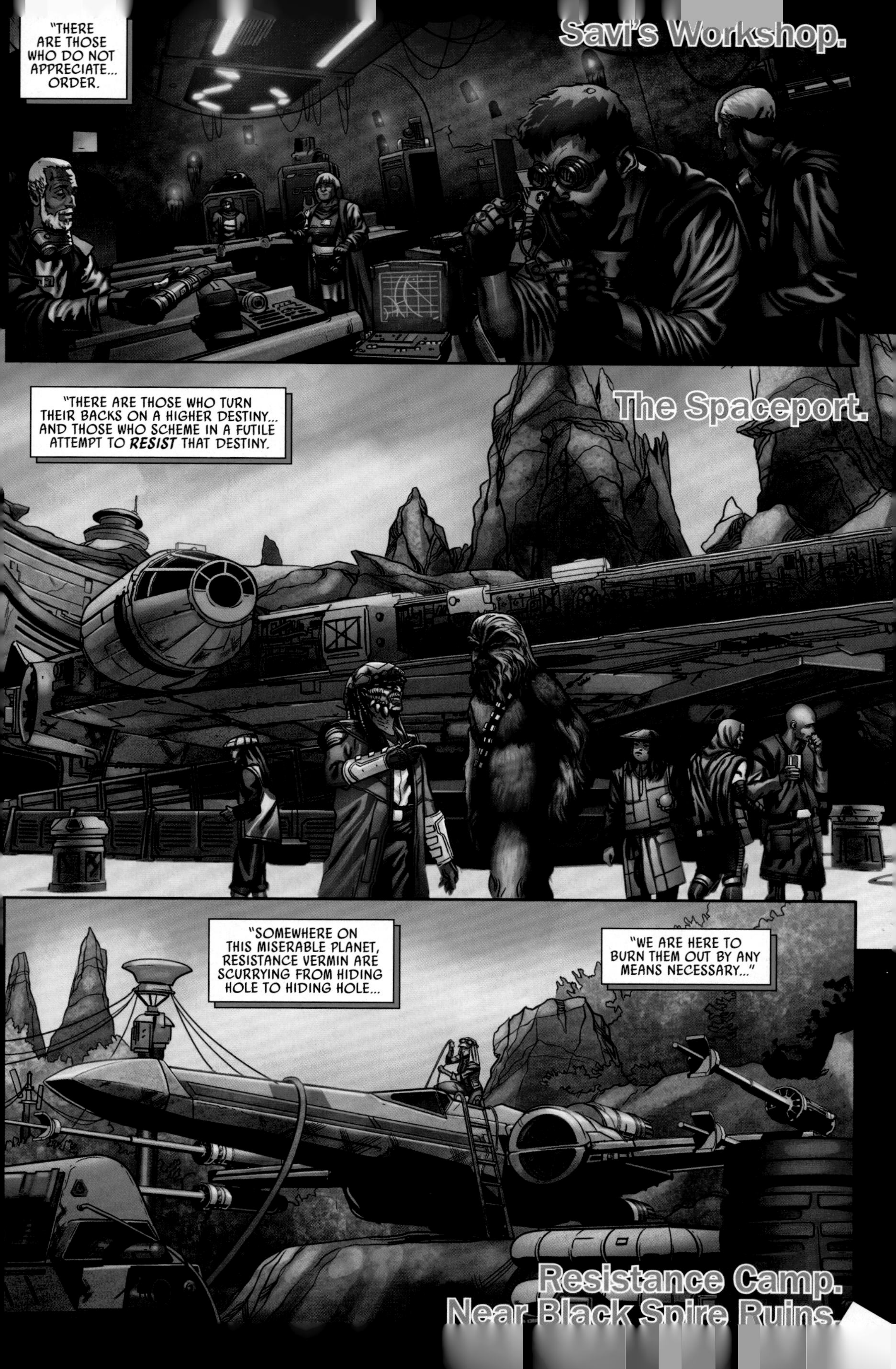
"THERE ARE THOSE WHO DO NOT APPRECIATE... ORDER.
Savi's Workshop.
"THERE ARE THOSE WHO TURN THEIR BACKS ON A HIGHER DESTINY... AND THOSE WHO SCHEME IN A FUTILE ATTEMPT TO RESIST THAT DESTINY.
The Spaceport.
"SOMEWHERE ON THIS MISERABLE PLANET, RESISTANCE VERMIN ARE SCURRYING FROM HIDING HOLE TO HIDING HOLE...
"WE ARE HERE TO BURN THEM OUT BY ANY MEANS NECESSARY..."
Resistance Camp. Near Black Spire Ruins.

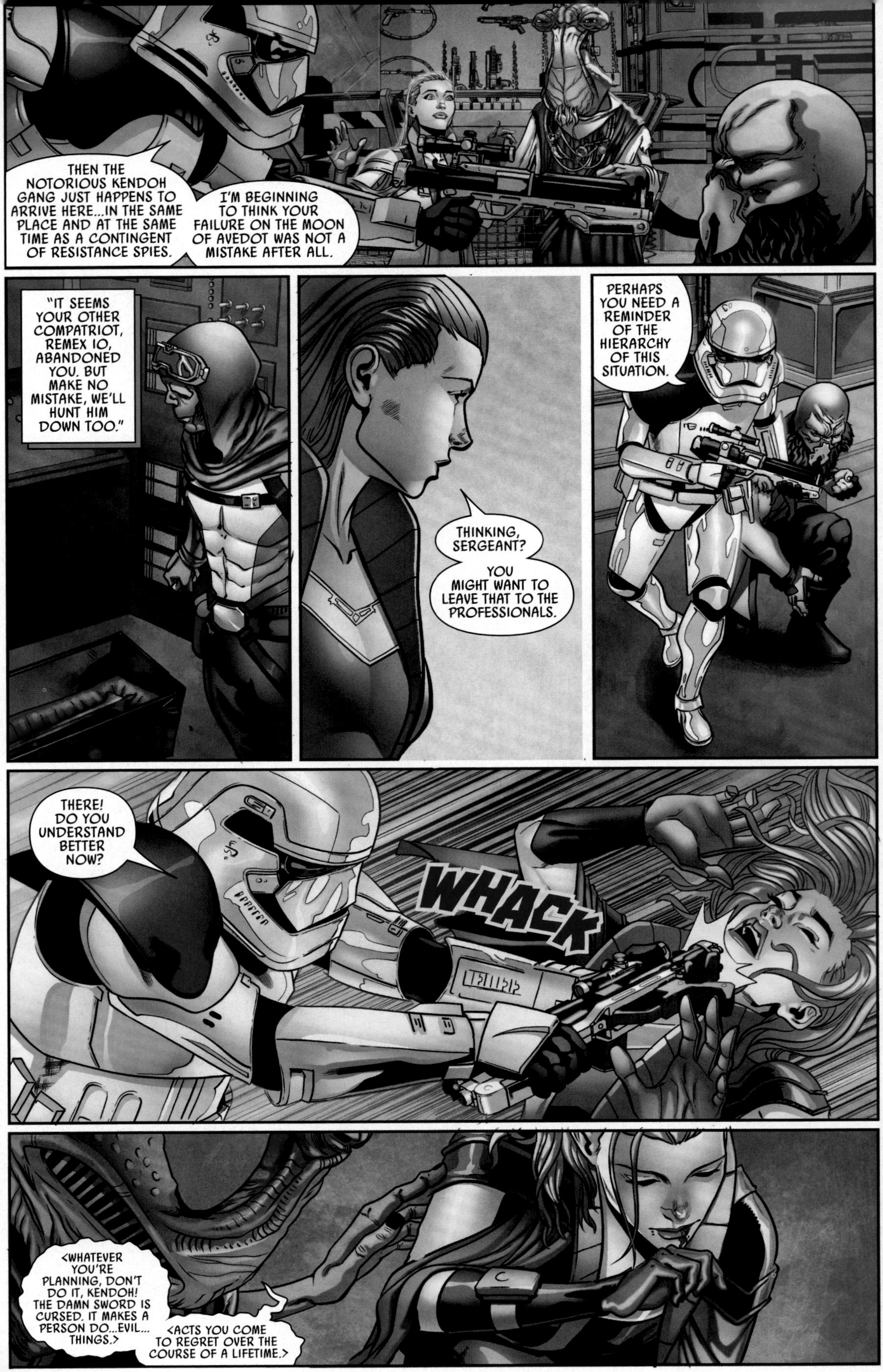
THEN THE NOTORIOUS KENDOH GANG JUST HAPPENS TO ARRIVE HERE...IN THE SAME PLACE AND AT THE SAME TIME AS A CONTINGENT OF RESISTANCE SPIES.
I'M BEGINNING TO THINK YOUR FAILURE ON THE MOON OF AVEDOT WAS NOT A MISTAKE AFTER ALL.
"IT SEEMS YOUR OTHER COMPATRIOT, REMEX IO, ABANDONED YOU. BUT MAKE NO MISTAKE, WE'LL HUNT HIM DOWN TOO."
THINKING, SERGEANT?
YOU MIGHT WANT TO LEAVE THAT TO THE PROFESSIONALS.
PERHAPS YOU NEED A REMINDER OF THE HIERARCHY OF THIS SITUATION.
THERE! DO YOU UNDERSTAND BETTER NOW?
WHACK
<WHATEVER YOU'RE PLANNING, DON'T DO IT, KENDOH! THE DAMN SWORD IS CURSED. IT MAKES A PERSON DO...EVIL... THINGS.>
<ACTS YOU COME TO REGRET OVER THE COURSE OF A LIFETIME.>

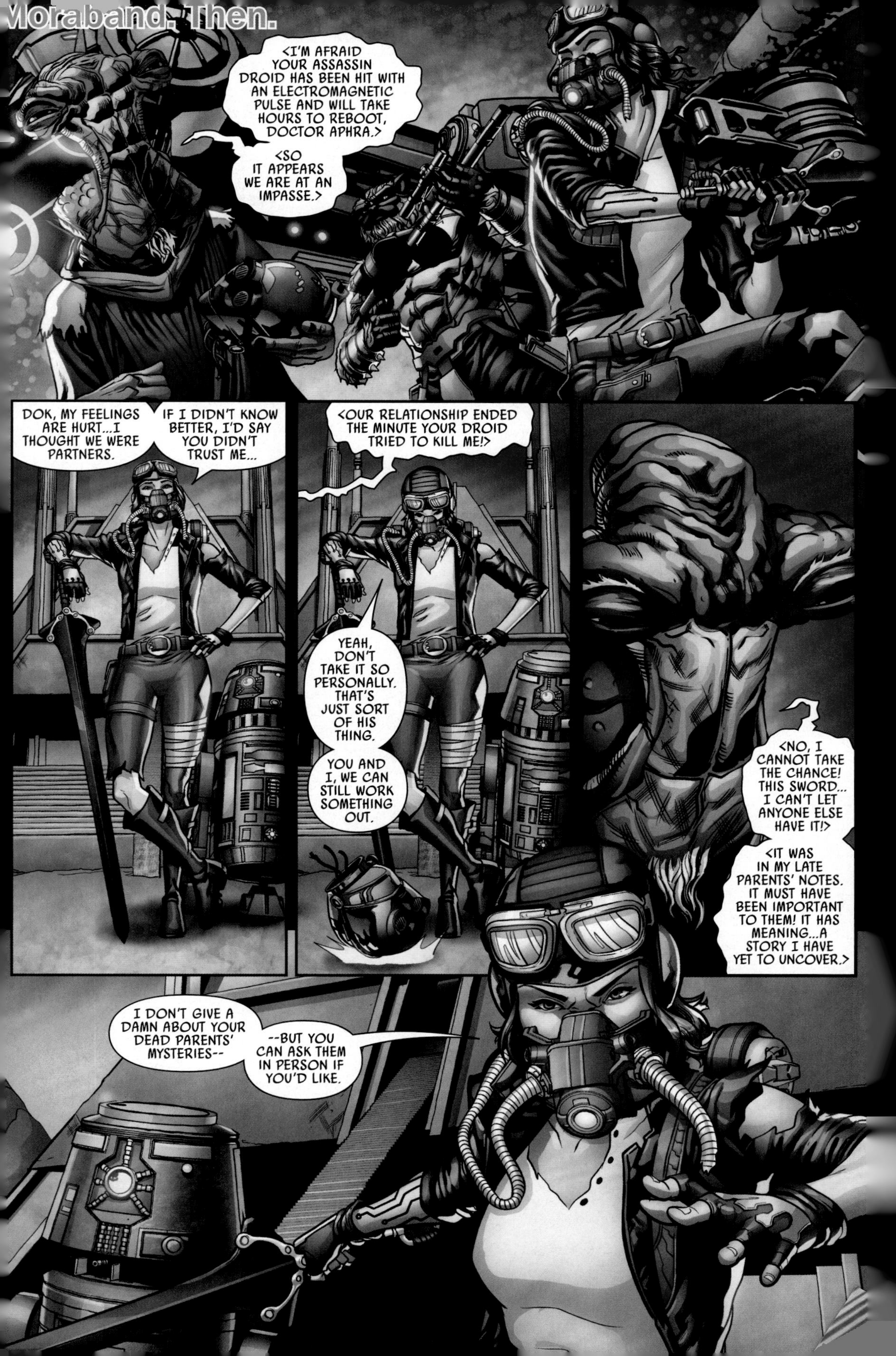
Moraband. Then.
<I'M AFRAID YOUR ASSASSIN DROID HAS BEEN HIT WITH AN ELECTROMAGNETIC PULSE AND WILL TAKE HOURS TO REBOOT, DOCTOR APHRA.>
<SO IT APPEARS WE ARE AT AN IMPASSE.>
DOK, MY FEELINGS ARE HURT...I THOUGHT WE WERE PARTNERS.
IF I DIDN'T KNOW BETTER, I'D SAY YOU DIDN'T TRUST ME...
<OUR RELATIONSHIP ENDED THE MINUTE YOUR DROID TRIED TO KILL ME!>
YEAH, DON'T TAKE IT SO PERSONALLY. THAT'S JUST SORT OF HIS THING.
YOU AND I, WE CAN STILL WORK SOMETHING OUT.
<NO, I CANNOT TAKE THE CHANCE! THIS SWORD... I CAN'T LET ANYONE ELSE HAVE IT!>
<IT WAS IN MY LATE PARENTS' NOTES. IT MUST HAVE BEEN IMPORTANT TO THEM! IT HAS MEANING...A STORY I HAVE YET TO UNCOVER.>
I DON'T GIVE A DAMN ABOUT YOUR DEAD PARENTS' MYSTERIES--
--BUT YOU CAN ASK THEM IN PERSON IF YOU'D LIKE.

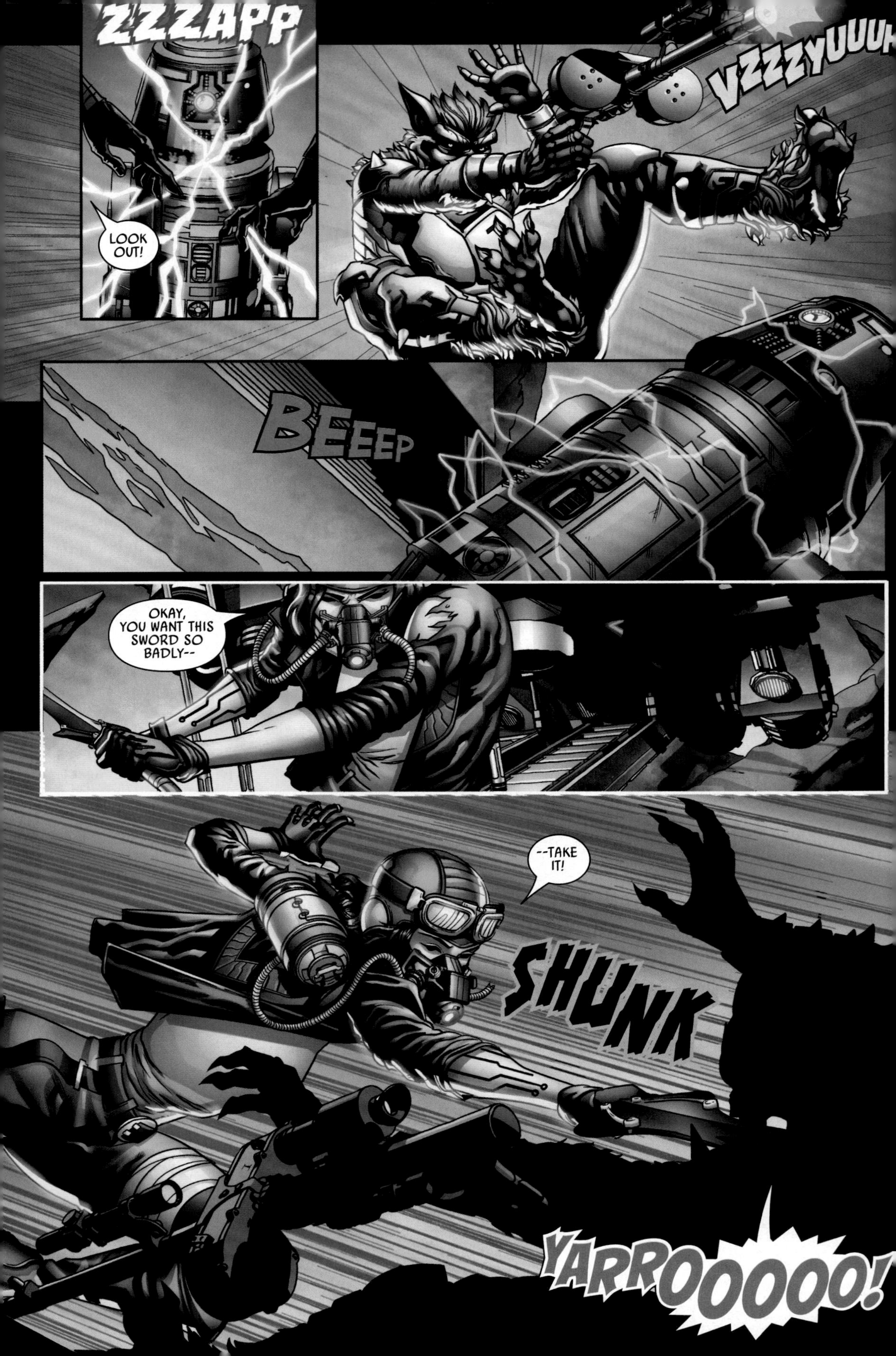
ZZZAPP
LOOK OUT!
VZZZYUUUH
BEEEP
OKAY, YOU WANT THIS SWORD SO BADLY--
--TAKE IT!
SHUNK
YARROOOOOO!

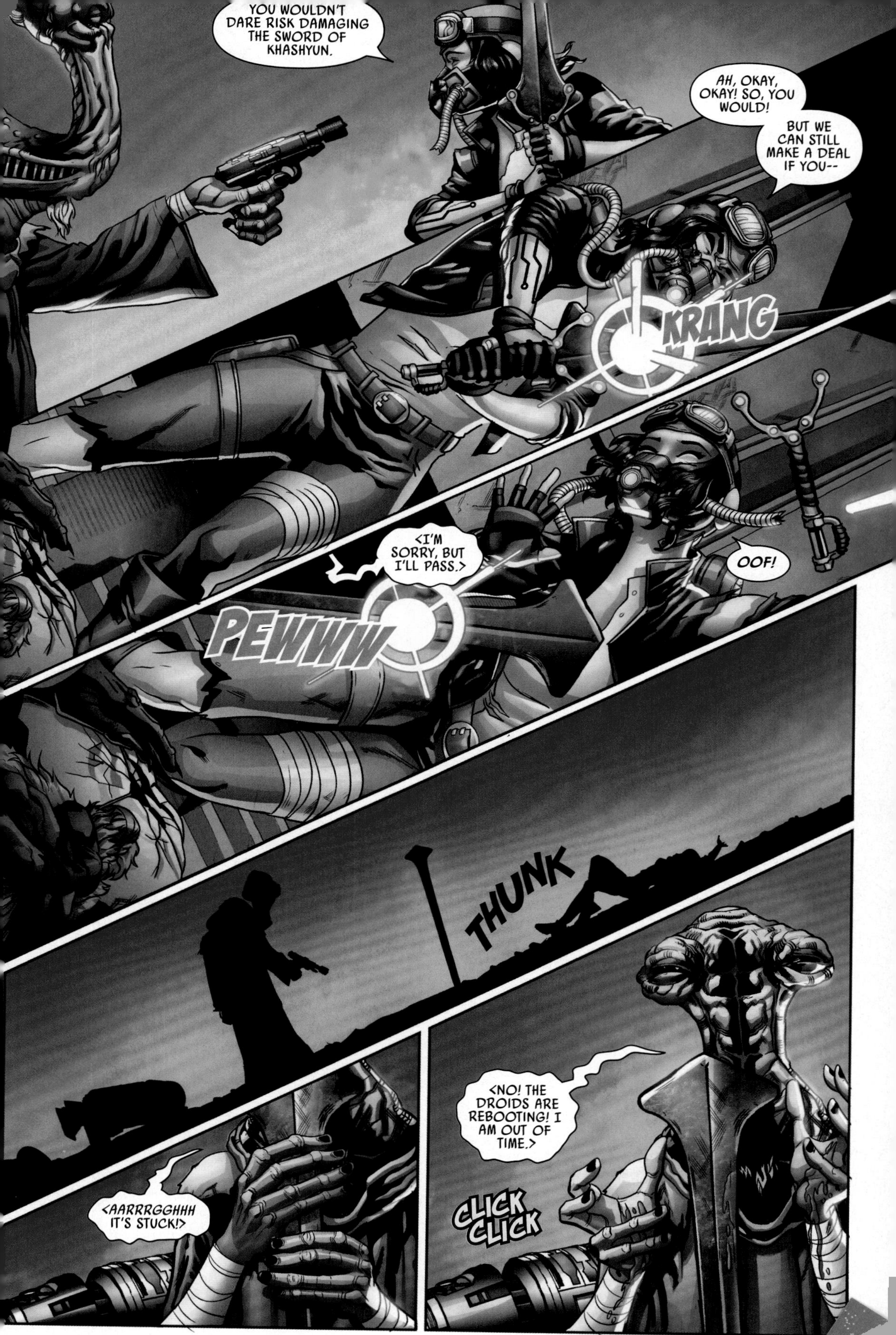
YOU WOULDN'T DARE RISK DAMAGING THE SWORD OF KHASHYUN.
AH, OKAY, OKAY! SO, YOU WOULD!
BUT WE CAN STILL MAKE A DEAL IF YOU--
KRANG
<I'M SORRY, BUT I'LL PASS.>
OOF!
PEWWW
THUNK
<NO! THE DROIDS ARE REBOOTING! I AM OUT OF TIME.>
<AARRRGGHHH IT'S STUCK!>
CLICK CLICK

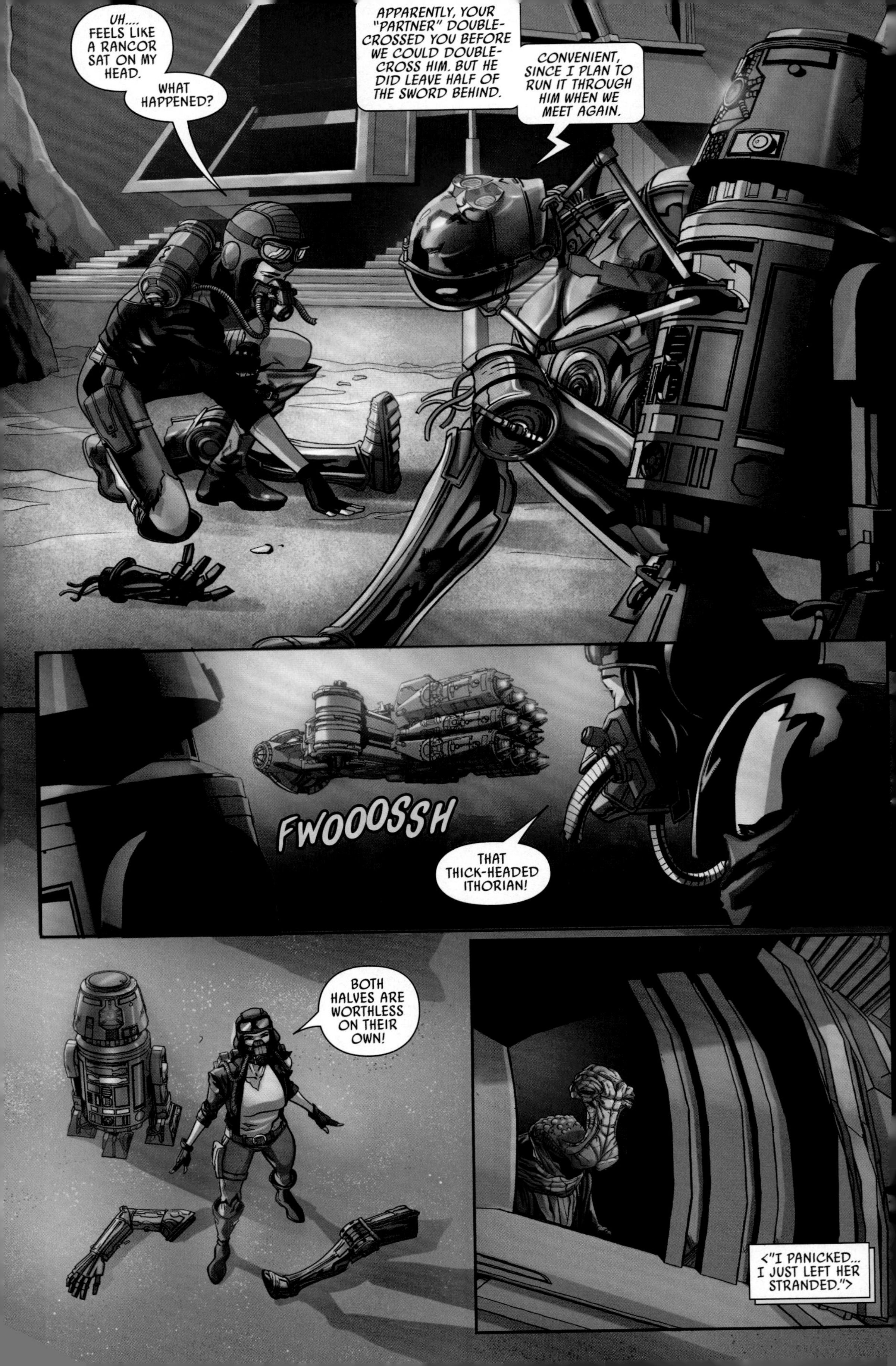
UH.... FEELS LIKE A RANCOR SAT ON MY HEAD.
WHAT HAPPENED?
APPARENTLY, YOUR "PARTNER" DOUBLE-CROSSED YOU BEFORE WE COULD DOUBLE-CROSS HIM. BUT HE DID LEAVE HALF OF THE SWORD BEHIND.
CONVENIENT, SINCE I PLAN TO RUN IT THROUGH HIM WHEN WE MEET AGAIN.
FWOOOSSH
THAT THICK-HEADED ITHORIAN!
BOTH HALVES ARE WORTHLESS ON THEIR OWN!
<"I PANICKED... I JUST LEFT HER STRANDED.">

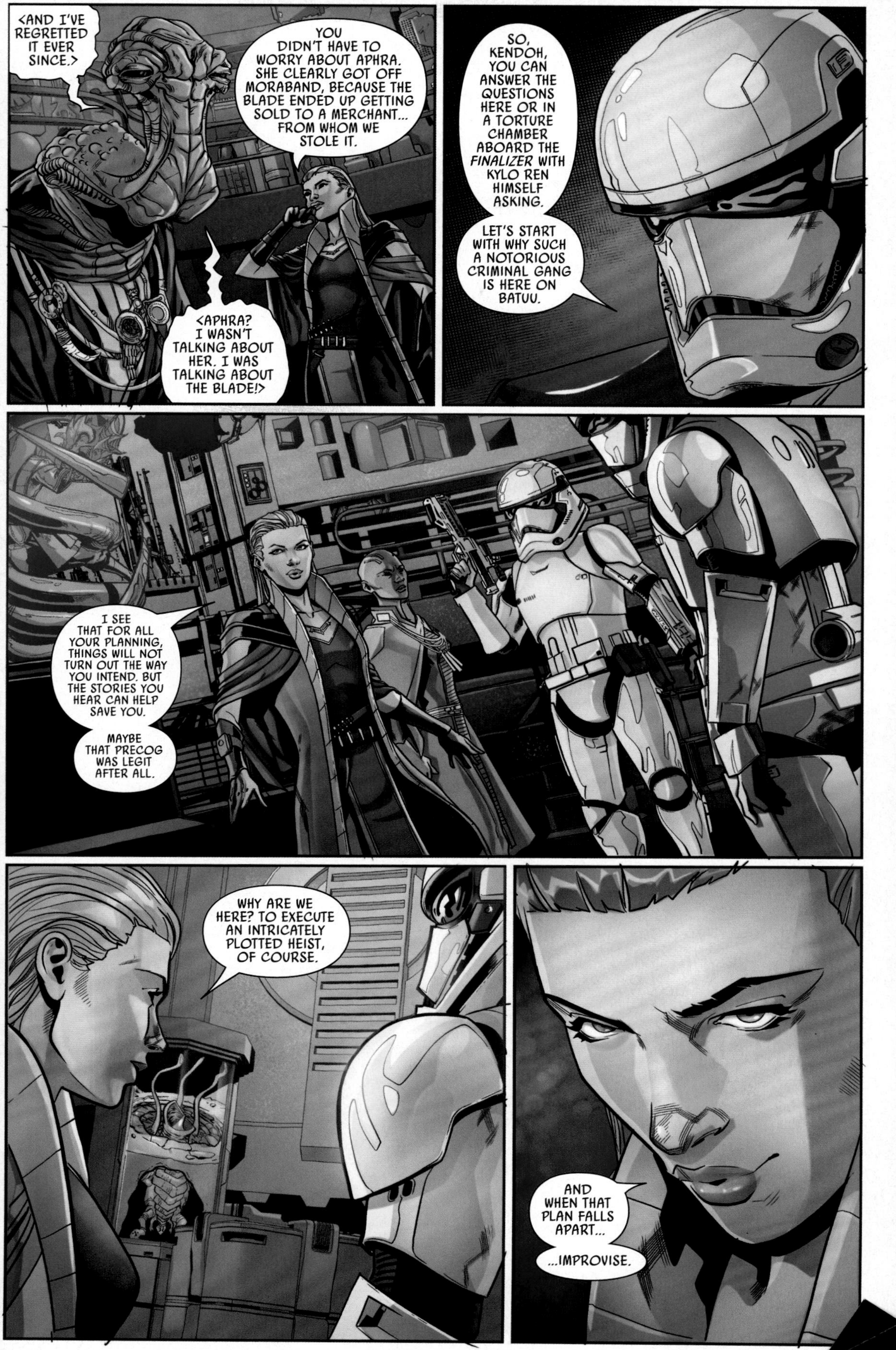
<AND I'VE REGRETTED IT EVER SINCE.>
YOU DIDN'T HAVE TO WORRY ABOUT APHRA. SHE CLEARLY GOT OFF MORABAND, BECAUSE THE BLADE ENDED UP GETTING SOLD TO A MERCHANT... FROM WHOM WE STOLE IT.
<APHRA? I WASN'T TALKING ABOUT HER. I WAS TALKING ABOUT THE BLADE!>
SO, KENDOH, YOU CAN ANSWER THE QUESTIONS HERE OR IN A TORTURE CHAMBER ABOARD THE *FINALIZER* WITH KYLO REN HIMSELF ASKING.
LET'S START WITH WHY SUCH A NOTORIOUS CRIMINAL GANG IS HERE ON BATUU.
I SEE THAT FOR ALL YOUR PLANNING, THINGS WILL NOT TURN OUT THE WAY YOU INTEND. BUT THE STORIES YOU HEAR CAN HELP SAVE YOU.
MAYBE THAT PRECOG WAS LEGIT AFTER ALL.
WHY ARE WE HERE? TO EXECUTE AN INTRICATELY PLOTTED HEIST, OF COURSE.
AND WHEN THAT PLAN FALLS APART...
...IMPROVISE.

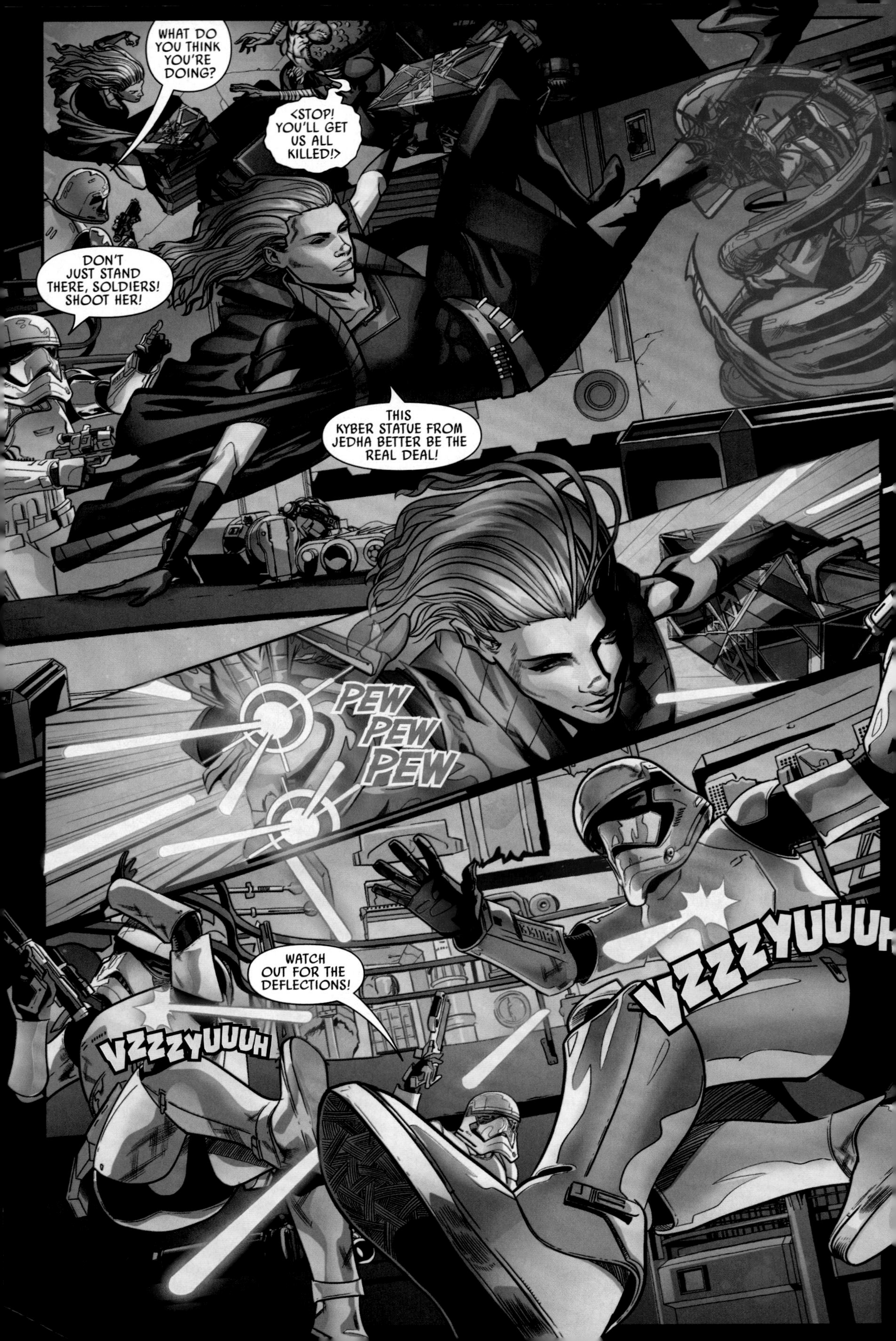
WHAT DO YOU THINK YOU'RE DOING?
<STOP! YOU'LL GET US ALL KILLED!>
DON'T JUST STAND THERE, SOLDIERS! SHOOT HER!
THIS KYBER STATUE FROM JEDHA BETTER BE THE REAL DEAL!
PEW PEW PEW
WATCH OUT FOR THE DEFLECTIONS!
VZZZYUUUH
VZZZYUUUH

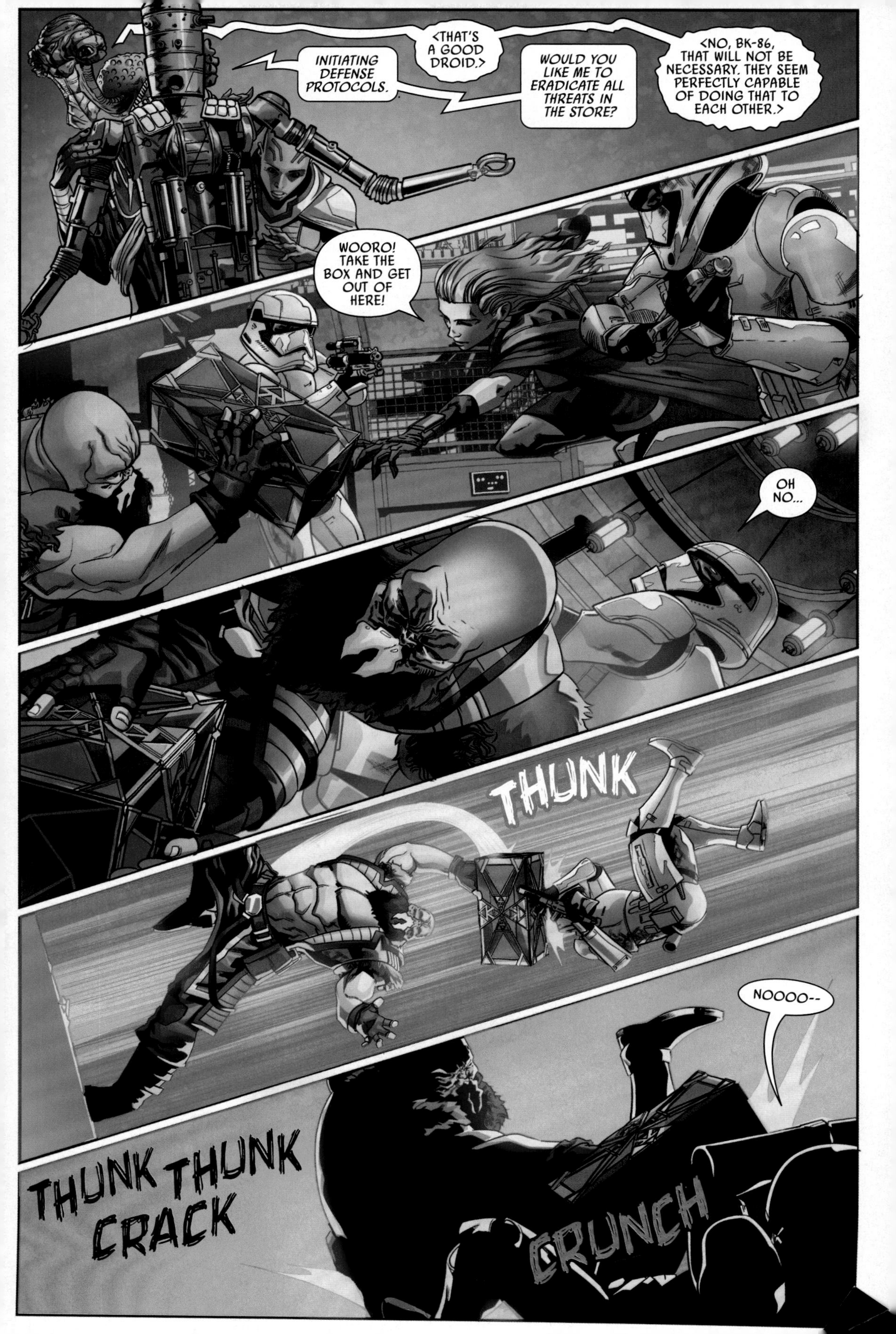
INITIATING DEFENSE PROTOCOLS.
<THAT'S A GOOD DROID.>
WOULD YOU LIKE ME TO ERADICATE ALL THREATS IN THE STORE?
<NO, BK-86, THAT WILL NOT BE NECESSARY. THEY SEEM PERFECTLY CAPABLE OF DOING THAT TO EACH OTHER.>
WOORO! TAKE THE BOX AND GET OUT OF HERE!
OH NO...
THUNK
NOOOO--
THUNK THUNK CRACK
CRUNCH

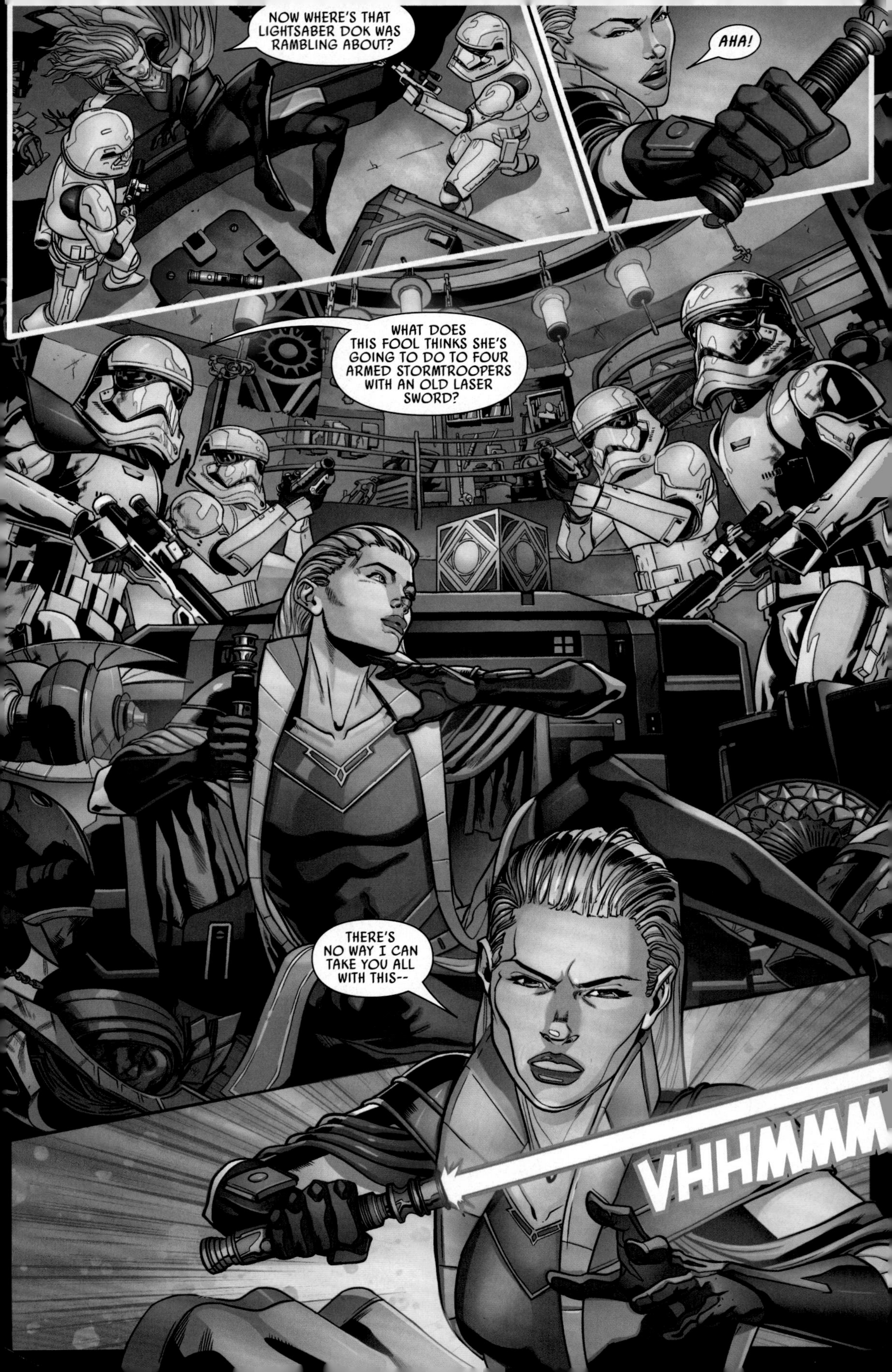
NOW WHERE'S THAT LIGHTSABER DOK WAS RAMBLING ABOUT?
AHA!
WHAT DOES THIS FOOL THINKS SHE'S GOING TO DO TO FOUR ARMED STORMTROOPERS WITH AN OLD LASER SWORD?
THERE'S NO WAY I CAN TAKE YOU ALL WITH THIS--
VHMMMM

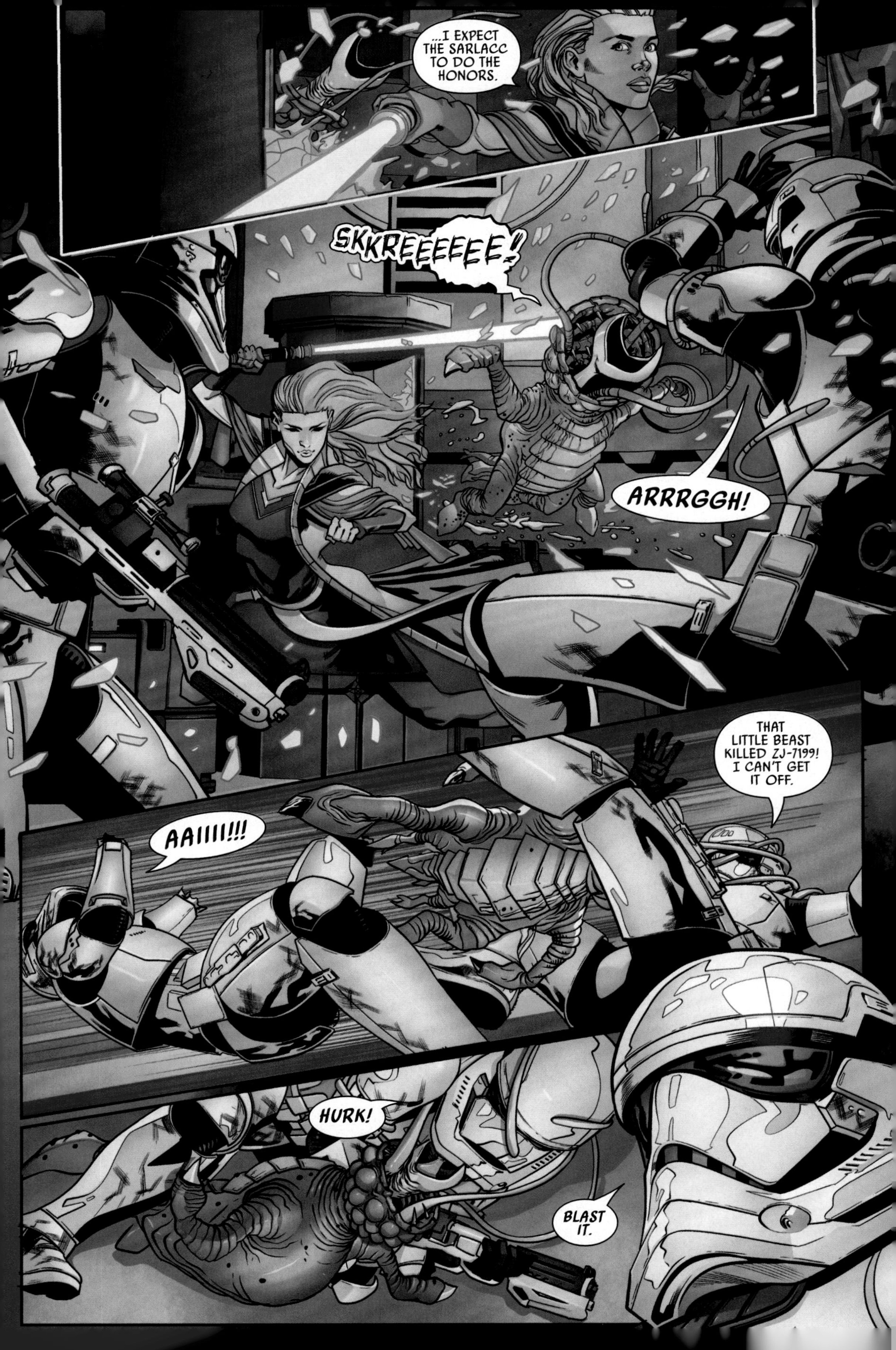
...I EXPECT THE SARLACC TO DO THE HONORS.
SKKREEEEEEE!
ARRRGGH!
THAT LITTLE BEAST KILLED ZJ-7199! I CAN'T GET IT OFF.
AAIIII!!!
HURK!
BLAST IT.

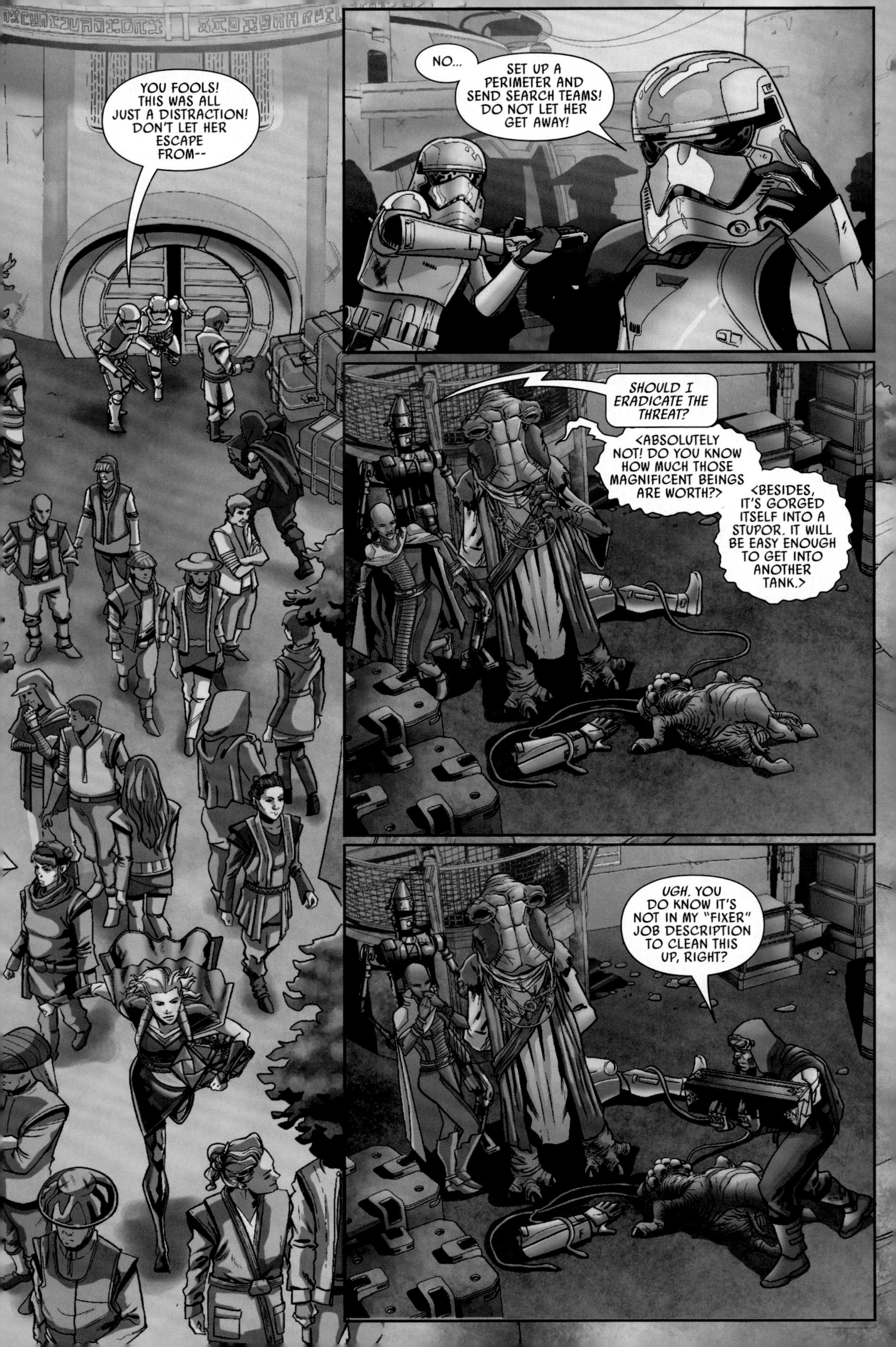
YOU FOOLS! THIS WAS ALL JUST A DISTRACTION! DON'T LET HER ESCAPE FROM--
NO...
SET UP A PERIMETER AND SEND SEARCH TEAMS! DO NOT LET HER GET AWAY!
SHOULD I ERADICATE THE THREAT?
<ABSOLUTELY NOT! DO YOU KNOW HOW MUCH THOSE MAGNIFICENT BEINGS ARE WORTH?>
<BESIDES, IT'S GORGED ITSELF INTO A STUPOR. IT WILL BE EASY ENOUGH TO GET INTO ANOTHER TANK.>
UGH. YOU DO KNOW IT'S NOT IN MY "FIXER" JOB DESCRIPTION TO CLEAN THIS UP, RIGHT?

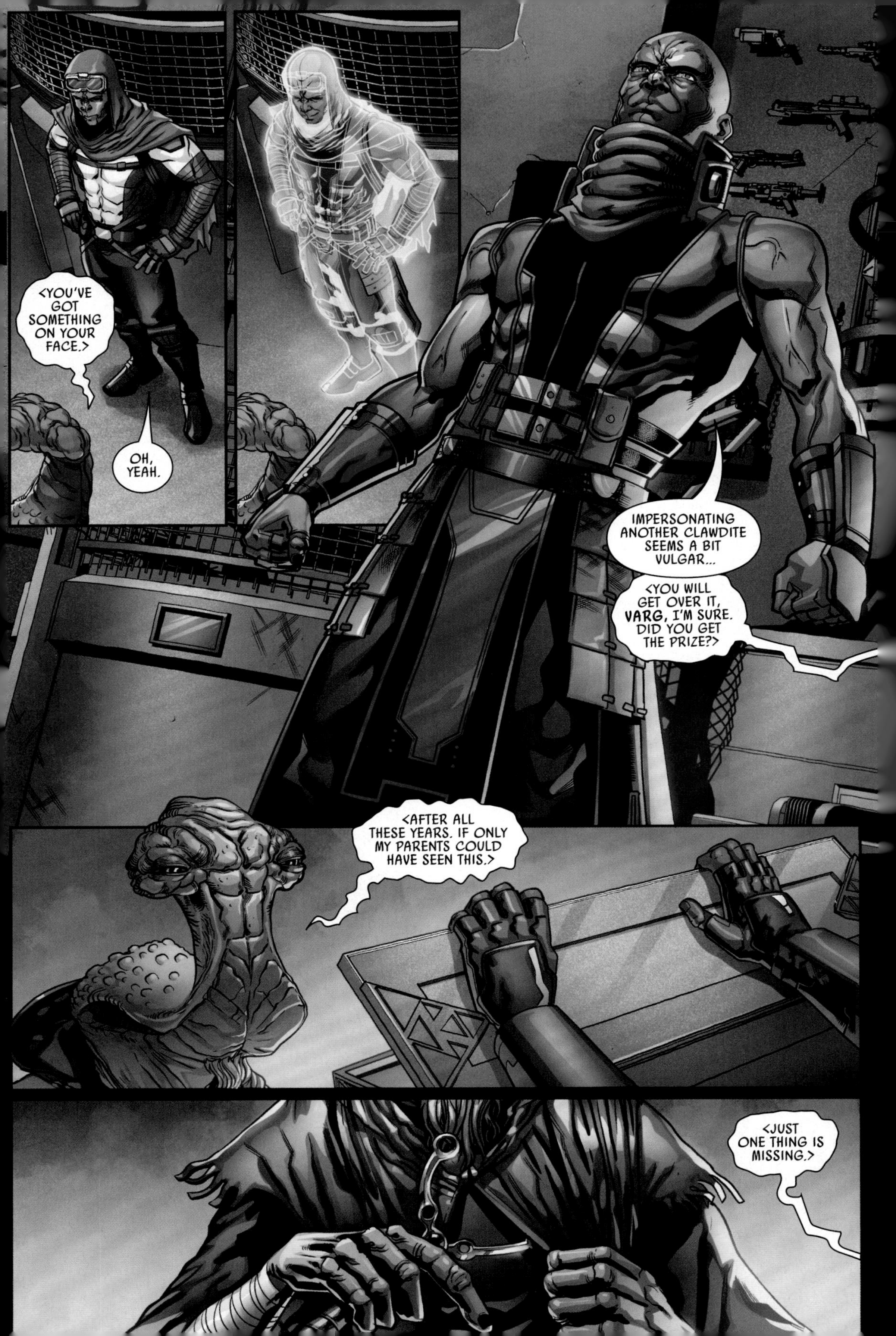
<YOU'VE GOT SOMETHING ON YOUR FACE.>
OH, YEAH.
IMPERSONATING ANOTHER CLAWDITE SEEMS A BIT VULGAR...
<YOU WILL GET OVER IT, VARG, I'M SURE. DID YOU GET THE PRIZE?>
<AFTER ALL THESE YEARS. IF ONLY MY PARENTS COULD HAVE SEEN THIS.>
<JUST ONE THING IS MISSING.>

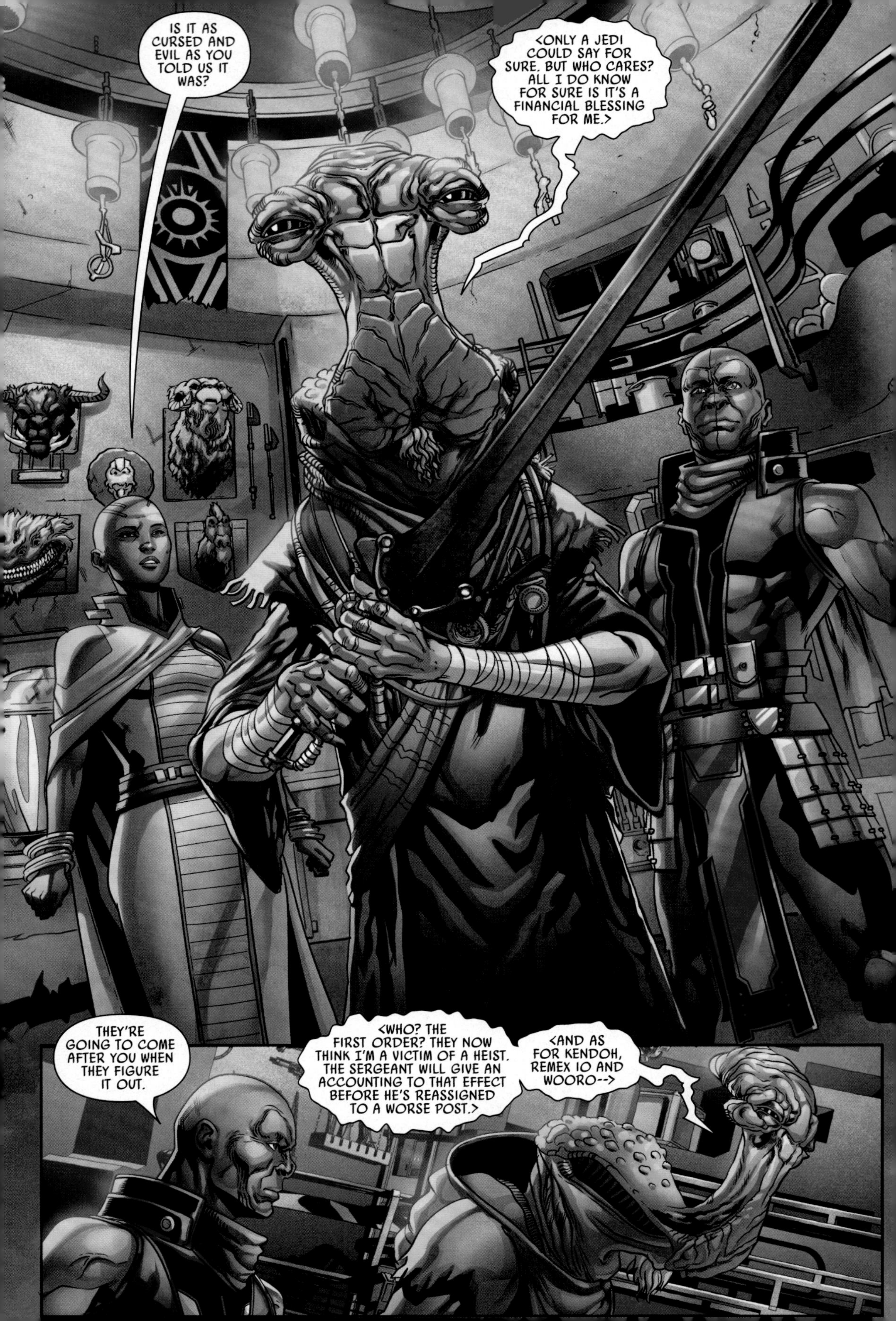
IS IT AS CURSED AND EVIL AS YOU TOLD US IT WAS?
<ONLY A JEDI COULD SAY FOR SURE. BUT WHO CARES? ALL I DO KNOW FOR SURE IS IT'S A FINANCIAL BLESSING FOR ME.>
THEY'RE GOING TO COME AFTER YOU WHEN THEY FIGURE IT OUT.
<WHO? THE FIRST ORDER? THEY NOW THINK I'M A VICTIM OF A HEIST. THE SERGEANT WILL GIVE AN ACCOUNTING TO THAT EFFECT BEFORE HE'S REASSIGNED TO A WORSE POST.>
<AND AS FOR KENDOH, REMEX IO AND WOORO-->

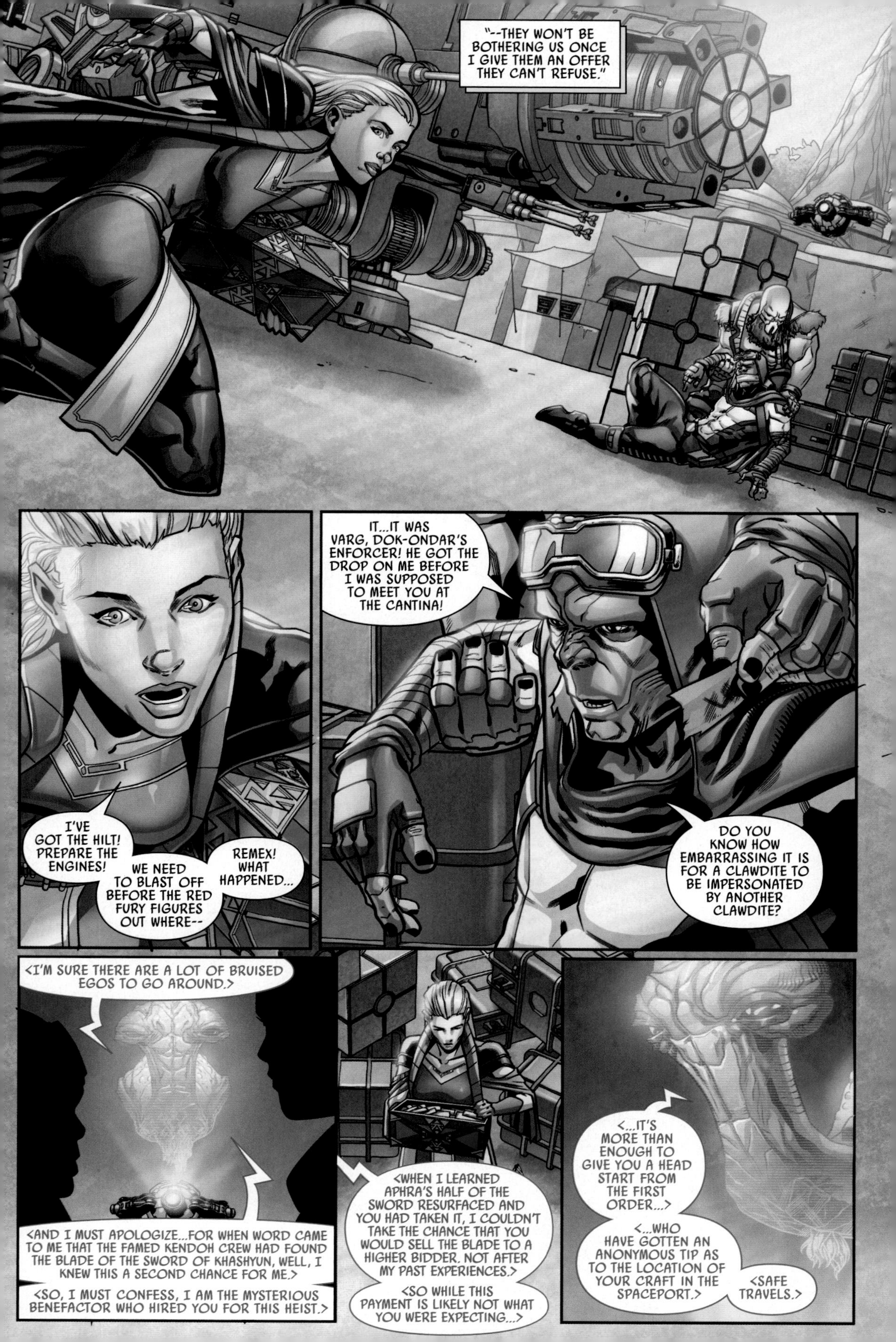
"--THEY WON'T BE BOTHERING US ONCE I GIVE THEM AN OFFER THEY CAN'T REFUSE."
I'VE GOT THE HILT! PREPARE THE ENGINES!
WE NEED TO BLAST OFF BEFORE THE RED FURY FIGURES OUT WHERE--
REMEX! WHAT HAPPENED...
IT...IT WAS VARG, DOK-ONDAR'S ENFORCER! HE GOT THE DROP ON ME BEFORE I WAS SUPPOSED TO MEET YOU AT THE CANTINA!
DO YOU KNOW HOW EMBARRASSING IT IS FOR A CLAWDITE TO BE IMPERSONATED BY ANOTHER CLAWDITE?
<I'M SURE THERE ARE A LOT OF BRUISED EGOS TO GO AROUND.>
<AND I MUST APOLOGIZE...FOR WHEN WORD CAME TO ME THAT THE FAMED KENDOH CREW HAD FOUND THE BLADE OF THE SWORD OF KHASHYUN, WELL, I KNEW THIS A SECOND CHANCE FOR ME.>
<SO, I MUST CONFESS, I AM THE MYSTERIOUS BENEFACTOR WHO HIRED YOU FOR THIS HEIST.>
<WHEN I LEARNED APHRA'S HALF OF THE SWORD RESURFACED AND YOU HAD TAKEN IT, I COULDN'T TAKE THE CHANCE THAT YOU WOULD SELL THE BLADE TO A HIGHER BIDDER. NOT AFTER MY PAST EXPERIENCES.>
<SO WHILE THIS PAYMENT IS LIKELY NOT WHAT YOU WERE EXPECTING...>
<...IT'S MORE THAN ENOUGH TO GIVE YOU A HEAD START FROM THE FIRST ORDER...>
<...WHO HAVE GOTTEN AN ANONYMOUS TIP AS TO THE LOCATION OF YOUR CRAFT IN THE SPACEPORT.>
<SAFE TRAVELS.>

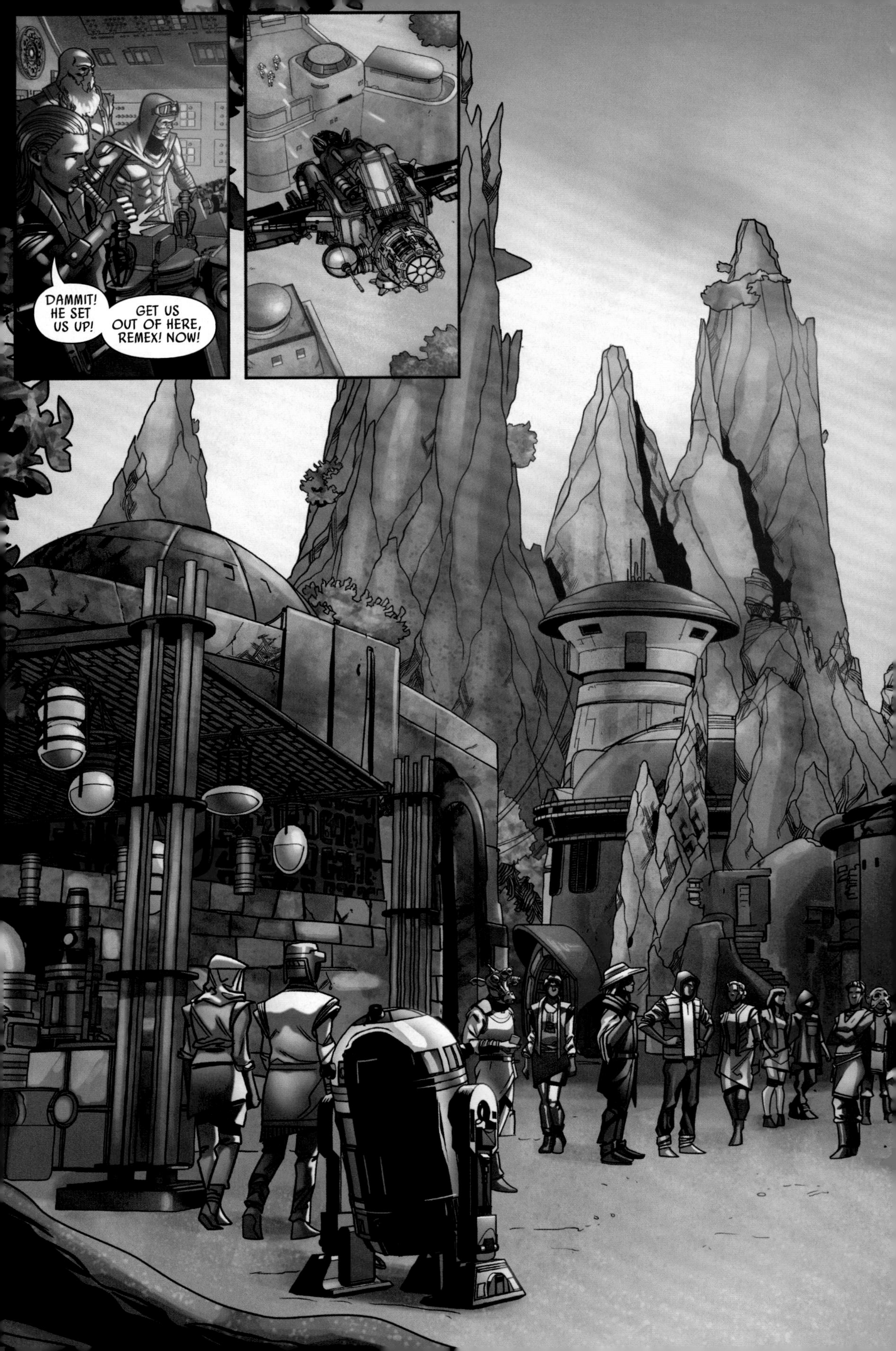
DAMMIT! HE SET US UP!
GET US OUT OF HERE, REMEX! NOW!

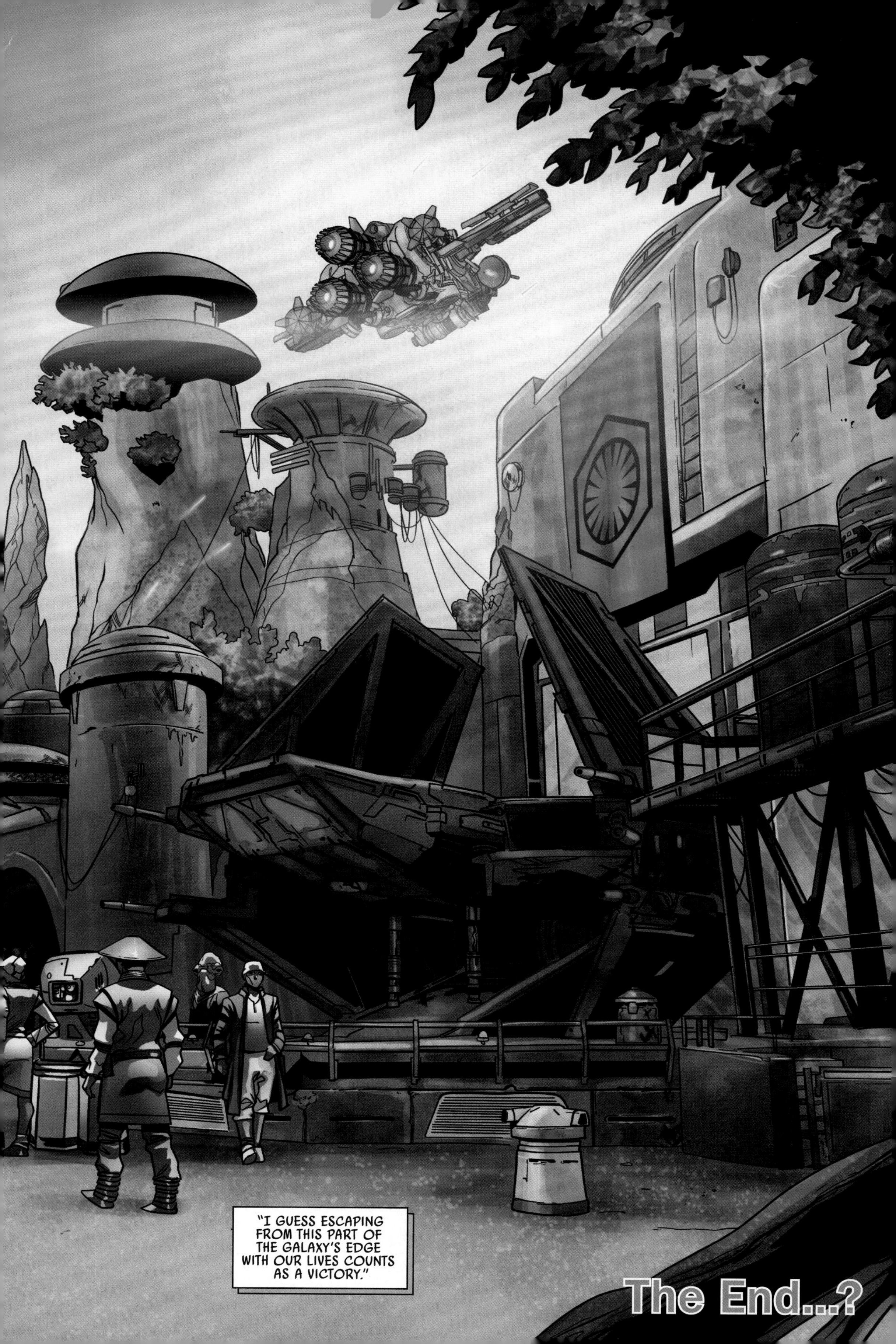

"I GUESS ESCAPING FROM THIS PART OF THE GALAXY'S EDGE WITH OUR LIVES COUNTS AS A VICTORY."
The End...?

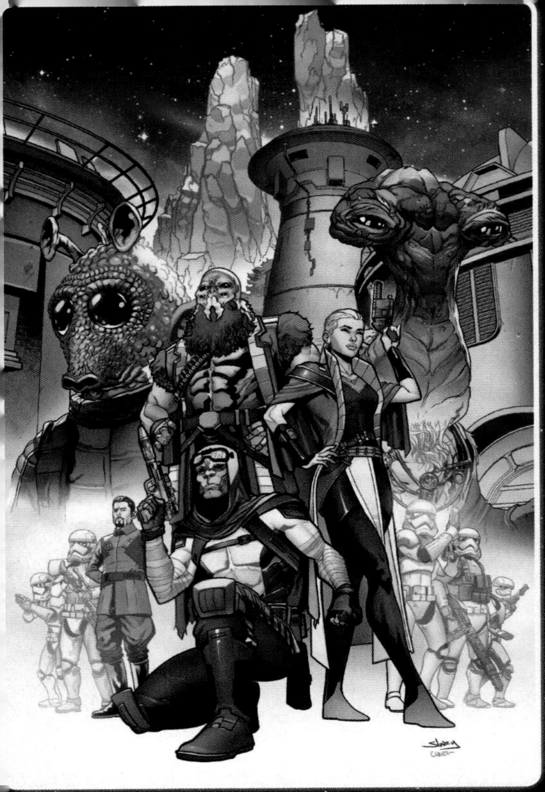

***STAR WARS: GALAXY'S EDGE* 2 Variant by**
WILL SLINEY & DAVID CURIEL

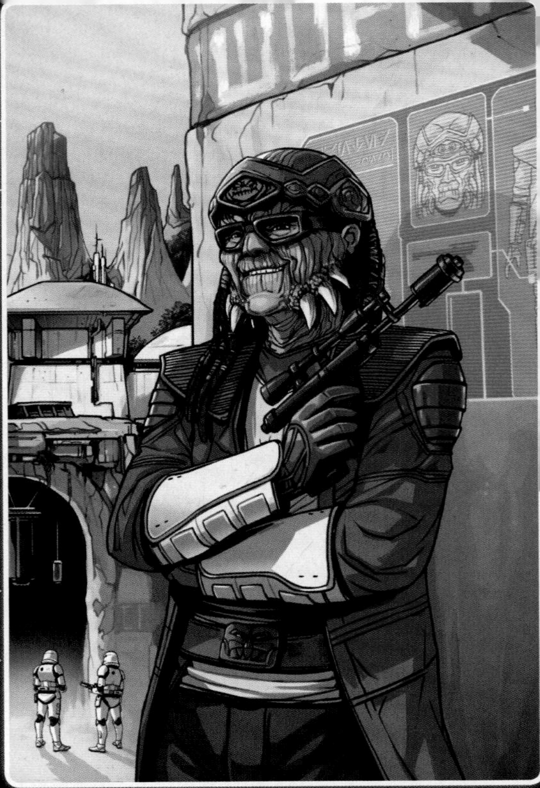

***STAR WARS: GALAXY'S EDGE* 3 Variant by**
CASPAR WIJNGAARD

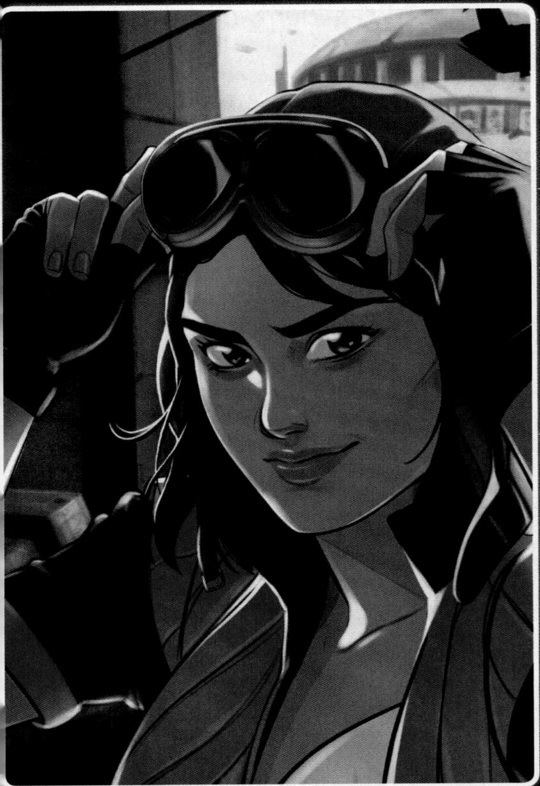

***STAR WARS: GALAXY'S EDGE* 4 Variant by**
STACEY LEE

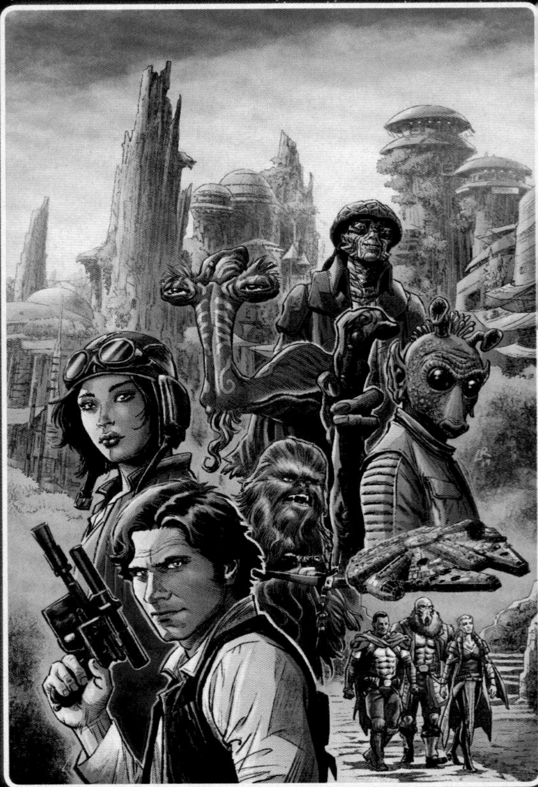

***STAR WARS: GALAXY'S EDGE* 5 Variant by**
LUKE ROSS & LEE LOUGHRIDGE

RELIVE THESE THRILLING STORIES FEATURING EXCLUSIVE NEW SCENES!

WENDIG
ROSS
MARTIN
MARVEL
STAR WARS
THE FORCE AWAKENS

STAR WARS: THE FORCE AWAKENS ADAPTATION TPB

ISBN: 978-1302902032

WHITTA
WALSH
SPICER
STAR WARS
THE LAST JEDI
MARVEL
RIVERA

STAR WARS: THE LAST JEDI ADAPTATION TPB

ISBN: 978-1302912017

ON SALE NOW
AVAILABLE IN PRINT AND DIGITAL
WHEREVER BOOKS ARE SOLD

TO FIND A COMIC SHOP NEAR YOU,
VISIT COMICSHOPLOCATOR.COM.

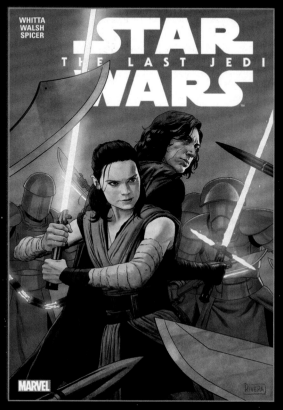

STAR WARS™

THERE ARE HEROES – AND VILLAINS – ON BOTH SIDES!

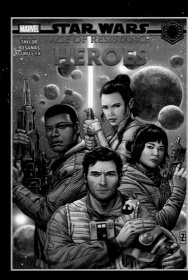

**STAR WARS: AGE OF
REPUBLIC – HEROES TPB**
ISBN: 978-1302917104

ON SALE NOW!

**STAR WARS: AGE OF
REBELLION – HEROES TPB**
ISBN: 978-1302917081

ON SALE NOW!

**STAR WARS: AGE OF
RESISTANCE – HEROES TPB**
ISBN: 978-1302917128

NOVEMBER 2019

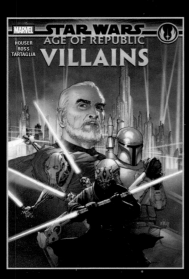

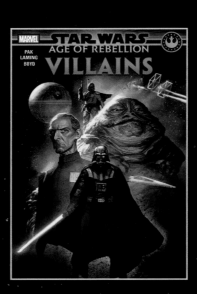

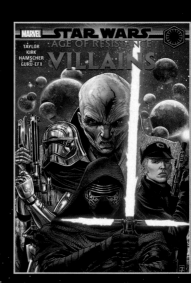

**STAR WARS: AGE OF
REPUBLIC – VILLAINS TPB**
ISBN: 978-1302917296

ON SALE NOW!

**STAR WARS: AGE OF
REBELLION – VILLAINS TPB**
ISBN: 978-1302917296

ON SALE NOW!

**STAR WARS: AGE OF
RESISTANCE – VILLAINS TPB**
ISBN: 978-1302917302

NOVEMBER 2019